# The Holocaust and
## the Crisis of
## Human Behavior

# THE HOLOCAUST AND THE CRISIS OF HUMAN BEHAVIOR

George M. Kren
and
Leon Rappoport

HOLMES & MEIER PUBLISHERS, INC.
NEW YORK • LONDON

First published in the United States of America 1980 by
Holmes & Meier Publishers, Inc.
30 Irving Place
New York, N.Y. 10003

*Great Britain:*
Holmes & Meier Publishers, Ltd.
131 Trafalgar Road
Greenwich, London SE10 9TX

Copyright © 1980 by George M. Kren and Leon Rappoport

Library of Congress Cataloging in Publication Data

Kren, George M. 1926–
   The Holocaust and the crisis of human behavior.

      Bibliography: p.
      Includes index.
      1. Holocaust, Jewish (1939–1945)   2. National
socialism.   3. Nationalsozialistische Deutsche
Arbeiter-Partei. Schutzstaffel.   I. Rappoport, Leon,
joint author.   II. Title.
D810.J4K687 1979      940.53'1503'924      79-23781

ISBN 0-8419-0544-4


Manufactured in the United States of America

# Contents

*To the memory of J. Glenn Gray*

Chapter I

# Dimensions of the Historical Crisis

Between 1941 and 1945, the Nazi government of Germany systematically killed millions of men, women, and children because they were Jews, Gypsies, or Slavs defined by racist ideology as threatening to Germanic ideals.[1] This event has come to be called "the Holocaust." Ever since it happened, the culture-makers of Western civilization—writers, artists, scholars, scientists, and thoughtful people generally—have wondered why it happened, how it happened, and what it means for human society.

These questions have led to documentation and soul-searching recorded in a seemingly endless literature. It is no exaggeration to suggest that by the end of the century, the accumulation of items concerning the Holocaust—books, films, poems, articles, stories—will equal or exceed the total number that have been produced about any other subject in human history.[2] Among all the material already available, however, there is no better expression of the hardly expressible challenge to meaning posed by the Holocaust than that written by Dwight Macdonald in 1945, when the ashes were still hot.

> Something has happened to Europe. . . . What is it? Who or what is responsible? What does it mean about our civilization, our whole system of values?
>
> The Nazis have not *disregarded* human life. They have, on the contrary, paid close attention to it. . . . There was no ulterior motive behind . . . [the Holocaust], no possible advantage to its creators beyond the gratification of neurotic racial hatreds. What had previously been done only by individual psychopathic killers has now been done by the rulers and servants of a great modern state. This *is* something new.[3]

The "something new" is the fundamental theme of this book, and elaboration of this theme depends first of all upon how the Holocaust may be understood as something new in human history.

1

## The Uniqueness of the Holocaust

It is generally acknowledged that the Holocaust was unique in quantitative terms, a matter of more innocent victims being deliberately killed per
unit of time than ever before. But this having been said, the events are then
very frequently shunted into the familiar stream of history wherein wars,
massacres, and persecutions are notoriously salient and apparently unchang-
ing, except insofar as applied science provides new possibilities for mass
destruction.

When viewed in this fashion, and accompanied with the proper citation of
other historical horrors (the religious crusades, the slaughter of the Albigensian heretics, the Turkish decimation of the Armenians, and even the British
invention of concentration camps during the Boer War), it becomes all too
convenient to see the Holocaust as "unique"—but normal, after all. The long
European tradition of anti-Semitism adds further plausibility to the idea that
killing off whole populations is an ugly but familiar fact of historical life. And
if anyone takes issue with this orderly view of things, they will usually be
patted on the head and sent off to do their historical sums, i.e., count the
casualties.

Such intellectually comfortable perspectives on the Holocaust must be
rejected on historical grounds. Psychologically, however, and especially
where the present work is concerned, it is essential to recognize very early on
that like all emotional defense mechanisms, the tendency to normalize
extraordinary events reduces anxiety only by falsifying reality. Arthur Koestler has said of this human propensity to explain away the intrinsically
incredible that it is like a "smug and smiling voice in us, which whispers in our
ear the gentle lie that we shall never die, and that tomorrow will be like
yesterday. It is time we learnt to distrust that voice."[4]

Distrust in this case may begin with correction of the popular myth that
traditional German anti-Semitism was a major cause of the Holocaust. The
myth goes as follows: Nazis began by elevating anti-Semitism to an article of
political and cultural faith. Action was first limited to simple abuse. Later,
with enactment of the Nuremberg laws, the Jews lost most of their legal rights,
and they were encouraged to emigrate on the condition of leaving all of their
possessions to the state. Later still, they were put in concentration camps.
Finally, mass killings were started in special extermination camps.[5]

This makes the death camps appear to be merely the last, atrocious rung on
the ladder of anti-Semitism. The Nazi euphemism "final solution" also
contributes to the appearance of a logical causal chain. What could be
simpler? Given the Nazi premise that Jews were an inferior race corrupting
humanity, it follows that with increasing Nazi power there would be an
increasingly harsh program of repression.

The only problem with this reassuringly neat analysis is that it is wrong.
Prior to the advent of Hitler, and even for some time after his appearance,

German anti-Semitism was not much different from what prevailed throughout Europe. Indeed, during the nineteenth century and for several years after World War I, Jews received better treatment in Germany than in Russia, Poland, the Habsburg Empire and its succession states, Scandinavia, and even France, where the Dreyfus affair made Jews targets for substantial abuse. In brief, anti-Semitism is a European tradition. It was never confined to Germany, nor was it more intense in Germany than elsewhere. Yet complete destruction of the Jews was never made a state policy, let alone attempted on a broad scale, anywhere except in Germany. Consequently, although historical anti-Semitism was clearly relevant to the Holocaust, it cannot be accepted as a primary cause.

The uniqueness of the Holocaust also stands out when the focus of inquiry is shifted from historical trends to the level of personal experience. All of the surviving victims who have been able to describe their experiences have their own idiosyncratic perspectives to convey, but the major theme they agree on is the uncanny atmosphere of the death camps. To call it a nightmare quality is inadequate; by all accounts it was another world in which everything previously considered human and meaningful was turned upside down. David Rousset, for example, said that the most fundamental reality about the camps was how they defied intelligent comprehension: "Ordinary human beings do not know that everything is possible." Just as a mystical experience may not be easily conveyed in words, even though it may forever transform the individual, Rousset indicates that those who have experienced the world of the camps are set apart from others in a fashion that is "impossible to communicate."[6]

It may well be true that the qualitative nature of the death camps and many other aspects of the Nazi genocide program must remain a mystery for those without firsthand experience. But this does not mean that intense qualities of experience generally reported by survivors should be ignored. On the contrary, it is only by attempting to work through various patterns of individual experience that certain crucial issues of meaning may be identified.

Some writers disagree, however. Faced with the extraordinary revealed horrors, their response has been to place the Holocaust in a religious or metaphysical context, treating it either as a massive testing of faith analogous to the sufferings of Job, or a biblical judgment associated with restoration of the Jewish homeland.[7]

Looking very broadly over previous reactions to the uniqueness of the Holocaust, therefore, it seems clear that two extreme alternatives have predominated, and both have served to block the way toward careful interpretative analysis. Thus, if the genocide is seen in the cold light of normal history, chiefly remarkable for the large number of innocent victims, then there is no special challenge to critical inquiry, and historians may conduct business as usual, gathering facts and examining how they may be articulated as explanations for specific actions. If, on the other hand, the Nazi genocide program is seen in the passionate light of mystical revelation, then it will appear to be manifestly beyond critical study.

Taken together, both of these viewpoints go a long way toward explaining why the essential human questions arising from the Holocaust have largely gone unanswered: Neither view leads to constructs of meaningfully human dimensions. At one extreme, human actions are overshadowed by impersonal historial forces (e.g., anti-Semitism); at the other, they are overshadowed by metaphysical principles (e.g., God's will). We reject both, and in doing so, accept as a necessary first responsibility the requirement to suggest a new context for discussion.

## Psychosocial Qualities of Mass Destruction

In order to comprehend the Holocaust as a human event, it must be placed on or alongside some kind of comparative human scale. The most convenient scale is always quantitative, but where very large numbers of people are involved in extraordinary situations, the quantity scale quickly becomes relatively meaningless—unimaginable; and worse yet, preoccupation with the abstractions generated by large numbers diverts attention from the fact that the qualities of mass destruction are not always and everywhere the same.

Masses of innocents have been killed throughout the ages, to be sure, and death is indivisible. It must be granted that apart from the variations of pain involved, it can hardly matter a great deal to victims whether they are machine-gunned to death, vaporized by nuclear bombs, burned up in incendiary raids, or gassed in murder camps. The meaning of mass destruction does not necessarily begin and end with the suffering of its victims, however. Particularly when broad segments of a whole civilization are involved in the process of destruction, its meaning extends to the psychosocial and technological forces that have produced it, as well as the specific motives and methods that have made it possible. The following discussion of major historical atrocities provides a general scheme for conceptualizing mass killings according to the essential psychosocial qualities involved: motives, methods, and emotions. At each of the four general levels of atrocious action described, the central questions are *why* the action happened, *how* it was carried out, and *what emotions* accompanied or followed it.

Conventional or "ordinary" atrocities constitute the primary level of mass destruction. The typical case occurs when soldiers capture a village or city and more or less spontaneously set about to pillage, rape, and murder. The reasons of such behavior are usually understood to be a mixture of high stress experienced by the soldiers and poor disciplinary control by their commanders. The methods employed in such cases are invariably primitive and impromptu, and the emotions involved are about the same. A sizable concrete example might be the "rape of Nanking" by the Japanese army in 1937, or the "rape of Berlin" by Soviet forces in 1945. In both these cases, historians have noted that although the troops involved seemed to be acting spontaneously out of blood lust, thirst for vengeance, and so forth, they were also in some instances acting in obedience to implicit or explicit high-level political policies. It is a fine distinction, however, and need not be of concern here, except that it leads directly to the second level of atrocious action.

Clear and deliberate acts of mass destruction, to which human passions are either incidental or irrelevant, constitute the second level. Historically, this level of horrors may seem very close to the first, but the distinctive feature of calculated or preplanned mass violence is that it *is* calculated. It is usually aimed at terrorizing large numbers of people into passivity or into active compliance with an imposed orthodoxy. In short, the reasons for such actions have to do with the assertion of power.

Abundant examples illustrating calculated mass terrorization can be found throughout recorded history, ranging from Old Testament and classical Greek epics to the great fire-bomb raids of World War II. The methods involved have varied from primitive weapons (e.g., putting every tenth person to the sword) to nuclear devices capable of eliminating whole cities at one stroke. Frequently, a careful selection of targets is an integral part of the method. Thus, people or places may be selected for destruction in order that their fate may have the maximum exemplary effect upon others—"pour encourager les autres," as Voltaire had it.

As for the emotions associated with calculated mass violence, it appears that for the most part they are not particularly extreme. Moreover, certainly until the end of the nineteenth century, killing large numbers of people was not easy work; it required a great deal of hard physical effort. In modern times, insofar as mass killing has become much more convenient, policy planning for such killing has become something of a corporate process, and policy implementation has become more and more of a technical process requiring professional experts. In these circumstances, emotional feelings about the victims seem to become virtually irrelevant. Of course, even the most professionally detached planners or field personnel may be gratifying some otherwise repressed aggressive impulses through their work, but superficially, at least, the general rule appears to be affective neutrality.

It is easy to imagine a troop of cossacks, for instance, riding into a town or city after a struggle, or perhaps just on payday, and proceeding to terrorize the population in line with their passions as well as with some sort of higher policy aim of their sponsors. One can also imagine that such groups might be deployable on a more systematic basis, say once or twice a week. But even this degree of routinization might become a bit tedious for them after a while. And certainly a systematic daily diet of required rape, murder, or torture would soon be perceived as hard duty. Evidence to this effect is available from the SS Einsatzgruppen—SS task forces—that operated in the Soviet Union. It seems plausible, therefore, to conclude that apart from unitary mass killings quite limited in time and space, atrocious actions sustained over longer periods and covering larger areas can only be accomplished in accord with a systematic strategy and routinized tactics. Such considerations, in turn, would require field units capable of operating effectively whether they "felt like it" or not; that is, without significant passion.

A third general level of mass destruction may be identified when people become victims not simply to gratify aggressive passions or to serve as a terrifying example to others, but because their immediate existence is perceived as a threat or stumbling block to the designs of those wanting them out of the way. Some of the massacres and "relocations" of American Indians had this rationale.

The emotions involved in such events may again be quite variable, but the general matter-of-fact attitude that prevails at the policy level was aptly expressed by Hans Frank, the Nazi governor of Poland, who said, "We ask nothing of the Jews except that they should disappear."[8] Idi Amin might have said the same thing in relation to his expulsion of all Indians from Uganda. It is precisely this simple but inhuman aim of forcing segments of populations or entire populations to disappear that defines this particular level of mass destruction.

Despite the modern psychopathic flavor of such actions, it must be acknowledged that inherent in them is a certain traditional political rationality. Thus, one may find examples extending back to the ancient Greeks and Hebrews, wherein relatively weak or completely defenseless people have been forced (often with extreme violence, if not literally by death) to disappear. In many relevant historical examples, it is apparent that the victims usually have been either a real or a potential danger to their oppressors. Either by occupying a certain space or by having demonstrated a potential for aggressive action, the victimized people may in fact be rationally construed as a threat to those who would eliminate them. This point deserves special emphasis because it defines the outer limit of the qualitative scale on which all mass violence prior to the Holocaust may be comprehended. Passion, calculated terrorism, and the liquidation of people who threaten to make trouble or who are just in the way of something believed to be more important than they are—these three levels of destruction are all understandable in the light of historical precedents and the accumulated knowledge of political rationality.

None of this can be applied in an explanatory fashion to the Holocaust. Comparison shows that the Holocaust must be conceptualized as a fourth and genuinely new level of mass destruction because the quality of violence it brought into being was manifestly different than anything that had occurred before. Unlike the American Indians or other native populations in colonialized areas of the world, for example, the Jews posed no physical challenge to Nazi authority. Unlike the Christian Armenians seeking independence from the Ottoman empire, they claimed no territory. And unlike the various groups of heretics slaughtered through the ages, the Jews as such posed no threat to prevailing religious or cultural orthodoxies. Indeed, there is even some evidence to the contrary, because SS and Wehrmacht records indicate that in various conquered territories, the manual and skilled slave labor of Jews made an appreciable contribution to the German war effort.

It is also false to conceive of the Jews as standing in the way of any particular economic, political, or military activity. Insofar as they were judged to be occupying an excessive number of professional or entrepreneurial positions in Germany and the conquered territories, they could be, and they were, easily forced out of these positions. Insofar as they were a troublesome physical presence, they could be, and they were, transported out of the way and exploited for material gain in the process. It is, moreover, quite clear that Jews and other groups such as the Gypsies were not killed in order to terrorize others, because the killing program was kept as secret as possible.

Finally, the Holocaust stands apart from all previous mass killings because the victims could do nothing to save their lives by capitulation, collaboration, or conversion. Historically, people killed as heretics usually had some opportunity to save themselves by renouncing their beliefs; American Indians could surrender and hope to eke out an existence on reservations; Armenian communities could sometimes negotiate or bribe their way to survival; even prisoners sentenced to Soviet arctic labor camps at least had some chance of remaining alive. But Jews caught in the Holocaust were ticketed for certain death. It was an explicit policy, furthermore, that those selected to perform work assignments in the death camps instead of being killed immediately were eventually supposed to be killed. No one was to be left alive to tell the tale.

Turning from the policies which defined the victims in a historically new fashion to the means employed for their destruction, it is obvious that the highly organized methods required to funnel millions of people into gas chambers constitute yet another unique aspect of the Holocaust. The gas chamber-crematoria technology and the procedures associated with it add up to unprecedented mass murder organized according to industrial production criteria of efficiency. Nothing is more revealing of this fact than the SS recycling program for the eyeglasses, clothing, gold teeth, and hair "produced" by the victims.

What were the emotions of those assigned to operational planning and execution of the Holocaust? So far as the SS headquarters and staff people were concerned, various sources of evidence all indicate that they were relatively indifferent. Practically all of the lower echelon clerks and officers had inklings if not direct knowledge of what was going on under the euphemisms of "anti-partisan warfare," "relocation," and "final solution," but their own anxiety about these notions, added to the official regulations forbidding discussion and rumors suggesting that people who knew too much or did not keep quietly in their place might wind up on the Russian front, combined in such a way that most of these people tried not to know about the meaning of their work. Consequently, with the occasional exception of staff officers who were required to visit one of the camps for some reason, and in some instances have testified or left diaries describing their shocked reactions, planning and organization went forward with about the same emotional tone as could be observed in any other military bureaucracy.

In the camps themselves, the activities of the SS were highly compartmentalized and routinized, and this allowed many of them to ignore what was going on and to repress feelings of anxiety and disgust stimulated by those events they could not ignore. Most of the SS assigned to the camps did not, according to the evidence, either seek out the assignment or enjoy it. The problem here, however, is that there is also much evidence of gratuitously atrocious mistreatment and torture being done by SS camp personnel. How can these two bodies of evidence be squared up with one another?

This question can only be dealt with properly in the context of a full-scale review of SS behavior. It must suffice to note that extraordinary, paradoxical emotions and behavior may occur in extraordinary situations. Many psychiatric sources suggest that when supposedly powerless, inferior beings are serious sources of anxiety and frustration for their oppressors, the oppressors are very likely to act out their rage reactions on the most convenient "objects" available.

Taking all the material together, however, the results of qualitative comparisons reveal the uniqueness of the Holocaust in human terms quite apart from the numbers involved and the metaphysical significance it may hold. The reasons leading to it, the methods by which it was accomplished, and the emotions associated with it were all manifestly different from anything that had ever happened before. If the qualitative difference between the Holocaust and prior acts of mass destruction can be named at all, the only appropriate term for it is *dehumanization*. Although modern mass violence must frequently appear dehumanized compared with what occurred earlier simply because of the instrumentalities made available by modern science, this consideration does not invalidate our description of the Holocaust, for the character of the mass death inflicted by bombings or missile attacks, nuclear or otherwise, is far different from the Nazi death program. In order to make even an approximate analogy, one would have to postulate bombs or missiles designed so that they would seek out and destroy only Jews. In short, the uniqueness of the Holocaust is underscored by the fact that it was a massively selective program conducted more like a large-scale industrial enterprise than anything else. The sinister phrase so often repeated by its operators, "I was just following orders," should be recognized, in this connection, as a perfectly valid indicator, for it is a statement of the ultimate corporate mentality; a mentality which could be extended even so far as to accept genocide as a legitimate social policy.

### Genocide as Social Policy

Although it is clear that the Holocaust was unprecedented with respect to the sociopolitical justifications that have been given for prior instances of genocide, this does not mean that in a formal sense, it can be judged to be simply "irrational." The death camps were in fact an unexpected but quite logical result of a racist, genetically oriented political philosophy that was based upon rational, consistent assumptions and was supported by various kinds of respectable scientific evidence. The rationality in question is difficult to perceive because it is obscured by much of the bizarre surface detail of Nazism as a mass movement—from the special uniforms of the SS and their primitive bonfire ceremonials to the intense emotionality of Hitler's speeches and the Nazi contempt for books and intellectual activity generally. Further-more, common sense emphatically declares that only psychotic and semipsy-chotic deviants consumed with apocalyptic visions could possibly conceive of an Auschwitz or a Treblinka and make the vision work. Such commonsense reactions are also seductive because they have the added attraction of allowing the Holocaust to be treated as a historical aberration, an incredible "accident" roughly equivalent to what might be expected if insane inmates were able to take over the operation of a mental institution.

Yet surface appearances and common sense can both be deceiving. Far from being irrational, the Holocaust can only be epitomized in terms of excessive rationality, an example of logical thought slipping the bonds of human feeling. Ultimately, and in an oversimplified fashion, the logic under-lying the Holocaust is somewhat analogous to the logic lying beneath some contemporary proposals advocating systematic, lawful euthanasia for very elderly, incurably ill persons in our own society. Like the Nazi program, this represents an effort to cope with perceived social problems by destroying people, preventing undesirable forms of life from continuing. Similarly, if some compulsory abortion and birth control proposals were to become law, then one would have a state policy aimed at preventing undesirable forms of human life from getting started.

Judged strictly on the grounds of pure rationality, what emerges as the central issue in such programs is the proposition that large-scale prevention of human life should be a state policy. Like cannibalism, moreover, what makes this proposition unthinkable is not that it is irrational; quite the reverse. It is the nonrational or feeling side of our humanity that rebels at the thought of killing masses of people for food, or to improve the quality of our population. The meaning of the death camps as a crisis—a unique event in history—may be seen more distinctly when it is understood that given certain premises, human extermination represented a logical social policy.

Evidence for this interpretation is scattered all through the fabric of the Third Reich. The Nazis raised eugenic considerations of folk and blood from the status of mere ideology to that of a sociocultural fetish.[9] If this were not the case, they would not have created a whole network of programs, besides the death camps, aimed at manipulating the genetic character of the German population. These included breeding centers (the *Lebensborn* program) where selected representatives of the ideal Aryan type came together solely for the purpose of conceiving children;[10] a compulsory sterilization program for those who were feebleminded or judged to be otherwise genetically undesirable; and, most important from our present perspective, euthanasia centers where mental or physical incurables who were judged to be both a drain on the resources of the state and a stain on the biological quality of its population were simply murdered.

The euthanasia program is of particular importance partly because, in conjunction with the breeding and sterilization efforts, it reveals how serious the Nazi leaders were about putting their eugenic philosophy into practice. Despite the fact that it was not primarily a racially defined program of administered death, it contained many of the same elements that would later appear in the Holocaust.

It is a matter of record that, beginning in September 1939 with an implementation order from Hitler, several killing centers were organized to dispose of mentally deranged and retarded individuals. In principle, of course, the idea of euthanasia or mercy killing is not new, and may be acceptable to many of us who can imagine that a quick death is better than a prolongation of life in conditions of total dependency or unrelievable pain. But while the Nazi program may have had such a rationale attached to it initially, it was not voluntary, and it quickly turned into an indiscriminate method for cleaning out the back wards in various medical institutions.

From the very beginning, the program was supposed to be carried out in great secrecy. Transportation of the victims to the killing sites was done in the guise of movement to centralized treatment facilities. And the relatives of victims were sent death notices certifying natural causes—the standard ones being heart failure or pneumonia. In this respect, some primary features of the Holocaust are apparent: secret operation orders and plausible cover stories concealing the real purpose of the death machinery.[11]

The most striking parallel, however, concerns methods of killing and disposing of the dead. Such procedures as shooting and lethal injections were tried but proved inefficient. According to Poliakov's description of the first gas chambers, it seems plain that they were a prototype for the much larger installations used later at places like Auschwitz and Treblinka:

> The method they devised was asphyxiation by carbon monoxide gas. The installations this required were simple—the euthanasia stations had a relatively insignificant "production." In each institution, there was a hermetically sealed room camouflaged as a shower into which pipes passed that were connected to cylinders of carbon monoxide gas. Patients were generally rendered somnolent by being given morphine, scopolamine injections or narcotic tablets before being taken in groups of ten to the gas chamber.[12]

In its own short life—by the middle of 1941 the euthanasia program had ceased to exist on an important scale for reasons mentioned below—approximately seventy thousand persons, including mongoloids, mental defectives, schizophrenics, and tubercular persons, were eliminated from the German population. While the program was going on, another parallel to the Holocaust emerged when it became clear that perfect secrecy was impossible. Despite the threat of severe punishment, some of those operating the program let word of it leak out. The inhabitants of areas near the killing facilities also became aware of what was going on when shipments of victims passed through local railway facilities and heavy smoke with a peculiar odor appeared in the neighborhood soon afterward. And it was, after all, one-way traffic. Consequently, when people began to raise questions after receiving unexpected death notices concerning close relatives, it was not difficult for influential clergymen, physicians, and lawyers to learn the truth.

The whole matter became a cause célèbre in August 1941, when the bishop of Münster courageously attacked the program from his pulpit. Earlier that summer, certain law and church authorities had submitted formal private complaints to government officials, but were ignored. Apparently impressed by the public outcry in August and feeling reluctant or unable to impose a strong repression, Hitler quietly let the euthanasia program be terminated.

The question arises whether a few years later, when there was equal if not greater public knowledge of the death camps, a similar public outcry might have been effective. There is no way to answer this because the situation was drastically changed by 1943. For one thing, the general population was by this time much more used to the idea of large-scale death, and for another, Nazi control over all German institutions, including the church, was much increased. The whole apparatus and climate of repression was simply of a greater order of magnitude than in 1940–1941. Those who considered public protest did not protest because by this time they were convinced that any such action would only lead to their speedy arrest and probable death.

The euthanasia program seems especially significant for at least two reasons. First, viewed with other Nazi efforts to actualize their eugenic principles, it shows that they took their rationalized racial purification policies very seriously. So much so, in fact, that these policies were first applied in practice by systematically killing Germans, not Jews. Second, the euthanasia program could not have failed to serve as a model for the later Holocaust. Some direct evidence for this point involves the reassignment of key personnel from the euthanasia program to the death camps.

Conceptually, the origins of the death camps may be traced to more remote sources than the particular eugenic ideals adopted by the Nazis. These ideals had emerged from the nineteenth-century eugenics movement, an offshoot of "social Darwinism," and the racist ideas characterizing this movement had impact throughout Europe and America. One need only consider, in this connection, many scientific studies of the time purporting to demonstrate the inferiority of Africans and Asians to Caucasians, and the specific ways in which the American immigration laws of 1921 and 1924 excluded Asians and subdivided Caucasians according to their presumed genetic desirability, in order to appreciate the prevalence of scientifically supported racist social policies.

This type of in-depth analysis of the scientific-intellectual roots of National Socialist ideology is readily available in other sources, however. It is enough to mention here that ideas of racial improvement or "purification" did not originate with the Nazis. Nor were they the first to extend the logic of racist thinking into politics. But they were the first to expand the politics of racism into a Draconian social policy which led, finally, to the Holocaust.

The dehumanized quality of the Holocaust, therefore, can be traced to the abstract, rationalized racial ideas that lay beneath much of the Nazi social program. Having assimilated into their ideology conceptual schema denying their victims full status as human beings and portraying them instead as the carriers of biological pollution, the high Nazis responsible for the death camps were able to construe their activities not as a wholesale slaughter of innocents, but as a heroic purging of bad genes from the population of Europe.

## The Concept of Historical Crisis

Ever since it occurred, the Holocaust has been a terrible, frightening enigma, an open wound in the body of Western culture, because it has stubbornly resisted definition and explanation according to commonly accepted standards of meaning. One proof of this is that Dwight Macdonald's questions, quoted at the beginning of this chapter, are as challenging today as when he first raised them in 1945. Another is that as succeeding generations of sensitive young people come of age in our society and "discover" the Holocaust, their reactions are always the same. Their questions—How are such things possible?—are always predictable, and the answers they find available are always inadequate, conveying little besides the warning that the human condition can be more terrible than they ever imagined.

In the face of these realities, which have persisted despite strenuous scholarly and intellectual efforts to the contrary, it must finally be concluded that the Holocaust will never be assimilated—given substantial meaning—in terms of the familiar, normative thought structures provided by Western history and culture. Reduced to its essentials, the problem here involves a gross disharmony or imbalance between the historical substance to be explained and the cultural forms available for its explanation. It is a problem of epistemology: one cannot measure pain with a ruler, or the temperature of a blast furnace with a fever thermometer.

Viewed in this context, the naive, how-are-such-things-possible questions most people ask about the Holocaust are ultimately correct, for according to the fundamental tenets of Western civilization, such things are not possible. This is crucially important. Practically no one can believe Auschwitz—let alone the full scope of the Nazi genocide program —unless in one form or another they see it with their own eyes. But many who did see it with their own eyes while it was happening have testified time and time again that they could not believe what they were seeing; their eyes could accept the images as real but their minds could not.

It is on the basis of these philosophical and psychological considerations, as well as the more conventional historical and psychosocial evidence for the uniqueness of the Holocaust, that elaboration of the concept of historical crisis becomes a fundamental necessity.

Formal use of the term "historical crisis" is usually reserved for extraordinary events such as the French Revolution of 1789. More concretely, it may be said that a crisis has occurred when events make such a profound impact on the way people think about themselves and the world around them that the apparent continuity of their history seems drastically and permanently changed. In the lives of individuals, such events are usually called life crises; when they happen to whole societies or civilizations, they must be recognized as historical crises. Moreover, like a personal life crisis, a historical crisis is compounded of events or situations which render accumulated past experience or learning quite irrelevant. In many respects, the effect of historical crisis is to turn the world upside down, as Dwight Macdonald indicated when he suggested that in post-Holocaust society, it was not those who break the law but those most obedient to the law who would be the greatest threat to humanity.[13]

Societies facing historical crises are usually thrown into a period of chaos until they can replace their traditional but now ineffective modes of conduct with new, more appropriate modes. It is, therefore, possible to define a historical crisis as involving any new situation of sufficient impact or magnitude to require serious, wide, and comparatively rapid changes in the normative behavior of a society. If these normative changes are at least minimally effective, they tend to become institutionalized as relatively fixed patterns of thought and action which resist serious change until another crisis situation occurs.

In addition to analogies based on obvious similarities between individual life crises and historical crises, however, there is a very important distinction to be made between them. When an individual, or a family, or even a corporation faces a crisis, the larger institutions of society will usually offer some ready-made guidelines for change in a more adaptive direction. There are available bankruptcy courts for failed corporations and counseling or psychiatry for failed personal lives. But when a society faces crisis, all of its routine internal guidance mechanisms—institutions of law and religion and education—become virtually useless; otherwise there would be no crisis.

Another specific aspect of historical crisis is that after it has happened the world appears in principle significantly different from what it was before. For example, the Protestant Reformation was a historical crisis not only because of the turmoil and conflict associated with it, but because of the new principle that human beings could and should define their relationship to God directly without an intermediary. And the French Revolution was a crisis because the principle that the king's legitimacy derived from God was replaced by the idea that people of a common nationality form a basic political unity having the right to govern itself and to overthrow authorities that do not express its general will.

Like individual life crises, historical crises may develop along different lines. Thus, it seems clear that crises may be primarily economic, like the Irish potato famine or the Great Depression; they may be sociopolitical, like the French Revolution; or they may be ecological, resulting from natural disasters or human alterations of the environment. In this latter connection, the anthropologist Peter Farb has described the arrival of the horse on the American continent as posing an important challenge to various Indian societies.[14] Most of them conceptualized horses as a valuable new form of transportation, integrated them into their way of life according to this primary function, and experienced a period of material and cultural growth. Others, however, saw the horse only as something new to eat and soon went into decline.

Large-scale social reactions to unique events obviously vary a great deal depending upon the event and the historical context in which it occurs, but in most cases scholars agree on the following general rule: people tend to look at the new in terms of the old, the present in terms of the past. The American Indians who first encountered steam locomotives called them "iron horses." Anthropologists note that in Africa, after tribes have their initial, serious contacts with the physical and social products of European civilization, there is a sharp rise in the practice of magic and witchcraft.

It is, therefore, generally accepted that superstition and anthropomorphism dominate the behavior of primitive people facing historical crises. But while this is easy enough for most of us to grasp when it is viewed from a remote historical or cultural vantage point, similar understanding is harder to achieve when crises occur closer to home.

As World War I recedes into the past, for example, analyses by historians and behavioral scientists show that the political and military leaders of 1914–1918 were essentially caught in a crisis of warfare. They did not understand that social and technological changes had created new conditions that made their past experience largely irrelevant. The result of their efforts to persevere in the present according to understandings of the past was a stalemate leading to mutual exhaustion, which ended only when one side acquired a new source of energy through the American commitment. Yet it has taken a long time for scholars to recognize this.

The historiography of World War I suggests still another general proposition concerning historical crises. Just as self-protective psychological mechanisms seem to prevent individuals from recognizing their own psychopathology, similar mechanisms apparently operate to prevent whole societies from recognizing their collective crises. The conventional literature on World War I suggests that the four-year stalemate occurred because of poor leadership. The military and political leaders of the time appear for the most part as essentially stupid, self-righteous, stubborn, aggressive, self-seeking, and shortsighted. The common view seems to be that were it not for these salient features of human nature, the war would probably not have begun. Or, once begun, it would not have lasted so long. Or, once ended, it would not have led to arrangements well suited to generate a second round twenty years later.

What can be made of such interpretations? The available evidence does indeed support judgments of stupidity, cupidity, neurosis, and all the rest. But even if these inferences can be justified by the day-by-day evidence, this does not mean that they must be accepted as definitive in a larger context. If our grasp of human history is to advance, it is necessary to get beyond conclusions based chiefly on the notion of human fallibility and frailty.

One way to do this is by recognizing that the war represented an industrial-technological historical crisis, and that obtuse, wrongheaded conduct is not unusual in the face of such crises. The war itself arose partly as a result of technological and socioeconomic innovations hardly understood by those who created them. Although the conduct of the war generally followed a narrow, repetitive pattern, this was less a matter of incomprehensible stupidity than of an entirely comprehensible belief in the validity of past experience and obsolete traditions, coupled with an equally naive if less extensive belief in science.

The naiveté in question was analogous to superstitious reactions in primitive societies, and was demonstrated in both the technical-military and socioeconomic spheres of activity. In the former, for example, the tank was seen as no more than iron cavalry; truck columns as no more than wagon trains; airplanes as mobile balloons and, later on, as airborne artillery. In the latter area, failures in understanding the socioeconomic implications of mass conscript armies and the mobilization of civilian populations necessary to support them were associated with the belief that peace would mean little more than a return to prewar conditions.

What happened, of course, was that systems of warfare and social organization had been irrevocably changed. These changes were accompanied by equally irrevocable changes in modal forms of conduct after the war as people at all levels of Western society began to think differently about themselves and the world than they had before. The era of mass social movements with charismatic leaders and programmatic political ideologies was to be formed on this foundation.

Applied to the Holocaust, the concept of historical crisis can as yet only be suggested rather than demonstrated, although the main thrust of the succeeding chapters is to show how the relevant cultural, historical, and psychosocial dimensions converge to require a crisis interpretation. Our thesis is that the Holocaust has been the major historical crisis of the twentieth century—a crisis of human behavior and values. If this has not yet been widely acknowledged, it is because the consequences of such a crisis—unlike economic, political, and ecological crises—tend to be impalpable, especially when they are masked by a language that seems unable to express them and a public rhetoric that seems unwilling to try. But these are matters that must await discussion in the concluding chapter, after diverse substantive material has been exposed to critical examination.

# Chapter II

# *Why Germany?*

The question is fundamental: Why, of all the countries in Europe where Jews have been the traditional victims of oppression, was it Germany alone that became the agent of an unparalleled genocide program against them? And since other categories of people were also destroyed in the death camps, it would be more accurate to ask: Why was it that systematic racial murder became a national policy in Germany and nowhere else?

One familiar response prevalent among Germans and non-Germans alike is denial. "It wasn't Germany, it was the Nazis! It wasn't even all the Nazis! Many just went along with anti-Semitism and racism because it was expected, and many Jews *were* communists. Really, it was only some of the high leaders and the SS who were responsible. Even among the SS, most of the youngsters joined up out of patriotism; out of enthusiasm. And for those who finally had to work in the death camps, it was terribly hard. They didn't volunteer for it, and they didn't enjoy it, but they had to follow orders."

The separate elements making up this line of exculpatory rationalization are by no means entirely false, although it has (quite properly in our view) been a matter for cynical humor ever since the victorious allied authorities first encountered it in 1945. Millions systematically killed and only a few thousand "war criminals" are to blame?

Estimates of the number of persons actually brought to trial as German war criminals vary a great deal. The Nuremberg war crimes tribunal began with a list of five thousand cases, out of which only two hundred and ten were tried. Each of the allied armies of occupation in Germany, however, conducted their own trials of military war criminals. The U.S. Army, for example, had an inventory of thirty-nine hundred cases from which five hundred were prosecuted. There were also war crimes trials in the countries that had been occupied by the Germans. Informed scholars now estimate the total number put on trial—not all were convicted—to be about fifty thousand.[1]

Yet despite its intrinsic interest, and whether it is approached legalistically or moralistically, the concept of national guilt, including the degree to which it was experienced or denied by Germans after World War II, can only obscure analysis of the fundamental question. So far as any judgment of guilt is concerned, the connection between German society and the Holocaust speaks bluntly enough for itself. This is a brutally simple matter. No amount of scholarly work or argument can change the fact that under the direction of its political leadership and with the support of its military, industrial, and human resources, Germany created the Holocaust. The question, therefore, is not whether Germany is responsible, but rather, how did it happen in Germany? Why did it happen? If it is argued that "the Nazis" were to blame, then what made Germany vulnerable to the Nazis? Serious reflection upon these issues invariably leads to consideration of three basic factors.

The first and most general of these factors is culture, the values and social practices making up the essential fabric of German society and distinguishing it from all others. The thesis to be developed here is that beginning as early as the fifteenth century, German culture has been characterized by an accelerating tendency to split private life from public life, private morality from public morality. Historically, moreover, the sociopolitical events that might have altered this pattern were all failures: Germany has never had a successful revolution. The sociopolitical and psychological consequences of this fact permeated all important aspects of German society and were directly related to the success of Nazi ideology.

The second major factor paving the way for Nazism was defeat in World War I and the implications this carried for at least two generations of Germans. No modern European society has ever gone through any experience comparable to what overtook Germany in the years from 1919 to 1933. Perhaps the closest parallel is what happened in the American South after the Civil War. Yet paradoxically, and quite unlike the American South or any other defeated modern society, in Germany the leadership and institutional framework of the military remained intact after their defeat. It is ironic that at a time when it seemed that the historical moment for social democracy had finally arrived in Germany, it transpired instead that partly because of the recalcitrant military, social democracy would only be significant as the doorway to National Socialism.[2]

Finally, the third and most concrete factor contributing to the German creation of death camps was Adolf Hitler. In a general way, of course, it can be debated whether or not Hitler's career should be viewed as a cause or consequence of German history, but in regard to the Holocaust there is nothing to debate because an overwhelming burden of evidence shows that Hitler was the major force behind it.[3] The origins of his anti-Semitism have been thoroughly investigated in recent psychobiographies and need not be a primary focus of discussion here. What demands close attention, however, was his uncanny ability to generate mass enthusiasm and manipulate influential people from all levels of German society. Yet it must be acknowledged that Hitler remains a hermeneutical dilemma; it cannot be claimed that he embodied all of German society, but it cannot be denied that he was an authentic voice expressing the dark side of German society.

## German Culture

Even in relatively benign circumstances, it is difficult to show how a historically evolving culture, with all its many facets and inevitable contradictions, can be related to any specific national activity or event. One might argue, for example, that the popularity of football in America is the expression of a cultural tradition glorifying violent, aggressive action, and yet be brought up short by the fact that football is hemmed in by all sorts of rules and regulations impeding violence, and that other less popular sports (rugby, lacrosse, hockey) are more violent. Cultural analysis, in short, is no simple matter. The idea that a culture popularly characterized by such giants as Luther, Kant, Goethe, and Mann, among others, should be completely dissociated from the book-burning Nazis is easy enough to understand. Those who perceive culture in relatively abstract, elitist terms see the Nazis only as a terrible, unfortunate manifestation of barbarism, a primitive anticulture phenomenon.

A more sophisticated, scholarly case for the separation of Germanic cultural traditions from the Nazis was produced by German historians in the years immediately following World War II. Working independently in the academic tradition known as historicism, Friedrich Meinecke and Gerhard Ritter both suggested that the Nazis were essentially a fluke or "accident" of history.[4] Meinecke in particular concluded that it was only through chance circumstances in the fragile structure of Weimar parliamentary democracy that the Nazis were able to attain national power. In many respects, the thrust of his work was to indict parliamentary government—which was, after all, an alien presence in the German political tradition—rather more seriously than the Nazis themselves. For his part, Ritter traced the origins of National Socialism to the French Revolution, arguing that Hitler's movement was un-Germanic, an offshoot of the European drive toward mass democracy which had no indigenous cultural roots in Germany. Both authors portray the Nazis as an aberration to be sharply differentiated from the genuinely German political tradition of lawful authoritarianism. This line of interpretation, beloved of conservative traditionalists who considered Hitler an upstart, celebrates Bismarckian Germany as the cultural ideal and leads quite directly to the popular psychological critique of German culture.

The psychological interpretation linking traditional German culture to Nazism is based on the premise that political behavior may be understood as a manifestation of personality structure. The theme elaborated by many psychohistorians is that Hitler's political style, as well as his program, spoke directly to the emotional needs of most Germans. Since most Germans were raised in accord with traditional authoritarian childrearing practices and educated in authoritarian school systems to take on adult roles in an authoritarian, i.e., Bismarckian, society, they were naturally uncomfortable and antagonistic toward anything except authoritarian political leadership. And when the *paterfamilias* mode of authority represented by Bismarck, the Kaiser, and ultimately General von Hindenburg finally failed, most Germans—by this interpretation—fell in with the youth gang mode of authority represented by Hitler. This summary description is oversimplified, but insofar as virtually all psychological interpretations of Nazism are based upon analyses emphasizing the authoritarian character of German childrearing practices, it is essentially accurate.

The heavy emphasis placed on childrearing makes the popular psychological interpretations of Nazism seem relatively superficial and unsatisfactory from the larger standpoint of cultural history. Important as they may be to individuals or generational cohorts, childrearing practices are only one aspect of culture. Although close attention to childrearing can serve many useful purposes, it can also distract attention from longer-term cultural trends. A common failing of most works primarily concerned with the effects of childrearing patterns is that they do not consider the historicocultural causes or sources of childrearing patterns. Instead, the patterns that prevail in the historical moment of interest are taken for granted as givens, and then frequently reified into such catch phrases as "authoritarian" or "permissive."

The extensive historical discussion of culture and individuality in Fromm's *Escape from Freedom*[5] is a conspicuous but only a partial exception to the critique given above. Although Fromm had much to say about the historical origins of modern authoritarianism, he treated the phenomenon itself primarily as a psychic defense mechanism for coping with the "fear of freedom" he postulated as a historically evolved characteristic of Western peoples. Consequently, apart from noting certain parallels between the child in the family, on the one hand, and humanity in historical epochs, on the other, Fromm offers very little substantive material on the origins of authoritarian childrearing.

Wilhelm Reich also made many references to the "authoritarian family" in his *Mass Psychology of Fascism,*[6] but this contained little historical material that was not embroidered into his arguments about sexuality, economics, and ideology. Both Fromm and Reich were generally concerned with cultural history and analysis and produced a number of important ideas that have remained relevant to contemporary social science. But with regard to authoritarianism, their work is so speculative and loosely mixed with matters of ideology that it is hardly useful.[7]

At least one other generic approach deserves mention. It is an extreme, all-inclusive opposite to the too narrow psychological interpretation, and its main theme has been that a romantic cult of irrationality running through the history of modern Germany reached its peak and culminated in the rise of Hitler. This theme has been expressed in such works as Lukács' *The Destruction of Reason,* Kohn's *The Mind of Germany,* and Viereck's *Metapolitics: The*

*Roots of the Nazi Mind.*[8] What these and other studies of the same type have in common, aside from their similar titles, is a protean interpretation of the underlying unity between the diverse intellectual, artistic, and socioeconomic dimensions of German history. This unity is most frequently named "irrationality": a state of mind associated with romantic, nature-loving primitivism, always tending toward authoritarian leadership and invariably contrasted to the more practical, realistic "rationality" supposed to be typical of democratic societies.

Philosophers have decried the irrationality of German philosophy, sociologists have condemned irrationality in German institutions, and artists have testified to its presence in German art. Witness this comment by the musician Bruno Walter: "It must be regretfully admitted that the home of music was at the same time the source of those hateful sentiments whose popularity helped National Socialism gain power."[9] This whole line of interpretation is persuasive enough if one accepts the implicit premise that Western parliamentary democracy is the only rational form of government, or, perhaps more directly relevant, that all forms of thought and expression deviating from the normative definition of rationality are, ipso facto, antidemocratic.[10]

Brought down to the concrete level of individual cases, particularly when applied to the alienated, sensitive youth and certain older intellectuals, the so-called irrationalism seen as permeating German culture undoubtedly does substantially explain some of the appeal of Nazism. But apart from an occasional heuristic value for larger problems, it is not clear how the irrationalism attributed to "the German mind" can contribute very much to understanding Hitler's practical (not to say "rational") successes in Germany and throughout Europe. Despite its elaboration by the more promethean analysts of Nazi Germany, irrationality remains, after all, essentially a value judgment that cannot be tied down to the major events of the Nazi era. It might be different if the Nazis had made war with spells and broomsticks instead of tanks, or tried to kill the Jews with Wagner recordings instead of putting them on trains to Auschwitz. Indeed, it is the absurd *disconnection* between such imagery as tanks and mysticism, railroads and romantic opera—always remembering, furthermore, that German tanks and railroads were second to none—that represents the fundamental paradox of German culture.

### German Ambivalence: The Public-Private Split

At the most general and obvious level of investigation, the task of cultural analysis is to identify consistent, univocal themes characteristic of a society. Where Germany is concerned, one such theme has centered upon the psychological pattern called authoritarianism, and another upon the more global philosophical tendency called irrationalism. Yet insofar as it is apparent that culture is never one-dimensional and all of a piece, analysis must penetrate beyond the modal, single-track themes lying close to the surface and attempt to identify the central core from which these themes emerge. In other words, the dynamics of any given theme cannot be grasped in isolation, but only in terms of its relationship with other themes. If such relationships can be traced through to their various intersects or juncture points, then cultural meanings can be perceived not only in modal social behaviors, but also at their sources in the historical tensions and contradictions that generate all important forms of cultural activity.

Based on this dialectical strategy of culture analysis, it would follow that the themes of irrationality and authoritarianism must be related to one another in terms of the German historical experience. One might argue that such a relationship begins to seem quite plausible if it is accepted that a simple way to cope with a threatening sense of irrationalism is to bury it under the practice of exaggerated authoritarianism. And it must be acknowledged that the anarchic mysticism characterizing early German history—that very same historical material that was later to reappear dressed as art in Wagnerian operas— suggests considerable support for this interpretation.

Yet the romantic irrationalism displayed in the work of Wagner and so many other nineteenth-century German artists and writers reveals at best only one side of German culture. The other side, the side necessary to fill out the dialectic, was present in the opera house as the audience.

It was this constant audience, not only for opera but also for the more readily available romantic art songs, that absorbed endless quantities of romantic-mystical art while at the same time embodying in themselves the rationality, efficiency, hard work, and repression of spontaneous emotionality that gave substance to the metaphors and stereotypes of German national character popular throughout the rest of Europe and America.

There was, moreover, a fundamental, dialectical split between the extreme public rationality and private romantic sentimentality typical of nineteenth- and twentieth-century Germany. It was dialectical because the two conflicting extremes were interpenetrating: each was necessary for the other to exist, and both existed together, whether consciously acknowledged or not, in the individuals, groups, and institutions making up the fabric of German society. All of this may be seen clearly and dramatically in the sharp contrasts between the substance of popular art, architecture, and culture-in-general in pre-1914 Germany, and the mechanistic, intensely rationalistic quality of its industrial-technological enterprises, its school systems, and its central government institutions, such as the bureaucracy and the army. Symbolically, the split can be perfectly represented by the contradiction between the exquisitely detailed sentimentality of the German art song and the cold material factuality of Krupp's steel and Zeiss's lenses. Indeed, there is no parallel to be found anywhere else in Europe or America to this clear separation between extreme private sentimentality, on the one hand, and extreme public rationality, on the other.

Before proceeding to discuss some of the historical roots of the public-private split, however, it is important to emphasize that although much of the relevant material has been cited by other authors in support of such concepts as authoritarianism and irrationalism, the theme we are proposing arises directly out of Holocaust experiences. Thus, its immediate reality was displayed many times by defendants at Nuremberg and later war-criminal trials. In response to massive evidence of inhuman activity, defendants invariably submitted evidence to show that they *were* good human beings: honest, law-abiding, sensitive, and concerned for the well-being of their families and subordinates. When asked how they could reconcile their murderous careers with their self-proclaimed humanism, the reply was almost always puzzlement and surprise: "Ah, that was the war, and obviously one had to do one's duty, no matter how hard."

Time after time, cases would end in an odd atmosphere of mutual bewilderment and skepticism. The judges and prosecutors could not see how the defendants could possibly expect to be believed given the blatant evidence against them ("they must be either fools or madmen, or think we are"); and the defendants could not see how their evidence of good citizenship and personal decency could be ignored ("they talk about justice but are only taking revenge on the losers").

Events like these illustrate precisely what is meant by the public-private split and why it is so essential to cultural analysis of the Holocaust. When the war criminals defended themselves by saying that they were just following orders, they were not lying, and they were not necessarily revealing anything as complex as authoritarianism or irrationalism, although these concepts are not entirely irrelevant. They were simply demonstrating a psychological reality that had grown, through at least a century, to be a pervasive aspect of German character structure, namely, the ability to make a sharp and to our eyes virtually schizophrenic distinction between public and private matters. But any critical inferences about gross psychopathology must be understood primarily as only reflecting the preferences of the distant observer.

Absurd as it may have sounded to others, for example, when Alfred Rosenberg's lawyer at Nuremberg tried to defend his client by arguing that Christian morality requires first and foremost obedience to established authorities, the preference or world view underlying this argument was directly in line with German historical experience. In this connection, Martin Luther's role in the German peasant revolt of 1525 is particularly instructive in that it is so apparently remote from the Holocaust.

Luther argued in his *On the Freedom of the Christian Man* that individual salvation was a purely personal matter, not subject to control from outside authorities. The peasant revolutionaries of the time used his statement as an ideological basis for their movement, but Luther reacted with angry indignation, insisting that in secular matters, the individual owed full obedience to constituted authorities. The whole contretemps was epitomized by his remark that even if captured and sold into slavery by the Turks, a Christian would not have the right to escape because this would deprive his master of his property.[11]

The point of these two examples is that the extraordinary split between the public and private domains of the psyches of many Germans must be grasped as an evolving psychological adaptation to their history, an adaptation which reached its high point in the decade preceding World War I.

Evidence for this interpretation might be detailed by analyses of relevant events, such as the dismal failures in revolutionary action in 1525, 1848, 1918, and 1944 (it is a cliché among many historians that the Germans have no talent for revolution). Brief mention of some salient trends should be sufficient, however. During the eighteenth century, for instance, after secular power had been established throughout Europe and Frederick the Great dominated the future Germany, he defined his philosophy of government with such famous comments as "I am the first servant of the state" and "I am not master to do as I please." This idea lines up closely with Luther's dichotomy between public and private functioning: the state begins to be construed as an organic entity superior to any individual, including the ruler, who must set his own private concerns aside in its favor. In so doing, the ruler also fulfills his duty by establishing a proper norm for everyone else. This attitude is especially noteworthy, because during a time when the Anglo-Americans and French were starting to define the state as the servant of the people, Germans were accepting definitions of the people as servants of the state.

The pattern becomes plainer as one moves forward in time. By the first decades of the nineteenth century, a romanticized conservative philosophy dominated German intellectual thought. Such writers as Stahl and Hegel treated the state (metaphorically, à la Hobbes) as a living organism, suggesting that in at least one dimension—the moral dimension—it could not be understood on a human scale. It was held that the state could not be judged according to conventional moral law, nor could it be made accountable to such law, because as a supraindividual entity, its activities went beyond the scope of ordinary human values.

But these two seminal ideas, that individuals owe service to the state, and that the state is above individual morality, went against the grain of the emerging middle class and helped pave the way for the revolution of 1848.

In Germany, the revolutionary and reformist actions of 1848 were mainly led by the new middle class and inspired by a body of liberal principles suited to their needs. When the revolution failed—partly because of internal wrangling among the leaders and their inability to rouse mass support—the repression that followed effectively eliminated the German middle class from any important role in political life. Consequently, the only force in Germany which might have opposed the notion of service to a state above moral law was crushed.

But the end of the middle class as a significant political factor did not mean the end of the middle class as such; quite the contrary. It grew and prospered as a political castrate. Excluded from genuine participation in government, middle class energies were directed—from our point of view diverted—into industry and the arts.

Nowhere else except in Germany does one find this consuming and widely popular middle class concern with quality technology on the one hand and cheap-jack aesthetics on the other. In this connection, the significance of Wagnerian art was that it encouraged emotional immersion in a primitive world entirely opposed to modern industrial reality. Wagner's world was a place where rational activities were denigrated and daemonic violations of moral law were justified by redemptive love. For example, it is their superior love which justifies the incestuous-adulterous relationship of Siegfried and Sieglinde; it is love that releases the Flying Dutchman from his curse; and it is love that covers the absurdities of Tristan and Isolde with a cloud of sentiment. Moreover, Wagner's villains are characters like Alberich, symbolically a Jew and a capitalist who may be seeking political power.

For the German bourgeoisie, intense, vicarious romanticism of this type seems understandable only as a neurotic counterpart to an overly organized and rationalized reality, a sublimation of political powerlessness. Active participation in political affairs might have provided a mellowing middle ground—a third estate of the mind where opposites could be integrated—but no such ground was available. Instead, the dichotomy between public and private areas of responsibility which began as far back as the sixteenth century hardened into a fixed cultural pattern which made obedience and industriousness the norm for public life, while encouraging indulgence in romantic kitsch as the norm for private life. The general outcome was that sense and sensibility were compartmentalized and insulated from one another; the novels of Hermann Hesse provide an outstanding expression of this phenomenon.

Those who attained discretionary political power as servants of the state encountered a different variation of the same basic dichotomy. The problem—and the eventual German solution—can be put in dramatic focus by examining Bismarck's experience. After going through a deeply felt conversion to the spirit of Christianity, Bismarck confronted the fact that in his public behavior as statesman, he had to violate the moral principles governing his private behavior as a Christian. He reasoned that when acting as servant of the state, a man was not bound by the same morality binding him as an individual. His official duty was to exercise stewardship for the state, and since the state could not be limited by ordinary moral law in the pursuit of its interests, neither could be the individual who was acting as a part of the state.[12] This perfectly rationalized public-private double standard was to become a cardinal principle for all modern bureaucrats, but it went deeper and was more pervasive in Germany than anywhere else.

When traced in outline, the public-private split appears necessarily as a linear sequential development tied to major events in German history. But at the end of the nineteenth century the formal dialectical quality of the split could be seen dramatically in the self-conscious effort of many young people to negate it, and thus to transcend it. Generally known as the German Youth Movement of *Wandervögel* (literally, "rambling birds") and based mainly on romanticized back-to-nature ideals combined with intense personal feelings of comradeship (*Bruderschaft*), the movement was similar in many respects to the hippie life-style or ethic that emerged in America during the 1960s.[13] Most of the young people involved in it, for example, were the best and the brightest children of German middle and upper middle class families. They grew up on Novalis and other romantics: "It is a hard saying, and yet I say it because it is the truth: I can conceive of no people more dismembered than the Germans. You see workmen but no human beings, thinkers but no human beings, priests but no human beings, masters and servants, youths and staid people, but no human beings."[14]

The origin of the movement was quite innocuous. According to Laqueur, in 1896 a poor twenty-one-year-old student at Berlin University named Hermann Hoffman formed a group to study shorthand in a grammar school on the outskirts of Berlin. He began leading this group on occasional hikes into nearby forests. The hiking trips gradually expanded, and finally reached a point where they were more important than the shorthand. By 1899 the group had progressed to a four-week journey through the Bavarian mountains. They had also developed an ethos centering on a rough-and-ready style, with no extraneous comforts and emphasizing a guitar-playing, folk-singing, campfire mystique.

When Hoffman left Berlin in 1899, his role as leader was taken over by a nineteen-year-old named Karl Fisher, who was more enthusiastic, disciplined, and demanding than the founder himself. Fisher increased the number and length of the trips and held more frequent meetings at home. Under his aegis the group adopted a special whistle to identify themselves, a greeting of "hail" (*Heil*), and a sequence of ranks through which members could be promoted.

In 1901 the group became a formal association with a constitution and the name *Wandervögel,* Committee for Schoolboys' Rambles. Local branches of the association were formed in other cities as former members of the original group began to move about the country. These branches consisted of small groups of young people organized around young adult leaders whose personal style or charisma made them effective leaders on the hiking trail and at home. The groups were held together both by their shared feelings of alienation from the adult world and by the continuing sense of *Bruderschaft* they derived from their adventures away from home.

Over the next several years the association grew steadily (eventually it included almost sixty thousand members) and published its own magazine and songbooks. One commentator noted that the general image of the *Wandervögel* was of "longhaired, untidy bacchants . . . who used to wander through the fields and woods strumming on their guitars their collective revolt against bourgeois respectability."[15]

As the organization grew, however, it began to take on a patriotic, nationalist flavor. Rambles through the forests were increasingly justified by claims that through such activities, youth might better come to know and love the true soul of Germany and the roots of its national culture. Spartan routines and quasi-pagan campfire ceremonials were justified as specifics against the corrupting love of comfort typical of the middle class. And running all through the rhetoric was an appeal to the primitive sources of German life—ideas of tribalism, Teutonic chivalry, and spontaneous, nonintellectual forms of action—which could be set against the formal norms of society.

The Youth Movement was initially a rather spontaneous reaction against the stultifying hypocrisy of a society in which private ideals and emotions were kept so sharply separated from public practices that most adults could be plausibly described by and to their own children as "dismembered" beings. The exaggerated glorification of nature and of simple naturalness in human behavior promulgated by the *Wandervögel* can only be interpreted as an attempt to expand and extend personal sensibility in a way that would finally allow feelings to be reintegrated with rationality.

This objective was never achieved; perhaps more important, it was never even seriously formulated or expressed in a programmatic fashion. (When concerned adults asked about their purpose, the youngsters in the movement often replied: "The absence of our program is our program."[16]) Yet the movement turned out to have too many important implications to be dismissed as an insignificant fad or adolescent gesture. And given the general character of German society in this period, the movement could certainly not be seen the way some social scientists later saw the American hippie phenomenon, as resulting from permissive childrearing and educational practices.

Apart from giving dramatic evidence of the depth of the public-private split in German society, the youth movement also expressed at least three stylistic values that were to become a part of Nazi ideology: (1) emphasis upon mystical nationalistic and racial theories; (2) glorification of romantic anti-intellectualism; and (3) idealization of charismatic leadership. This third point is particularly noteworthy because as the "Führer principle," it was to become a central feature of Nazi doctrine. The passionate loyalty that young people in the youth movement gave to their group leaders, who typically took the role of friendly but demanding older brothers, was psychologically very similar to the loyalty that Hitler would later receive from his followers and from most young people in the Nazi state.

## World War I

### Deprivation

It is widely acknowledged by many historians that the peace terms imposed upon Germany at the close of World War I were so impractical and unreasonably punitive as to virtually guarantee that another war would follow. Indeed, at an abstract level, many scholars view the two world wars as essentially the same struggle, two episodes of the same war separated by a twenty-year armistice. The general conditions this state of affairs produced in Germany between 1919 and 1933 were directly related to the rise of Nazism and, subsequently, to the feasibility of the Holocaust.

Among all of the many ruinous effects of the war, however, there were two in particular that have only recently begun to be recognized by psychohistorians as providing the psychosocial foundation for Hitler's climb to power. The first and most obvious of these effects was material deprivation. The victorious allies deprived Germany of its economic and military power and all that went with them, and creation of the Weimar Republic deprived Germany of its traditional form of government: it was left as an authoritarian state stripped of its authority. In this connection, one thinks again of the defeated American South, where night riders began to exercise authority by terror when no legitimate means were available. The Free Corps and assorted bands of bully-boys were a roughly equivalent phenomenon in postwar Germany.

But beyond traditional generalizations concerning material deprivation, contemporary research has been able to identify a traumatic pattern of psychosocial deprivation experienced by a whole generation of German youth during and immediately after the war. Peter Loewenberg's study of this problem, "The Psychohistorical Origins of the Nazi Youth Cohort,"[17] presents carefully detailed evidence showing that the food deprivation, the absence of fathers who later returned in defeat, and the chaotic sociopolitical conditions created unfulfilled psychic needs in the youth and children of 1914–1920. When they faced the threatening uncertainties of economic depression as young adults ten years later, they became the most enthusiastic of Hitler's followers. He offered them exactly the blend of charismatic leadership, violent action, defensive rationalization, mysticism, and oral-aggressive imagery that could reintegrate the unresolved trauma of their wartime childhood, but now placing it in the context of need fulfillment and revenge. In short, Hitler's extraordinary influence upon young people, and many of their elders as well, can be traced to the fact that he served as the instrument for their catharsis.

Hitler's legendary charm, "animal magnetism," "hypnotic eyes"—all often cited as components of his notorious ability to sway individuals in both small groups and mass audiences—have become a serious focus of study for psychohistorians. Binion, for example, has discussed this phenomenon in detail and has concluded that Hitler's charisma was especially potent for Germans because his rhetoric evoked and promised to resolve the unresolved psychosocial traumas endemic to German society, particularly those psychic needs resulting from the effects of World War I.[18]

The precise Freudian arguments for these conclusions are readily available in the sources mentioned above, and the basic premises concerning the effects of traumatic experience are widely enough accepted in the psychiatric community and among informed people generally as to require no further didactic discussion. However, it is instructive to observe that current psychohistorical studies have been able to develop substantial documentary evidence confirming some of the more speculative or intuitive analyses first expressed by an earlier generation of psychohistorical writers. Thus, in the 1942 article "The Legend of Hitler's Childhood," Erik Erikson reviewed material from Hitler's popular autobiography *Mein Kampf* to show how his public version of his childhood was directly related to the developmental psychodynamics typical of most Germans.[19] And Wilhelm Reich, who elaborated the ideas for his *Mass Psychology of Fascism* in the 1930s, concluded that the Nazis succeeded where the Communists failed because the latter ignored the psychological needs that were felt so urgently by so many Germans. Making this point, Reich begins with an excerpt from a political speech by the early Nazi leader Otto Strasser:

*"Your [Marxists'] basic error is that you reject or ridicule soul and mind and that you don't comprehend that which moves everything."* Such were their arguments and exponents of Marxism had no answer. It became more and more clear that their political mass propaganda, dealing as it did solely with the discussion of *objective* socioeconomic processes at a time of crisis . . . did not appeal to anyone other than the minority already enrolled in the Left front.[20]

But if the work of Loewenberg, Binion, and the pioneer psychohistorians of an older generation can now be seen as converging to explain the psychosocial basis of Hitler's extraordinary appeal to so many Germans who came of age in the 1920s and 30s, including his more obvious attractiveness to older rural people and the urban bourgeoisie, it remains to be considered how and why he could also gain the loyalty of many tough war veterans. The earliest Nazis were almost all unhappy veterans who felt betrayed by their government. In later years, it was men like these who rose to middle and upper echelon positions of power in the Nazi state.

## Heroic Nihilism

The German veterans of World War I were, at least twice over, grandly disillusioned men. They were disillusioned first because like so many of the soldiers in all the armies of 1914–18, their romantic ideals about war ("We set out in a rain of flowers to seek the death of heroes"[21]) were shattered by the disgusting realities of life in the trenches. And they were also disillusioned because, unlike the allied veterans who returned to victory parades and reasonably quick integration to civilian society, the Germans returned defeated and feeling betrayed by a society undergoing such hardships that no attention could be spared for them. On the contrary, these veterans were mainly perceived as only one more problem adding to the already excessive burden of urgent tasks facing a fragile caretaker government presiding over a crippled economy. Hence the second disillusionment was the discovery that to have survived the war meant less than nothing.

In the face of this situation, which was permeated throughout by a strong sense of alienation, many of the returned veterans were reluctant to trust anyone who had not shared their experience. And among the various leaders to emerge from their ranks, those who were best able to evoke battlefield ideals of comradeship, perseverance despite intense stress, and a still-strong striving for victory were the most successful. The chief remaining values held by the veterans were those of the war. Their youthful prewar standards of conduct had been destroyed in the trenches. Then, in the chaos and blame following the war, the only alternative values involved radical materialism: either socialism or dog-eat-dog capitalist competition. To adopt either of these alternatives would be to deny the meaning of their wartime experience, which had made personal loyalty and duty to country the sovereign standard. It was in response to appeals emphasizing these ideas that many veterans joined units of the Free Corps.

These paramilitary units were unofficially organized to suppress internal disorders and to fight for the disputed territories claimed by Poland and the new Baltic states. According to the peace terms of 1919, the German army had to be largely disbanded, but in view of the uprisings occurring in various parts of the country, as well as the aggressive actions of Poland in Silesia, stronger military forces were needed. Consequently, an unofficial government policy encouraged the formation of small private armies commanded by former officers with sufficient personal appeal to recruit men and lead them in combat without the authority of official rank or recognition. Veterans found a style of life emphasizing personal courage, loyalty, and even considerable freedom from the control of established political authority. In short, the Free Corps served as an optimum subculture for nurturing the growth of what may be termed "heroic nihilism."

In this general context may be seen a definitive source for the emerging model of the existential hero as one who establishes his identity through adventure and danger experienced in the company of others like himself. Giving loyalty mainly to select leaders rather than abstract causes, and maintaining a faith based on that courage-in-action which can justify any other personal failings, this disillusioned "new man" was bred in the trenches and could be found in paramilitary and elite regular forces throughout postwar Europe. The British had them in the notorious Black and Tans, the French in the Foreign Legion, the Russians in the Kolchak Army, and the Germans in the Free Corps.

On the surface, the keynote to their existence seemed to be violent action as an end in itself, but closer analysis of memoirs and novels produced by writers describing this way of life (T. E. Lawrence, Ernst Jünger, Antoine de Saint-Exupéry) reveals that it was something more than a perverse love of danger. It was a relatively understandable love for a general atmosphere which allowed individuals to affirm themselves vis-à-vis fate, God, governments, and all other people who lived their lives in thrall to such abstractions. This "heroic nihilism" was a kind of antivalue value system, which can be better understood by reading de Sade and Nietzsche than social science studies of alienation. *Thus Spake Zarathustra* is illustrative: "Ye say it is the good cause which hath hallowed even war. I say unto you: It is the good war which halloweth every cause."[22] And the novelist Hermann Hesse presented the romantic, antirational aspect of heroic nihilism in the midst of a scene depicting senseless killing:

What we are doing is probably mad, and probably it is good and necessary all the same. It is not a good thing when man overstrains his reason and tries to reduce to rational order matters that are not susceptible of rational treatment. Then there arise ideals such as those of the Americans or of the Bolsheviks. Both are extraordinarily rational, and both lead to a frightful oppression and impoverishment of life, because they simplify it so crudely. The likeness of man, once a high ideal, is in process of becoming a machine-made article. It is for madmen like us, perhaps, to ennoble it again.[23]

The nihilism at issue should not be mistaken for a passing form of semiadolescent alienation, although its surface manifestations may sometimes be interpreted this way. Such phenomena as the death's-head insignia worn by many SS units, the Viva Muerte slogan of Franco's Spanish foreign legion, and the Kill for Peace signs displayed by some American troops in Vietnam are all representative though not necessarily definitive of heroic nihilism.

Whether the idea of heroic nihilism is accepted as a valid theoretical statement or merely as a convenient metaphor, however, the main point is that Hitler's style and rhetoric were directly in line with the deep psychosocial concerns of German veterans. He provided the means for them to focus their alienation from civilian society and their repressed guilt feelings about the lost war in a program of sociopolitical action that was more a matter of life style than of politics. This explains, in good part, the rapid growth of the Nazi paramilitary *Sturmabteilung* (SA; "storm troops"), which was largely composed of veterans.

The most extreme members of the SA were to become the original cadres for the fanatic SS organization. Moreover, the official motto of the SS, *My honor is my loyalty*; the blood oath to Hitler the person rather than to any abstract program; and many of the other mystical trappings that Himmler created for his Nazi elite can be seen as fitting the pattern identified as heroic nihilism.

## Hitler

The third general factor that helps explain the Nazi rise in Germany and the ensuing Holocaust is Hitler himself. Despite the prevailing skepticism about "great man" theories of history, when it comes to Nazi Germany the central role of Adolf Hitler is indisputable.[24]

A wide range of material is usually discussed in relation to this conclusion, but the central theme in most conventional histories is that the political, social, and economic disruptions resulting from the lost war created a cockpit in which all moderate forms of leadership became impossible, and Germany was transformed into a battleground between extremists of the far right and far left. Hitler emerged as the leader of the far right, and attained total power, because despite his neurotic character, he was an intuitive political genius, a clever opportunist who could capitalize on unpredictable events as well as the traditional values and latent and manifest discontents of the German people. Conventional history, therefore, treats Hitler's rise as a fluke made possible by extraordinary conditions. And Hitler himself is recognized as extraordinary insofar as, by a combination of luck, audacity, intuitive shrewdness, and charismatic oratory, he managed to take power. The terrible events that eventually followed as World War II and the Holocaust are then usually attributed to Hitler's accelerating irrationality, since no rational leader, tyrant or otherwise, would have acted as Hitler did.

This sort of general historical conclusion is, for psychohistory, the fundamental problem requiring analysis. As one major psychohistorical writer has argued, "To conclude that a person's conduct—for example, Hitler's orders to kill all the Jews of Europe or his decision to invade the Soviet Union—was 'irrational' should not terminate a discussion; it should rather initiate the most serious inquiry."[25]

Serious inquiries of exactly this type have been going on for several years with results that are now sufficiently clear for brief summary and discussion. The mass destruction of the Jews was Hitler's inspiration and his alone. The accumulated evidence on this point is virtually irrefutable. But how did Hitler come by this inspiration? How was he able to make it come true? Answers to the first question are provided by psychobiographical studies of Hitler's early life which probe the deep emotional sources of his later behavior. The second question involves Hitler's uncanny ability to sway giant audiences and manipulate individuals. In this connection, the sociopsychological character of his relationship with the German people has been a major focus of study.

The main chronological facts of Hitler's life prior to his political career are not in dispute. He was born in Braunau, Austria (1889), to an authoritarian father he later hated and an indulgent mother he adored, raised in lower middle class circumstances in Linz, and early inclined toward the arts, especially painting and architecture. His father died when he was fourteen and his mother four years later. He then moved to Vienna, where he lived on his own in modest but relatively comfortable circumstances, thanks to a small inheritance, an orphan's stipend, and loans from an aunt. Failing to gain entry into art school after two attempts, he adopted a semibohemian life-style, and except for selling occasional paintings and postcard art, allowed his life to drift while preoccupied with romantic, solitary daydreams. In 1913 he moved to Munich and joined the army at the outbreak of war in 1914, which he saw as a heaven-sent means of rescue from obscurity. After four years of hard combat service in which he received two decorations for bravery, he was gassed in 1918, hospitalized, then released and permitted to reenlist for training as an army political instructor. In 1920, out of the army for good, he joined the very small German Workers Party, and was soon in control, having renamed it the National Socialist German Workers Party. From this point onward he was fully involved in political activity. Along with other right-wing groups including General Ludendorff, he attempted a coup d'état or putsch against the Bavarian state government in Munich in 1923. It failed, and he spent the next year in prison, planning a new strategy and writing his memoirs *(Mein Kampf)*. Ten years later he became chancellor of Germany.

Concerning Hitler's hatred of the Jews, the major psychobiographies vary in the emphases they place upon different events, but the following themes are salient.

1. As a teenager in Linz he absorbed a great deal of anti-Semitic literature. (It has been said of Austrians in Linz during this era that their anti-Semitism seemed easier and more natural than even their beer drinking.[26])

2. The death of his mother after painful suffering from breast cancer that was treated by a Jewish physician was a traumatic experience in which the physician took on the ambivalent status of a father figure.

3. During the years in Vienna after his mother's death, and the disappointment of being rejected from art school, he became further immersed in racist, anti-Semitic writings and grandiose fantasies of power.

4. From adolescence onwards, certain ambiguities in his father's genealogy led him to fear that his paternal grandfather might have been a Jew.

5. His treatment as a gas attack casualty in 1918, ten years after his mother's death, reintegrated this trauma, which he now perceived in visionary terms as his beloved motherland Germany dying at the hands of foreigners because she had been corrupted internally by "Jewish poisoners." (Hitler's writings and speeches often portrayed Germany as the loving *mother*land; he apparently identified his father with corrupt, oppressive Austria.)

Bare as it is, this outline of the outstanding psychological facts of Hitler's life up to the time he entered full-time politics is enough to show the steady, potent, frequently threatening, and at least once, with the death of his mother, intensely traumatic Jewish presence in Hitler's consciousness. From early adolescence through the end of his young manhood, Jews or Jewishness (as popularly conceived in anti-Semitic literature) seemed to be either literally or symbolically woven into the pattern of his anxieties and fantasies.

Many of the details of this pattern have been filled in by careful psychobiographical research, and the major studies have interpreted the psychodynamics of Hitler's personality accordingly, using psychoanalytic theory to coordinate his experiences to his behavior. The results are impressive.[27]

Stierlin, for example, attributes Hitler's fierce anti-Semitism directly to the mechanism of displacement, arguing that hatred of his father was shifted over to Jews. They were a socially acceptable "safe" substitute object, and the suspicion that his father might be half Jewish adds to the plausibility of this interpretation. Indirectly, however, Stierlin suggests that Hitler's anti-Semitism was also nurtured by his unconscious status as his mother's "delegate."

This thesis is based on Stierlin's professional psychiatric experience with teenagers and young adults who, he claims, may often act out the fantasies of one or both of their parents. That is, the children serve as surrogates, or delegates, for their parents.

In Hitler's case, Stierlin sees his indulgent mother passing on to her son all of her own repressed hostilities and fantasies of power or revenge (she was treated badly by her husband and by fate as well, since her first three children all died in infancy or childhood). She lavished attention on her surviving boy who could be her one clear object of success and symbolic instrument of power. There is considerable evidence to show that young Hitler's childhood and adolescent fantasies were of grandiose projects in which he, as military leader, master artist, builder, or king, would change and reform society, bringing it toward the simple peasant virtues represented by his idealized mother. Absorbed as he was in anti-Semitic propaganda, it is easy to imagine that he would early identify Jews as corrupters to be cleaned out. And his later fanatic passion on this point becomes comprehensible when the connection between the Jewish physician and his mother's slow, painful death can be seen to provide a substantive basis for his neurotic metaphorical representations of Germany's condition following the war. It is also noteworthy that Hitler frequently spoke of Jews as being a "cancerous growth" in the German body; his choice of political analogies and metaphors in general clearly resonate to what we now know of his mother's death.

Stierlin also appeals to his theory of "delegation" to account for Hitler's extraordinary ability to manipulate the emotions of his German audiences. Briefly, the suggestion is that Hitler acted as the delegate of the German people; he expressed their collective fantasies and repressed desires, and by doing so, earned their intense loyalty.

Like the theoretical arguments offered in support of the thesis that Hitler was his mother's delegate, the idea that he was, in addition, the delegate of the German people also depends upon psychoanalytic interpretations that can hardly be evaluated against any criterion except general plausibility. Insofar as the evidence of Hitler's life does not contradict Stierlin's conclusions, which seem reasonable enough as theoretical speculation, the work must be acknowledged as providing useful insights. On the other hand, informed scholars question whether interpretations based on theories relevant to psychiatric treatment of disturbed or delinquent American teenagers ought to be directly applied to the case of Hitler. Moreover, because the available material on Hitler's mother is relatively thin, conjectures based on her apparent behavior must be treated very cautiously. There is, finally, a perfectly reasonable possibility that Stierlin has got the relationship between Hitler and the German people all wrong. Instead of him acting as their delegate, a persuasive argument may be made that he manipulated them to serve as his delegate, especially where the more fanatic of the young Nazis are concerned.

Standing in sharp contrast to Stierlin's tendency toward loose speculation,

Binion's psychobiographical work on Hitler is very concrete.[28] On the basis of firm and detailed documentary evidence, he maintains that Hitler's anti-Semitism had its emotional roots in the trauma caused by his mother's death. Binion further suggests that the attending Jewish physician may have made an error in treating her but that Hitler repressed his hostility toward the doctor. Later, when the treatment he received as a gas casualty brought on a second trauma which reactivated the first, Hitler linked his mother's death to the German defeat and focused responsibility for both the painful personal and public events of his life upon Jews in general.

Binion explains Hitler's unique ability to influence the German masses as based upon the close analogy between Hitler's individual trauma over the loss of his mother and the German collective trauma over loss of the war. That is, Hitler fused the collective national trauma with his own personal experience. Thus inspired, he knew intuitively what to say to his audiences and how to say it in such a way that he could reach their deeply repressed emotional feelings.

These interpretations bear directly upon the major questions of concern to psychohistorians and follow from very explicit evidence related to the traumatic themes in Hitler's life. Binion's theoretical assumptions are based upon well-established psychiatric knowledge about the effects of traumatic experiences.

Waite has produced a comparatively broad, eclectic psychobiography of Hitler. Although both he and Binion seem to be in fair agreement about the major traumas, Waite differs most specifically by emphasizing Hitler's abnormal sexual development as an important causal factor in his behavior.

It is well known that Hitler's sex life was bizarre. As a young man, he repressed direct sexuality and projected his erotic energy in grandiose fantasies. In his thirties, he was consistently attracted to young, childlike women who clearly resembled his mother. They could, therefore, be more easily dominated than mature women but at the same time serve as a symbolically representative mother figure. Waite's review of the material concerning Hitler's relationships with women makes it quite clear that he had an intense, unusual effect on them, probably because of his odd sexual demands. Just what these were remains a matter of debate, but the fact is that virtually every one of at least several young women who were close to Hitler at one time or another either attempted or succeeded in committing suicide.

The sources of Hitler's sexual peculiarities are generally considered to lie in his unusual relationship with his mother. Her indulgence of him throughout his infancy and childhood, coupled with the obviously unresolved conflict with his father, who died as he entered puberty, is in keeping with many case histories of people with disturbed adult sex lives. Waite goes an important step further, however. Based on a controversial Soviet medical report on Hitler's dead body which showed that he had only one testicle, Waite argues that this condition was responsible for much of Hitler's pathology. Although the condition occurs frequently enough in otherwise normal males to be generally considered a minor anomaly rather than a medical problem since there is no serious loss of sexual potency involved, it can be a source of severe anxiety to teenage boys. The general thrust of Waite's argument is that in Hitler's case, this condition was responsible for his sexual repression and consequent inability to benefit from any normal form of direct sensuality. His intense grandiose ambitions, then, can be seen as an effort to compensate for a basic feeling of inferiority and isolation. In this connection, his irrational hatred of the Jews, with its specific sexual references to Jews as seducers of innocent young German women, also falls into place as a projective defense mechanism.

Waite's view of Hitler's influence over the German people also differs somewhat from the interpretations mentioned earlier. Along with Binion and Stierlin, he says that Hitler instinctively knew how to arouse the latent fears, guilts, and desires of the people because their values and prototypical experiences were literally or symbolically close to his own. But Waite adds that Hitler's diffuse (i.e., unintegrated) identity allowed him to perform as a consummate actor who could deliberately manipulate his behavior to take advantage of circumstances and the desires of his audiences. In short, Hitler was quite aware that he had a genuine dramatic talent for presenting himself as all things to all men. Whether or not this capacity should be attributed to shared trauma with the masses, as Binion's work suggests, or to a diffuse identity structure, as Waite argues, must remain an open question.

Quite obviously, many of the differences between the Hitler psychobiographers cannot easily be reconciled, and it is likely that some will never be resolved. Yet the convergences are, overall, much more significant than the differences. The relevant studies all show that Hitler's career was more closely parallel to that of a charismatic religious leader than of any conventional political leader. His feelings about the Jews in particular had the quality of a religious passion; they were deadly serious convictions intimately associated with crucial events in his life, and it is no exaggeration to suggest that his Jew-hatred was probably the most consistent central dimension in his chaotic personality.

When considered in relation to the other general factors—the cultural tradition of separation between private and public values, and the ruinous effects of World War I—Hitler's role as the essential third force which specifically guided Germany down the road to the Holocaust is unmistakable. Without him, there might well have been a second world war, and there could have been an authoritarian, anti-Semitic regime in Germany, but there could not have been a Holocaust. Without his burning hatred of the Jews to energize this massive death program, and without the instrumental power he attained through the SS organization, there is no important indication that European Jews, Poles, Gypsies, and others would have suffered anything more than their traditional hardships.

Ultimately, then, the answer to the question "why Germany?" can be schematized very simply as a three-factor sequence. First, Germany was culturally vulnerable to authoritarian and romantically anti-intellectual leadership. Second, Germany was pushed into profound political, economic, and social confusion by the consequences of World War I. And third, these conditions nurtured the rise of a fanatic leader who ended by using Germany to actualize his murderous racial hatreds.

Because of its detached, formal quality, this conclusion may seem to offer an easy path toward exoneration of German society from serious responsibility. It does not consider, for example, the concrete reality in which ordinary German people either participated, acquiesced, or closed their eyes to the horrors of the Nazi state. But the thematic problem examined in this chapter is only the beginning, not the end, of our analysis. It provides the very general and therefore rather impersonal and abstract historical and psychosocial considerations that are the necessary framework for the more specific investigations which follow.

# Chapter III

# The SS: A Unique Institution

"I insist on a height of 1.70 metres. I personally select a hundred or two a year and insist on photographs which reveal if there are any Slav or Mongolian characteristics. I particularly want to avoid such types as the members of the 'Soldiers' Councils' of 1918–19, people who looked somewhat comic in our German eyes and often gave the impression of being foreigners. To insure the right spirit of sacrifice I insist on their paying for their own black trousers and boots, which cost forty marks."

Heinrich Himmler, describing the selection of SS recruits in 1937[1]

Captured here in a trivial instance is a perfect illustration of the countless absurdities underlying the basic character of the SS. Only Himmler, operating with his peculiar combination of pseudoscientific, medieval, and petit bourgeois thinking, could unblushingly announce that in addition to the correct genetic endowments, prospective SS men would also have to prove their motivation by paying for their own pants. It is just this sort of thing—bizarre, gratuitous triumphs of bad taste joined with extraordinary power—that make the SS an endlessly fascinating object of study, because by all the accumulated standards of common sociopolitical wisdom, it should never have become anything more than a fringe group of eccentrics and psychopaths.

Intellectually, study of the SS leads one into a bottomless pit of contradictions, a Wonderland in which very few things turn out to be what they seem to be. This is particularly frustrating at the outset, when it is discovered that every apparent step forward toward intelligent explanation ultimately requires two or three steps backward. Thus, almost every generalization about the SS ends up being drowned in so many exceptions and qualifications that logical analysis begins to seem impossible. Strangely enough, however, it is from this confusion that a primary thesis emerges which does make sense: rational study of the SS seems impossible chiefly because the organization was never really based upon consistent principles defining either its structure or its function.

It cannot be studied as one examines government institutions in parliamentary democracies, by tracing their evolution from enabling legislation through executive implementation procedures; nor can it be examined as one might scrutinize a private national or supranational institution, by reviewing its initial statement of purpose and subsequent activity. Instead, since all the important developmental phases of the SS were originally surrounded by secrecy or obscurity—many of the the leaders were themselves never really quite sure what was happening outside their own immediate domains—it is first of all necessary to establish some general principles to serve as guidelines for study.

The two methodological principles that appear appropriate to the subject matter may be called the "Alice in Wonderland" rule, and the "psychiatric model" rule. The former is quite easy to explain: like Alice going through the looking glass, anyone who goes into the world of the SS soon discovers that it is nonsense to search for sense where it does not exist. In a world where the price of pants might be given equal status with arbitrary notions of heredity, and where similar anomalies occurred so frequently as to be typical rather than exceptional, one can make no headway without first relinquishing many conventional notions of sociopolitical causality.

For example, in the ordinary world it may be assumed that people will only be killed if there is some reason for it; in the SS world of the camps, people would not be killed if there was some reason for keeping them alive. The Wonderland principle is illustrated more concretely by the sign that was attached to the main gate of the Dachau concentration camp: *Arbeit Macht Frei* (literally, "work makes free"). Similarly, the accumulated lore of the SS world can be epitomized in such aphorisms as: Security is only found through risk; Medical help is given to those who seem most healthy; Personal identity must be obscured in order to be maintained.

The psychiatric rule for study of the SS is much more complex because it signifies a mode of investigation developed as a means of understanding disturbed or irrational behavior. Yet because of the contradictions, diversity, and absence of unity or integration in the SS, the institution can best be approached as a psychiatrist approaches a schizophrenic patient exhibiting bizarre symptoms—that is, by cautiously examining gross behavior in accord with the limits and pressures defining its historical context, and hence its meaning. The paradoxical nature of all available evidence on the SS, moreover, literally forces the adoption of a psychiatric viewpoint, because aside from theology, psychiatry is the only organized mode of thought suited to the interpretation of active paradox.

## Origins

Although the SS was an extraordinary organization because it became an the SS was not only the primary security and enforcement organization in Germany, it was also policing all other such forces, including much of the military. Consequently, in tracing the history of this institution, one is dealing with the growth of an amorphous creature which never remained long in a stable condition. Instead, having once been established in the body of the Nazi state, it grew like a cancer, expanding steadily until at the very moment of national collapse in 1945, the SS had reached its maximum state of development.

The cancer analogy is particularly appropriate because the SS began in such a small way, virtually as an afterthought in the mind of Adolf Hitler. The name of the organization is in itself evidence of a trivial beginning: *Schutzstaffeln*, "protective squads," indicating the function for which it was created.[2] During the winter of 1922–1923, when Hitler was gaining significant recognition as a political figure and street fighting with leftist groups accompanied many of his public appearances, he decided to form an elite personal bodyguard. It was a small force of men selected for their personal loyalty who could be depended upon to provide him with more efficient protection than the more casual members of the SA (*Sturmabteilung*; "assault details," or "storm troops," as they came to be called).

According to his recollection of this decision in 1942, what he had in mind was a very small organization of men—perhaps twenty in every major city—who could be trusted to perform any duties demanded of them.[3] It would be different from the SA, which already existed as the paramilitary component of Hitler's party. Composed mainly of war veterans who later served in Free Corps units, and led during most of its formativehistory by Ernst Röhm, a former wartime officer and charismatic Free Corps commander, the SA was not particularly reliable and owed personal allegiance more to Röhm than to Hitler. Since Röhm considered himself a political leader as well as a fighter, and since many in the SA thought of it as a private army which might become the national army of Germany, if not the government itself, it was a difficult organization to control. And so the quality of the SA made the idea of the SS even more attractive.

The SS originated in March 1923 when Julius Schreck selected eight men from the SA to become a bodyguard for Hitler under the title *Stabswache*. After an expansion in May of that year the unit participated in the unsuccessful Munich Beer Hall Putsch of November. In 1926 Joseph Berchthold took over command of the SS and at a rally in July of that year Hitler publicly proclaimed the SS as his elite organization. After a dispute in 1927, Berchthold was replaced by Erhard Heiden, who now sported the title *Reichsführer* SS. Heinrich Himmler became *Reichsführer* SS in January 1929 and was to lead this organization until its and his death in 1945.[4]

Himmler apparently was given this position as a political maneuver by Hitler, who needed someone he could trust to keep an eye on the growing SA.

structure. Thereafter, the SS languished for a time under Himmler, who was satisfied during this period to establish himself as a relatively mild-mannered diplomatic member of Hitler's inner circle, and to elaborate a special SS code of racial purity mixed with medieval conceptions of chivalry and honor. The one area of practical action for Himmler was recruiting. Starting with 280 men in 1929, by the end of 1930 the number was up to 400, plus 1,500 part-time members; by 1932 the total was approximately 30,000.

Symbolic of the internal struggle to come, conflict between the SS and SA broke out in Berlin in 1931. The Berlin SA organization had grown strong and independent with the support of the Strasser brothers, Nazi party leaders who took the "socialist" part of national socialist doctrine seriously enough to begin questioning Hitler's views. Always sensitive to critics who might develop an independent power base of their own, and aware that the Strasser brothers were accomplishing this with the Berlin SA, Hitler appointed Kurt Daluege commander of the Berlin SS. Daluege was an early follower who had been the original organizer of the Berlin SA but had then taken a less active role because his job as supervisor of the Berlin municipal garbage dump interfered with full-time politics. When the Strassers took over the Berlin party headquarters, evicting Joseph Goebbels (Hitler's man) from the premises, Daluege led his SS men against the SA, trying to force them out. This effort failed; the police were called in to maintain order, and a legal suit was filed which eventually restored the disputed premises to Hitler's control.

At about the same time, the byzantine political maneuvers so characteristic of the Nazis were such that a new working arrangement was developing between Hitler and the SA. Ernst Röhm, who had left the SA several years earlier in order to take a military advisory post abroad, returned in 1931 and negotiated a new arrangement with Hitler.[5] Röhm was to again serve as national commander of the SA. Apparently as part of their deal, the SS was to be kept subordinate to the SA; this was not very difficult to arrange because Himmler had meanwhile kept the national SS organization out of conflict with the SA.

Thus, Himmler was able to accept Röhm's new position of power without any serious embarrassment. In retrospect, it appears that during this time Himmler wanted above all else to concentrate on building up the SS as a racial and cultural paramilitary elite. To this end, between 1931 and 1934 he acted with deference and mild amity toward Röhm, proclaiming that he accepted the priority of the SA.

For their part, Röhm and the central activists of the SA never seemed to suspect that the black-uniformed SS, led by an inoffensive young man with no combat experience, a former agriculture student and dreamer with Wander-vögel overtones, could possibly constitute a significant threat to their tough SA. Himmler's preoccupation with racial theories, along with his special efforts to recruit the sons of the aristocracy into the SS, must have confirmed the SA view of this organization as being little more than a self-glorifying elite good enough to parade before the public but with no stomach for serious action.

This interpretation is also supported by the stereotyped images of the typical SS and SA man prevalent at the time. The former was a relatively well-educated, athletic, and somewhat romantic young man with an enthusiastic but simple belief in Hitler's leadership. It is noteworthy that after the Nazis attained national power in 1933, the SS began to attract an increasingly large number of well-educated young men, including a surprising number holding doctorates. The economic confusion in Germany during the depression of the early 1930s undoubtedly pushed many of the educated toward the SS, because it appealed to young men trapped by economic circumstances in positions that offered little scope for their energies and no outlets for their ideals. In more general terms, a remarkably durable essay by Erik Erikson suggests why so many young people could eagerly embrace personal loyalty to Hitler as a meaningful ideal. Writing in 1942, Erikson interpreted Hitler's appeal as being analogous to the charismatic attraction that a rebellious older brother may have for younger siblings:

> Psychologists overstress Hitler's father role. Hitler is the adolescent who never even aspired to become a father in any connotation, nor, for that matter, a Kaiser or a president. He does not repeat Napoleon's error. He is the Führer: *a glorified older brother,* who replaces the father, taking over all his prerogatives, without over-identifying with him: he calls his father "old while still a child" and reserves for himself the new position of the one who remains young in possession of supreme power. He is the unbroken adolescent who has chosen a career apart from civilian happiness and "peace"; a gang leader who keeps the boys together by demanding their admiration, by creating terror, and by shrewdly involving them in crimes from which there is no way back.[6]

The young SS recruit, then, was typically (1) someone sophisticated enough to appreciate that traditional state institutions, including the army and organized religion, had failed to prevent the troubles following World War I; (2) physically tough enough to meet the requirements demanded of him; (3) romantic enough to accept authoritarian leadership emanating from a charismatic heroic figure; and (4) egotistical enough to fancy himself as one of a chosen, racially pure elite destined to tear down a corrupt society and put a new one in its place.

The bonds of comradeship were particularly intense and are still described in glowing terms by SS veterans. "We were," said a former concentration camp commander, "Germany's best and hardest. Every single one of us dedicated himself to the others. What held us together was an alliance of comradeship. Not even the bonds of marriage can be stronger. Comradeship was everything. It gave us the mental and physical strength to do what others were too weak to do."[7]

After detailed study of the SS, Tom Segev concluded: "To join the SS was to become part of an elite, an aristocracy, a religious order, a secret society, a gang, an army and a family all at the same time. ... At times the SS was something of a mentality, at times a way of life."[8]

The normative or average SA man of the 1930s was very different. Usually ten or fifteen years older than his SS counterpart, a veteran of the war or the

Free Corps, a family man with roots in his community, he was typically only interested in changing German society so as to obtain a greater share of its wealth for himself. Hitler had a certain charismatic appeal for these men, but not nearly as much as he had for the youth. These old fighters, after all, had seen too many men blown up in the trenches or beaten in back alleys to be swept off their feet by rhetoric. In short, compared with the typically more romantic, younger idealists of the SS, the SA was an organization of middle-aged realists. And while many of them were simply fighters and opportunists, the SA also contained men who were sincere in their belief that a national form of socialism was needed in Germany and who therefore put more trust in the Nazi party programs than in the person of Hitler. In general, then, their questionable loyalty and their capacity for violent action made the SA men loom as a constant source of threat to Hitler's leadership.

### Early Growth: The Identity Crisis of 1934

The first major turning point in the heretofore undramatic life of the SS occurred in June 1934, when it acted as Hitler's personal strike force against the leadership of the SA and other political factions that might have challenged Hitler's authority. The political and psychosocial circumstances leading up to the murder of Röhm and the subsequent domination of the SA by the SS are important not only because they reveal how this relatively small force, commanded by the apparently meek, idealistic Himmler,[9] could suddenly take power from the much larger, tougher SA, but also because the action itself can be seen as prototypical of how the SS would continue its growth in the future. Its impeccable status as Hitler's personal elite guard made it his preferred instrument for action at moments of crisis. As it continued to serve him well time after time, he steadily funneled more resources into it, until the SS finally became the ideal Nazi state within the Nazi state. The performance of the SS in the so-called Röhm putsch of 1934, therefore, apparently established the foundation for its later institutional identity as the personification of Nazi ideals.

The actions against Ernst Röhm and his colleagues grew out of long-standing personal rivalries and doctrinaire conflicts within the Nazi hierarchy. After Hitler became chancellor in 1933, these internal conflicts could no longer be avoided. First, Röhm and the SA leaders were anxious to legitimize their organization at the expense of the army and civilian police. But after allowing the SA to enjoy a period of untrammeled street action by authorizing them to act as police auxiliaries in 1933, Hitler realized that the organization was becoming uncontrollable. Second, the SA had grown to an active 500,000 men, thus giving Röhm the capability to make a revolution of his own. Röhm's public speeches, moreover, threatened further "revolutionary action" at the same time that Hitler was trying to play down the theme of revolution. Third, and perhaps most important, the conservative elements in

Germany—military, industrial, and financial leaders represented by President Hindenburg—were demanding that Hitler curtail the activities of the SA as a condition for their support.

Thus, after becoming chancellor with a promise to Hindenburg that he would maintain the traditional structure of German society, Hitler was forced to choose between the revolutionary national socialism advocated by Röhm and the conservative nationalism sought by the older elites. Under the surface of this straightforward political situation, there were also strong psychological factors operating. To the extent that Hitler truly despised the military-industrial-bureaucratic German establishment and blamed it for the loss of World War I, he was in genuine harmony with the spirit of the SA. But to the extent that he was also a practical politician who desired a new mantle of respectability in order to maintain his national position, he was anxious for the approval and support of those who had formerly held him in contempt. In addition to this fundamental conflict, considerable evidence indicates that Hitler had ambivalent personal feelings about Röhm. On the one hand, he admired him for being a courageous man of action, a charismatic military leader who could inspire other men to loyalty and self-sacrifice. On the other hand, Hitler was apparently repelled by Röhm's notorious homosexuality. Röhm was the heroic nihilist war lover par excellence—so it is not surprising that he provoked mixed feelings of admiration and fearful dislike in Hitler.

By spring 1934 it was clear that Hitler's initial compromise strategy—imposing some curbs on the SA as a means of reassuring the conservatives—had failed. The conservatives were not satisfied and the SA was solidifying behind Röhm's demands for a greater share of the spoils of office. Röhm had already frightened the army leaders by asking for a position in Hitler's cabinet which would allow him to dominate the nation's military policies. A definitive choice could no longer be postponed. Yet any decision to wipe out the SA threat entailed a further danger for Hitler: what source of power could he use against the SA which would be strong enough to accomplish the task and still be relied upon not to turn against him once the SA were under control?

The army generals were bitterly opposed to the SA, and with their disciplined 100,000-man force they might easily arrest key SA leaders before serious resistance could be organized. But the army was also an unreliable instrument. As professional soldiers, the army men were reluctant to soil their hands with a job of domestic repression; the SA was aware of the army opposition and had sources of information about its activities; and, once the army had removed Röhm and the SA, what would prevent it from removing or dominating Hitler and the rest of the Nazi Party? Retrospectively, Hitler's judgment seems quite correct, since the historical evidence shows that along with most of the other conservative elements in German society, many of the ranking army leaders believed that Hitler was only a brief national phenomenon who could be brushed aside once he had served the purpose of destroying the communist-socialist threat.

Aside from the army, the only other significant forces available were the SS and the civilian police apparatus. Himmler had been busy expanding the SS while continuing to make a show of deference to Röhm, but the rivalry between the SS and the SA increased as both organizations conducted raids and arrests and shared in running the early concentration camps. Röhm had meanwhile produced a plan for "democratic" reform of the army, thus frightening the generals still further at the very same time that Himmler and Göring were beginning to view him as their primary competitor. Göring wanted control over the military, but Röhm had a stronger claim and blocked his way; Himmler wanted control over internal security, but Röhm's SA stood in the way here too.

Throughout the latter part of 1933 and the beginning of 1934, all the factors so far noted—Hitler's ambivalence toward Röhm, the army fear of the SA, and Göring's and Himmler's desire to eliminate their chief internal rival for power—combined to generate an extraordinary climate of intrigue. Historical sources vary in their accounts of what went on because the available evidence is both sketchy and unreliable. The main actors in this drama were all past masters at lying to their contemporaries, and retrospective war criminal trial testimony and memoirs are questionable for similar reasons. All accounts agree, however, on the bizarre atmosphere of threat, uncertainty, and violence. Within the Gestapo, for example, it is reported that rival SA and SS squads plotted against one another to such an extent that members of the different factions working in the same office building were afraid to visit the toilet alone. In one extreme incident, the SS guard detachment at a secret concentration camp fired at a police investigating team sent out by Göring.

By spring 1934, as Hitler still wavered in his attitude toward Röhm, Göring and Himmler decided to act. The SS assumed control over the secret state police, the *Geheime Staats-Polizei* (Gestapo), in April, and Reinhard Heydrich, a former naval intelligence officer serving as Himmler's deputy in charge of the Nazi party security bureau (the *Sicherheitsdienst,* or SD), started a systematic campaign to discredit Röhm.[10] While SS units stepped up their combat training, using arms supplied by the army, Heydrich inflated genuine reports indicating SA plans to overthrow Hitler and fabricated further information to this effect. For his part, Himmler complained that SA men had tried to assassinate him because of his loyalty to Hitler.

Hitler reacted to all this information by arranging a private conference with Röhm on June 5, during which Röhm agreed to a drastic reduction in SA activity. It was announced shortly afterward that the entire SA would be furloughed for the month of July and that Röhm himself would leave immediately to take a long rest cure in a sanitarium at Bad Wiessee near Munich.[11] Despite this apparent compromise, time began to run out for Röhm on June 21. A few days earlier, Franz von Papen, the conservative-nationalist vice chancellor, had given a speech attacking the changes in German life being imposed by the SA wing of the Nazi party. Hitler replied defensively in speeches of his own, but on the twenty-first he also conferred with President von Hindenburg and General of the Army von Blomberg, who demanded decisive moves against both Röhm and the "socialist" Gregor Strasser.

At this point, the available evidence is again quite ambiguous: it is known that Blomberg ordered the army to an alert status on the twenty-fourth, canceling all leaves. Heydrich generated a flood of rumors and faked documents indicating an imminent SA attack upon the army, which was believable enough for many army officers to begin keeping loaded weapons handy. Goebbels reported from Berlin that instead of preparing to go on leave, SA units were planning to take over all government buildings. It is also known that Hitler telephoned Röhm requesting a meeting with him and the top SA leadership at Bad Wiessee, which Röhm thought would be the occasion for a genuine reconciliation, although some sources suggest that Hitler set this up in order to capture all the SA leaders in one swoop.

In any case, events moved very quickly. Throughout the twenty-eighth and twenty-ninth, Hitler received a steady stream of either partly or completely false reports from Berlin and Munich emphasizing that the SA was finally moving directly against him. Enraged and resolved on immediate action, he flew from Bonn to the Munich airport at two o'clock on the morning of the thirtieth, where he was met by an army guard detachment and several carloads of SS men and old party comrades. The local SA commander was brought to the airport, stripped of his insignia, and placed under arrest. After arranging for the arrest of other local SA leaders, Hitler drove with his followers in a small column of vehicles to Bad Wiessee. Gun in hand, he went through the pension where Röhm and his cronies were still asleep, routing them from their beds with charges of betrayal. Despite their protestations of innocence, the captives were quickly transported to the Munich jail. Hitler then returned to Munich party headquarters, sent word to Göring in Berlin that he should continue the SA purge, and before taking off by plane for Berlin, he ordered a special SS squad to shoot all the prominent local captives except Röhm.

Together in Berlin, meanwhile, Göring, Himmler, and Heydrich set their previously planned operation in motion. Lists of names—including SA leaders, conservative opponents, radical socialists, and personal enemies—were given to special SS and Gestapo squads formed specifically for this "counterrevolutionary" mission. The squads operated freely for the next three days, killing some of their victims wherever they were found, taking others for one-way rides in the country, and holding many under arrest in police and SS barracks until their execution was approved by higher authority. SS and Gestapo units throughout the country took their cues from Berlin and joined in to eliminate their local opponents.

Hitler officially halted the killings—which he referred to as the "Röhm putsch," and which came to be known more colloquially as the Night of the Long Knives—on July 2. Röhm was finally killed on this date, but only after arguments from Göring and Himmler convinced Hitler that this was necessary. It is not clear whether Hitler wanted Röhm kept alive as a counterforce against the power now shifting toward the army, or whether he was moved by personal feelings for his early revolutionary comrade, but his final decision was that Röhm should be given an opportunity to shoot himself, and then be killed if he refused. In the end, he did refuse and was summarily shot in his Munich cell.

Approximately eighty additional prominent persons perished along with Röhm during the three-day purge. Aside from SA leaders, these victims included the conservative generals von Schleicher and von Bredow, Gregor Strasser, Gustav von Kahr, who had opposed Hitler's putsch in 1923, and two prominent associates of von Papen. The total number of lesser persons killed or kidnapped into concentration camps has never been established, but some estimates run into the thousands. Hitler's subsequent public statements explained that the purge was necessary in order to forestall a broad-front conspiracy against the government by radical and conservative dissidents. On July 3, a law passed by the Reichstag referred to the events of the prior three days as being "justifiable acts of self-defense by the state," thus precluding any judicial investigations of the killings and demonstrating that Hitler could in fact now safely deal with his opponents outside the formal legal structure.[12]

This summary of the Röhm purge should indicate why it stands as a definitive turning point in the life of the SS. By eliminating or coopting the leadership of the SA and placing the remaining membership under the administrative command of the SS, Himmler, aided by Heydrich and supported by Göring, succeeded in reducing the former parent body of the SS to a mere caricature of what it had been. Steps were also taken to transform the SS itself from a loose collection of improvised organizations into a powerful internal security force. The secret police (Gestapo), the party security and intelligence group (SD), the concentration camp guard units (*Totenkopf-verbände*; Death's Head units); and the general service troop battalions (*Verfügungstruppen*, which later became the Waffen SS) were now all officially grouped together under Himmler's direction.

It is ironic that although the SS was later identified primarily with the dreaded concentration camp system and the death camps, its connection with the camps was initially almost a matter of chance. Not long after Hitler had become chancellor, in 1933, the Reichstag passed an enabling law giving the government authority to round up and hold in protective detention all persons suspected of being "subversive elements." To implement this law, which was aimed mainly at communist, socialist, and some Jewish groups, who were all defined by Nazi ideology as subversive, the SA and SS were deputized to act as police auxiliaries. In the state of Prussia alone, approximately twenty-five thousand persons were arrested during March and April 1933. They were held in all sorts of makeshift facilities, including abandoned army barracks, civilian jails, and SA and SS headquarters buildings. The conditions of their captivity were atrocious and soon became something of a public scandal.

When news of apparently indiscriminate murders at the Dachau camp leaked to the public, Himmler had the commander of the camp dismissed and replaced him with Theodore Eicke, a former SA officer who had transferred to the SS and had the reputation of a tough disciplinarian.[13] Utterly ruthless, extremely energetic, and totally devoted to the Nazi ideology, Eicke quickly reorganized Dachau along the lines of a brutal military punishment facility. Within a few months, he turned it into a "model" concentration camp which ran so efficiently that Himmler promoted him early in 1934 and soon after put him in charge of consolidating and reorganizing all of the other camps along the Dachau model. Eicke later participated prominently in the Röhm purge, and was the one selected to kill Röhm. Having earned such perfect SS credentials as a man of action, Eicke became a central figure in SS field operations. He was, successively, architect and overlord of the concentration camp system; commander of the SS Death's Head units; and then trainer and field commander of Waffen SS regiments recruited from among the concentration camp guard detachments and put into frontline combat during the invasion of France in 1940.

Viewed from a more general perspective, however, the most significant thing about the early growth and identity crisis of the SS is its improvisational, chance character. The cold, tough efficiency it demonstrated during both the Röhm purge and the development of the concentration camp system was not the result of careful training or the selection of sadistic psychopaths as key personnel. On the contrary, it is clear that the SS gained its identity as the elite guardian of the Nazi movement because it contained men who first of all were able to prove their total devotion to Hitler by turning on their own former comrades, and secondly, were able to perform difficult, unprecedented tasks, such as running the concentration camps, in a highly disciplined fashion. This is not to say that the brutality of the SS was insignificant, or that its personnel was not deeply indoctrinated with the Nazi ethos. But its brutality was for the most part kept under strict control. Eicke himself enforced this principle when he took over Dachau in 1933 and either punished or dismissed a number of the SA and SS guards who were corrupt or lax in their discipline.

What may be seen, therefore, beneath the popular daemonic imagery which already surrounded the SS by the end of 1934, is the psychosocial reality of a young organization with a core leadership of men who could accept ruthless discipline and operate with ruthless efficiency in service of the ideas personified by Adolf Hitler. Those such as Eicke, who came out of the SA, had to be willing, as most of the SA were not, to subordinate their lives and careers to Hitler's efforts to create a new Germany. And those who joined later were first pledged to and indoctrinated in this purpose and then tested rigorously to make certain that they would carry it out in practice.

In line with the Wonderland premise suggesting that nothing is as it seems to be, it finally becomes apparent that the bedrock identity of the SS formed by the end of 1934 had comparatively little to do with atrocious behavior against revealed enemies of the state such as Jews and communists; these actions could be performed rather easily and many hands were available for the work. There were relatively few, however, even among old Nazi party members, who could be relied upon to act without mercy against ordinary Germans or former comrades, and who could translate the spontaneous brutalities of the concentration camps into a sustained, routine program of deadly repression.

## Growth to Power

With the SA effectively eliminated, the SS entered a period of growth and development which lasted for eight years. During the initial half of this period (1934–1938) three important factors contributed to its success.

As a consequence of the Röhm purge, the public image of the organization and the psychology of its members changed. Along with personal loyalty to Hitler, the SS had earlier symbolized a mixture of romantic Germanic tradition, social change, and quasi-religious ceremonials. But now loyalty to Hitler—even to the point of fratricidal murder—was a matter of demonstrated fact which overshadowed everything else. Hitler confirmed this by providing the SS with full support in all affairs except those which threatened to provoke serious conflict with the army. Thus, by the beginning of 1936 Hitler decreed that the Gestapo branch of the SS was to be an autonomous national entity, subject to no traditional legal supervision. All members of the SS were also placed beyond conventional law: Himmler set up internal "courts of honor" to adjudicate any disputes or accusations involving his men. Among the general public, therefore, the SS were viewed quite literally as Hitler's men, and their black uniforms became a genuine object of fear throughout the country.[14]

The second major factor underlying the growth of the SS was an extraordinary public relations campaign designed to establish it as the elite institution of national socialist Germany. Himmler accomplished this partly through speeches and news stories emphasizing inherently superior racial characteristics as a selection criterion for recruits, but he also offered honorary command ranks, including the right to a uniform, to influential persons in the Nazi party and to members of the traditional ruling classes. Himmler had earlier incorporated the German equestrian associations into the SS, thereby gaining yet another base of support among the aristocracy.

In 1934–1936 the campaign was extended to prominent industrialists who were known as "friends of the *Reichsführer* SS," while larger numbers of common citizens could show their sympathies by becoming "sponsoring members." All of these people had to validate their commitment by making financial contributions in amounts proportionate to their status. The campaign created hundreds of thousands of sympathizers in the general population. If some of them were simply opportunists seeking to protect their interests against government interference, all were good for raising money and many were at least moderately sincere believers. Among the military-age aristocracy, for example, the SS gained numerous recruits who were given preferential assignments. In all these matters of public relations, it may be noted, the Wonderland premise seems perfectly confirmed by the manifest absurdity of the contradictions involved. This deadly, threatening elite—bound in blood to their Führer and following their own law—peddled jobs, hawked honorary commissions, and hustled contributions wherever they could be found.

Yet another important component in the growth of the SS was a rigorous officer training program begun in 1935. Heydrich had earlier organized the first SS leadership school at Bad Toelz in 1932, but it did not become significant until command was given to former army general Paul Hausser three years later.[15] Prior to 1935, moreover, there had been no significant leadership problem: most of those given higher ranks were selected from among the "old fighters," men who had served faithfully before Hitler became chancellor. These men had the usual mixed army-Free Corps background and a loyalty proven in spilled blood. With expansion, however, and the decision to train the general service SS units along stricter military lines, came the need for many new junior officers.

Hausser turned out to be the ideal man for the job. A staff officer in World War I who later resigned from the army to become active in monarchist politics, he was a believer in both the tough Prussian tradition of training and the idea of a superior aristocracy. The former view led him to emphasize iron-hard discipline, while the latter allowed him to share the romantic mystique so important to Himmler. The result was a unique training program combining exercises in total obedience, compulsive attention to detail, dangerous tests of individual courage, and ideological indoctrination—including Himmler's brand of Teutonic elitism as well as standard National Socialist political and racial values.[16] Only after an initial period of testing in this system was the cadet given the privilege of taking the dramatic SS oath of loyalty to Hitler.

The officers produced by this system were far from being simple-minded robots. Instead, they formed a corps of "true believers" who were effective leaders because, in addition to convictions about their own superiority to other men, they felt a common racial bond with their troops and were imbued with a medieval sense of noblesse oblige toward them. Furthermore, since most of these officers had virtually surrendered their sense of personal identity to Hitler and the SS, they were rarely troubled by any of the personal doubts which can divert men from putting total energy into their work.

The expansion of the SS proceeded smoothly all through the later 1930s. In addition to playing at the byzantine politics engaged in by all the top Nazi leaders, Himmler elaborated rituals designed to transform the SS into a quasi-religious order, while Heydrich acted as the perfect executive assistant, supervising day-to-day operations, and Hausser continued to train the troops, organizing a second training school at Brunswick after outgrowing the facilities in Bad Toelz.

As recruits were attracted in larger numbers, rigorous racial selection criteria were followed (an officer candidate needed a pure Aryan family tree dating back to 1750). Young men with aristocratic titles or origins were placed in headquarters assignments or given troop commands; a substantial number of intellectuals, including many with doctorates, as well as doctoral candidates, were attracted to the SD, the security service; and experienced civilian police personnel with appropriate qualifications were absorbed into the Gestapo. The Death's Head concentration camp guards continued under the command of Eicke, but many of the older, original SA types were increasingly out of place in the "new" SS. Those who were clever enough, or had friends in high places, either moved up to better positions or found themselves sinecures. But those who could not adapt themselves to the tight discipline and fanatic zeal now required were quietly eased out.

Himmler and Heydrich also made steady progress toward their goal of putting all important police and internal security functions under SS domination. Insofar as German legal traditions conflicted with the SS drive toward centralized police power, these traditions were circumvented by the promulgation of new government decrees concerning "enemies of the state." With enemies of the state defined to include almost anyone who might be thought of as attempting to thwart the will of the people, and with formal new authority to place such enemies in "preventive detention" (concentration camps) the SS police power was virtually complete. The only important remaining countervailing force was the army, and once again chance events worked in favor of the SS.

Ever since the elimination of Röhm, the army leaders von Blomberg (minister of war) and von Fritsch (commander in chief of the army) had enjoyed warm personal relations with Hitler. As they learned more of his plans for aggressive use of the army, however, both generals became more critical. Hitler began to rely more heavily on the support of Göring and Himmler, who encouraged him to view the SS apparatus as a mechanism for preventing dissident army attitudes from gaining currency among the public. Thus, by the beginning of 1937, in addition to its other functions, the SS was also checking on the army. Such activity became more significant as the army expanded and was reequipped with new weapons, because a stronger army meant a stronger potential threat against Hitler's personal power. And this contradiction became clearer when von Blomberg and von Fritsch tried to discourage Hitler from the planned moves against Austria and Czechoslovakia.

There now occurred another one of those bizarre events so typical of the Nazi regime. During a routine police interrogation, a criminal who made a practice of blackmailing homosexuals indicated that von Fritsch was one of his victims. Himmler obtained the information and took it to Hitler, who called it filth which should be destroyed. But Heydrich retained the material, hoping to use it on some future occasion. Almost two years later, in January 1938, the widower von Blomberg married for the second time, and Hitler attended the ceremony. A few days later, Gestapo officers discovered that the young Madame von Blomberg had a police record as a common prostitute.[17] This time Göring carried the information to Hitler, who reacted with a profound sense of personal betrayal (he had kissed the bride's hand) and a feeling that the army was disgraced. Von Blomberg was pressured into resignation, but the essential question became the choice of his successor. Göring and Himmler now used the old charges against von Fritsch to keep Hitler from appointing him war minister, even though he was the only logical military candidate for the job. (One could not replace a man dismissed for marrying a whore with another man who might be a homosexual.) It therefore appeared that Göring would achieve his ambition to be named war minister, and that Himmler's SS, which had been prevented from expanding to a more significant military role by army opposition, would be allowed to grow much stronger.

Hitler disappointed them. Instead of selecting Göring, he took over the ministry himself, reorganizing it under the new name "High Command of the Armed Forces" (*Oberkommando der Wehrmacht*), and forcing von Fritsch and a number of other senior generals to retire. Consequently, although Göring and Himmler did not gain their objectives in this affair, the army leadership suffered a severe blow to its credibility and was thereafter much more cautious about opposition.

(Some weeks later, when general attention was distracted by the Anschluss with Austria, a high-level army court of inquiry cleared von Fritsch of the homosexuality charge. It seemed that there was indeed a von Fritsch who had been blackmailed for homosexuality, but he was a retired army captain, not the general, and the Gestapo had known this all along.)

### Adaptation to War

When Germany began to function as an active warfare state in 1938–1939—absorbing Austria, occupying Czechoslovakia, and gearing up for the attack on Poland—the SS also began to function as a warfare institution and its character changed again. One major dimension of this change was defined by new security responsibilities. In addition to promulgating the Nazi program in Germany, the SS was now charged with securing control over the newly occupied territories.

In Austria, locally organized SS groups were assimilated to the Reich SS, and efforts were organized to repress political opposition, imprison or kill old enemies of party leaders, and force the emigration of Jews. In Czechoslovakia, the range of SS activities expanded to include a substantial number of clandestine operations. Directed by Heydrich, and administered through the SD, these activities accelerated the Sudetenland crisis and were later instrumental in the occupation of the whole country. Heydrich also organized the notorious Gleiwitz incident, which served as Hitler's justification for invading Poland: one day prior to the German attack, SS men dressed as Polish border troops faked a raid upon the German radio station located near the border town of Gleiwitz.

War also gave Hausser's new men of the armed SS their chance for action.

Attached to the regular army for straight military duty, company and battalion-sized SS units participated in the occupation of Austria and Czechoslovakia, and regimental-sized SS units operated with the army in Poland and France. From such small beginnings, a military shock-troop role emerged as yet another dimension of SS activity.

Among the units assigned to march with the army were small "special detachments" (*Sonderkommandos*) and "task forces" (*Einsatzgruppen*), made up of SD and security police personnel. Their ostensible function was to seize intelligence information and police records, round up troublemakers, and in general serve as advance parties for the larger security organizations to follow. More fundamentally, however, these units were set up to carry out varied forms of dirty work that the army might refuse.

Of all these developments, the military and quasi-military foreign operations were the most significant. While the absolute numbers of SS men involved were relatively small, the psychological impact they created can hardly be exaggerated. To the outside world, including populations in occupied territories, the swift brutal actions which quickly came to be associated with the black uniforms were the hallmark of Nazi terror. And to the majority of home-based SS, who were still pursuing routine domestic duties, the dramatic actions of their frontline colleagues were grounds for serious envy. Citations and promotions were manifestly easier to gain if one were at the front.

Within the SS, therefore, the idea took hold that a man could best prove his courage, loyalty, and all-round worthiness by participating as directly as possible in Hitler's foreign conquests. This idea was at least partially fostered by the general contempt that the army and SS had for one another. All during the earlier growth of the SS, and especially after the outbreak of war, both common SS troops and their officers became increasingly sensitive to army jibes casting doubt on their abilities to perform as "real" soldiers. Hitler himself was apparently sympathetic to this view. His earlier directives to Himmler and statements to army leaders had stipulated that the armed SS were only to serve as internal security troops. But starting in 1939, he steadily approved larger military roles for SS men on grounds that they deserved such opportunities to publicly justify their elite status.

It is not surprising that the armed SS units trained and inspired by such military purists as Paul Hausser and Felix Steiner enthusiastically sought combat duty. A more peculiar result, however, was that many intellectuals concentrated in the SD also felt compelled to seek or accept active service abroad. This led to one of the more bizarre developments in the history of the SS: many of the command positions in the *Einsatzgruppen* organized for the Polish campaign went to "soft," highly educated professionals. And these men, who typically thought of themselves as being above the seamier side of Nazism, now unwittingly became directly involved in the first large-scale murder programs.

Kept secret from all except the innermost circle of Hitler's followers, these programs evolved from the general plan to treat Poland as a German colony. The Polish population was to be reduced to a source of common labor, and the Jews were to be concentrated in specially designated reserves or ghetto provinces. Some of Himmler's more imaginative staff suggested plans for a miniature Jewish state to be controlled by the SS and systematically exploited for the benefit of Germany. There was also talk of setting up an exclusive SS province where retired SS men might settle in the role of warrior-farmers to procreate the new species of Nazi elite. Amid all the fantasies, however, one immediate reality stood out: if the Poles were to be completely subjugated and reduced to the level of colonial natives, then all sources of their cultural identity must be eliminated. And this in turn would require destruction of the Polish intelligentsia.

Consequently, as Heydrich primed the new *Einsatzgruppen* for action, he gave secret verbal orders that Polish lawyers, doctors, businessmen, teachers, landowners, priests, and government officials were to be rounded up and killed. As for the Jews, they were to be terrorized into local provincial ghettos, and then transported out to a few special reserves.

The two programs went forward with a vengeance as Poland was conquered. Although small in numbers (there were five *Einsatzgruppen*, each including approximately one hundred fifty men) the task forces received some help from armed SS units, and, more importantly, found that many Poles were eager to aid in actions against Jews, while many *Volksdeutsche* ("racial Germans") were pleased to join in actions against the Poles. Some of these racial Germans organized their own vigilante groups which were later incorporated into the SS.

The secrecy surrounding all this activity led to considerable confusion among the various occupying authorities. Some of the army generals (most notably Ulex and Blaskowitz) who were in command of the occupation forces were appalled by reports of the SS atrocities. They compiled evidence and accused the SS units of arbitrary, disruptive brutalities which would dishonor the entire Wehrmacht. Similarly, some of the old Nazi party activists who had been awarded military government posts and were responsible for the economic exploitation of Poland found their efforts frustrated by actions of the *Einsatzgruppen*. They too protested but, like the generals, were also ignored.

From a psychiatric perspective, the killing operations in Poland put the SS across a new psychological threshold. Although not all of its members were fully aware of what was going on, the organization per se had now moved far beyond any conventional military or security service functions. From this point onward, the SS was increasingly compelled to invent its own rationale of self-justification. Himmler himself seemed quite aware of this. Addressing an armed SS regiment after their military participation in the campaign against France, he emphasized that a different but no less heroic duty was being performed in Poland: "In many cases it is much easier to go into battle with a company of infantry than it is to suppress an obstructive population of low cultural level or to carry out executions or to haul away people or to evict crying and hysterical women."[18] In this speech he also spoke of the "special toughness" required to shoot or drag away people by the thousands.

At first glance, Himmler's behavior appears illogical: why should he speak of the actions in Poland when they were supposed to be kept secret? And why should he address a fighting unit of what was now called the Waffen SS about the nonfighting activities of rear-echelon task forces controlled by Heydrich through the SD? The answer seems to be that Himmler feared disintegration of his unitary "order" ideal as various branches of the SS expanded and adapted to their diverse wartime activities. By 1941 these activities included internal security, racial affairs, espionage, ownership of industrial enterprises, and military combat. Each of the relevant SS departments had its own organizational superstructure and chief who was responsible to Himmler, but as each grew in size it began to develop its own distinctive character—as might be expected from branch organizations having different functions and, therefore, different priorities, needs, and operating procedures. The branches were, moreover, commanded by ambitious men who competed for power unrestrained by any institutional traditions or conventional moral scruples.

The Waffen SS provides an important case in point. Expanded to form two divisions and one regiment for the 1940 campaign in France, it established a relatively good combat record. In 1941, with the addition of one more division and numerous detachments, many of the Waffen SS commanders began to define themselves increasingly as a pure military elite, different from the regular army and from the rest of the SS as well.

This special identity of the Waffen SS could be justified in many respects, and was taken quite seriously by SS men, including Himmler, who complained about it. Yet recent studies have shown that although Waffen SS units did function primarily in a military role, they also participated in substantial civilian massacres and killing of prisoners as the regular army did not. Moreover, there was a steady interchange of personnel between the Waffen SS and other branches of the SS. Thus, another psychiatric riddle in the odd life of the SS may be seen here, because even though its military branch claimed a separate identity, it remained at the same time, for all practical purposes, an integral part of the larger organization.[19]

In general, then, by 1941 the successful expansion of the SS had generated internal strains and polycentric tendencies which threatened but never destroyed its integrity as a single institution. From this point until the end of the war, however, Himmler kept working against these strains by shifting personnel through different branches, playing department heads off against each other, jealously guarding his special relationship with Hitler, and making direct emotional appeals for unity.

### Doing and Dying: The Death Machine

The final period in the life of the SS (1942–1945) was marked by events strange enough to outstrip any form of literary or psychiatric imagination. For example: (1) As Germany wins military victories, the SS grows in power; as military defeats mount up, the SS grows even more powerful. (2) After the genocide actions have reached massive levels, some SS leaders seek an accommodation with the Jews. (3) While acting as chief custodian of the racial purity ideal, the SS enforces policies emphasizing the inferiority of East Europeans, yet at the same time it recruits Ukrainians and Russians into auxiliary units and argues for their recognition. (4) Originally constituted as an elite composed of handpicked volunteers, the SS is by 1944–1945 hoodwinking and coercing Germans and foreign nationals to join. (5) Despite their blood oath and shared crimes, some SS leaders end by plotting against Hitler.

The chronology of events underlying these contradictions is complex and confusing. Those who commanded various components of the SS were, as usual, working at cross-purposes while they conspired against one another and against other institutions in the Nazi state. However, two important developments combined to set the character of the SS in the final period of its existence.

The first originated in the SS role as guardian of Nazi internal security and racial ideals. Its consequent responsibility for the genocide operation—first in Poland, later in Russia, and later still in the specialized death camps—laid an indelible imprint upon the whole organization.

The second change occurred as the SS assumed a military role, and its fighting units proved to be so successful in combat that even army leaders approved plans for their expansion. This expansion progressed very rapidly (from two divisions and a handful of special units in 1941–1942 to thirty-nine divisions in 1945), but it was done at the cost of intense strain on the leadership and resources of the entire SS.

## The SS Role in Genocide

Hitler's decision to destroy the Jews of Europe only became a real plan of action in the spring of 1941. It apparently grew out of his thinking about the attack on Russia, for it was initially programmed to go into effect as the Wehrmacht occupied Soviet territory. For this reason, it remains questionable whether the genocide policy would have developed as it did if the war had not been extended to Russia.[20] Psychologically, moreover, it is clear that the Nazi leaders felt a greater freedom to turn their rhetoric into reality in Russia than anywhere else.

*Einsatzgruppen* patterned after those which had already operated against the Polish intelligentsia were now organized to follow on the heels of army combat units and destroy the "Jewish origins of Bolshevism." Four battalion-sized killing groups were raised to serve with each of the German armies poised for the invasion. Trained under the direction of Heydrich, who saw to it that the real nature of their mission was not immediately revealed, the groups were composed of men drawn from all components of the SS, including recently absorbed civilian police. They were told that they were going to operate against partisan groups and communist cadres in the occupied areas. A similar explanation was given to the army generals, who were pleased that line troops would not have to be detached for these security duties.

The four men selected to command the *Einsatzgruppen* were equally unaware of their ultimate missions. Arthur Nebe, a lawyer and head of the criminal police in Germany, volunteered as a commander in order to earn a military decoration and gain the good opinion of his chief, Heydrich. Otto Ohlendorf, another lawyer, was the idealistic head of an SD department who irritated many high-level Nazis by reporting upon corrupt government and party practices. He had earlier refused assignments to serve in the East but now accepted to avoid accusations of cowardice. Dr. Otto Rasch was an SD functionary in East Prussia who apparently accepted this new assignment because he thought it would advance his career. And Walter Stahlecker was an "old fighter" who had run afoul of Heydrich and been transferred to the foreign office. He hoped that field duty in the Soviet Union would smooth the way for a return to a position in internal security.

There is no evidence to show that either the commanders or lower-echelon personnel of the killing groups were specially selected brutes or sadists:

> The Jew-liquidators in fact were a curious collection—highly qualified academics, ministerial officials, lawyers and even a Protestant priest and an opera singer. Even among the rank and file, enthusiasm for Heydrich's duty in the East was so small that he had to comb all the Gestapo, Kripo, and SD offices to obtain the necessary personnel. He was even compelled to scratch men out from the *Ordnungspolizei* and Waffen SS; a Berlin Police Battalion was disbanded and distributed by platoons to the individual *Einsatzgruppen*.[21]

During their training, the groups were steadily indoctrinated with racist propaganda identifying Jews as the source of communist ideas and leaders. The commanders received inspirational visits from Heydrich, who gradually exposed more and more of what he expected of them, but who still cloaked his talks in euphemisms and rationalizations.

According to later testimony by Ohlendorf, just prior to the start of the Russian campaign Heydrich passed a verbal order from Hitler to the effect that communist officials, activists, Jews, and gypsies must be regarded as "persons who, by their very existence, endanger the security of the troops and are therefore to be executed without further ado."[22]

All through the summer and fall of 1941, as the Wehrmacht rolled across Russia, the killings proceeded apace, so that by winter the four *Einsatzgruppen* claimed a total body count of almost 500,000. And this figure was attained without benefit of the mass killing techniques soon to be introduced in the death camps. On the contrary, these killing groups murdered their victims in relatively primitive, face-to-face situations.

It was typical for detachments to enter towns and villages immediately behind army assault units. Then, using various subterfuges, they concentrated together as many Jews as possible and set them to work digging the trenches which would serve as their grave. When all was ready, and the immediate area was cordoned off from casual passersby, the shootings would begin. Groups of ten to twenty men, women, and children—often whole families—were counted off, sent forward to stand in the trench, and shot down with automatic weapons. In some of the larger population centers, killings would go on for several days and Waffen SS units were sometimes called upon to provide assistance.

The sheer horror of these actions took its toll on the killers, however. Despite all of the indoctrination, the sensory impact of the activity over-whelmed defensive rationalizations. Grisly dreams involving the sights and sounds of slaughter were the most frequent symptoms reported by the *Einsatzgruppen* personnel. Note the persistent, almost compulsive visual and auditory imagery in the following retrospective statements:

> In this grave lay, among others, an old man with a white beard clutching a cane in his left hand. Since this man . . . showed signs of life, I ordered one of the policemen to kill him. He smilingly replied: I have already shot him seven times in the stomach. He can die on his own now.
>
> One of the men snatched the baby . . . gripped it by the legs and smashed its head. . . . It went off with a bang like a bursting motor tyre. I shall never forget that sound as long as I live.[23]

In reaction, many of the killers turned to heavy drinking or drugs or arranged transfers to different units. Others, such as General Nebe's chauffeur, committed suicide; still others, such as SS General von dem Bach-Zelewski, suffered nervous breakdowns requiring hospital treatment.[24] During a tour of the "front," Himmler himself became ill to the point of collapse after watching two hundred Jews being killed at Minsk. One witness to this scene claimed that as a consequence of his experience, Himmler set in motion plans to find new methods of killing which would be less disturbing to the killers.[25]

Of the four original *Einsatzgruppen* commanders, Stahlecker was the only one to remain long in Russia, where he was killed by partisans in 1942. Ohlendorf stayed for a year before obtaining a transfer to the ministry of economics in Germany. Nebe went on sick leave after five months in Russia and never returned. And Rasch lasted barely four months before going on leave, after which he too contrived to stay in Germany. By the spring of 1942, moreover, similar forms of attrition had also occurred among lower-ranking personnel. The units were not very large to begin with, and after wintering in Russia they were worn down physically as well as psychologically.

But now a large new source of manpower was brought into play. An antipartisan army organized to function as SS auxiliaries was recruited from dissident ethnic groups in Russia. Traditionally anti-Semitic, bitterly anti-communist, and often totally illiterate, the men of this SS private army numbered approximately 200,000 at the end of 1942. For them, counter-guerilla warfare and killing Jews was a natural mixture of duties requiring little encouragement from their SS masters. By the middle of 1942, therefore, mass killing was no longer the exclusive burden of a few small *Einsatz* units.

Simultaneous with the genocide program in Russia, the SS began a different, more carefully organized effort to eliminate Jews in Poland. It was here that the gas chamber technique was first put into operation on a large scale and eventually perfected to such an extent that body disposal became a greater technical problem than killing.

The evolution of the SS system for production-line murder deserves careful study as a story in itself. In order to accomplish quiet liquidation of the millions of Jews concentrated in various Polish ghetto areas, a group of "experts" who had run the euthanasia program in Germany were transferred to Poland. Placed under the orders of SS Brigadier General Odilo Globocnik, the most prominent of the former euthanasia authorities was an SS captain named Christian Wirth. With the help of his expert staff and the powerful support of Globocnik, Wirth established the first of the new model death camps at Chelmno in the fall of 1941. His mission was to liquidate the Jewish ghetto at Lodz.

By December 1941, the operation was in full swing: Jews selected for death were packed into the back of large vans, which then drove from the camp to a nearby forest while carbon monoxide exhaust fumes were pumped into the back. When the vans arrived at previously prepared burial pits, a special *Sonderkommando* composed of other Jewish prisoners unloaded the bodies. Wirth is generally acknowledged to be the originator of this whole scheme, and he is said to have been particularly proud of his innovative use of prisoners to do the heavy, atrocious work of handling bodies.

Clumsy as it was by later standards of killing (the gas vans were fallible instruments requiring frequent maintenance service), the Chelmno operation enhanced Wirth's reputation for expertise sufficiently for Globocnik to put him in charge of a new, larger-scale death camp at Belzec. This was the place designated for elimination of the Jews in the Lublin ghetto, and it was the first camp to employ permanently installed gas chambers. According to a description by Gerstein who visited the camp in 1942, Belzec had gas chambers disguised as communal bath facilities.[26] Ukrainian guards supervised by SS men were able to pack as many as 750 persons into each chamber. Then the doors were locked and fumes from a large diesel engine were circulated through the chambers. When observers peeking through a special window thought all the victims were dead, Wirth's Jewish *Sonderkommando* sorted the bodies, removing rings, gold dental work, and hidden currency or jewels before carting them to burial trenches. The victims' hair and clothing were also saved. All gold, jewels, and currency was supposed to go to the SS treasury, although *Sonderkommando* prisoners were often able to retain some; hair was used to make felt boots and slippers, and the clothing was held for later distribution to slave laborers.

Another visitor to Belzec was Dr. Wilhelm Pfannenstiel, professor of hygiene at the University of Marburg and a lieutenant colonel in the SS. His postwar testimony is an example of the mentality that prevailed among many of the SS "middle management": "I wanted to know in particular if this process of exterminating human beings was accompanied by any acts of cruelty. I found it especially cruel that death did not set in until eighteen minutes had passed." He was also concerned with the SS operating personnel:

> I must say they were not wicked people in themselves, because they visibly suffered under the duty they had to perform. They told me personally that they wanted to be relieved at any cost. . . . I may have said, on that occasion, something to the effect that every one of us must do his job. . . . There can be no question of my having wanted to urge these people on to continue taking part in the killing of thousands more human beings. They had to do that anyway. It must be pointed out here that these SS men were themselves guards who took no part in the killings. The dirty work itself was done by Jews detailed for the purpose (and who, of course, did this because by this means they wanted to save their own lives).[27]

However hard the "duty" of service in the death camps may have been, there was apparently no great difficulty in finding the personnel required for expansion.

Under the overall supervision of Wirth and Globocnik, two additional camps with larger carbon monoxide gas chambers were soon opened at Sobibor and Treblinka. These facilities were used for the Jews of Warsaw, and operated along the same lines as Belzec. The SS officer who commanded Sobibor, and later Treblinka, was Franz Stangl. His story is particularly instructive because, like many others who operated the death camps, he claimed afterward (in 1970, while serving a life sentence in Germany for war crimes) that he had no choice in the matter.

As a civilian police officer, he was inducted into the SS shortly after the Nazis assumed power, and later assigned to administrative work in the euthanasia program. Early in 1942 he was ordered to Poland, where General Globocnik put him in charge of building what he thought would be a supply camp at Sobibor. Upon receipt of orders placing him under the command of Wirth, who was then commander at Belzec, Stangl reported to the Belzec camp and learned the truth: "Oh God, the smell. It was everywhere. Wirth wasn't in his office. I remember, they took me to him . . . he was standing on a hill, next to the pits . . . the pits . . . full . . . they were full. I can't tell you; not hundreds, thousands, thousands, thousands of corpses . . . oh God. That's where Wirth told me—he said that was what Sobibor was for. And that he was putting me officially in charge."[28]

Stangl protested; Wirth ordered. Stangl went to Lublin to protest to Globocnik but was unable to see him and returned to Sobibor. He claims to have considered deserting and rejected it for fear of what might happen to his family. In the end he decided to stay and keep trying for a transfer.

When the camp was nearly completed, in May 1942, Wirth arrived unexpectedly one day and quickly organized the trial gassing of twenty-five Jewish prisoners. From then on, the killing went forward rapidly. Stangl's reaction: "At Sobibor, one could avoid seeing almost all of it—it all happened so far away from the camp-buildings. All I could think of was that I wanted to get out. I schemed and schemed and planned and planned."[29]

To no avail. In July, Globocnik ordered him to take over Treblinka and his attempts to be transferred failed again. While at Treblinka, he said, he avoided direct contact with the killings as much as possible, and only tried to see to it that the operations ran smoothly. When questioned on this point, he explained that he was able to function by compartmentalizing his thinking: since he had no wish to harm the Jews, and the killings were not his fault, he felt no responsibility or guilt, only disgust and horror at being forced to oversee such terrible activities.

When a prisoner revolt forced closing of the camp, Stangl was pleased; he was transferred to Italy, where he became a supply officer working with Italian civilians. He got on so well that at the end of the war some of his Italian friends helped him escape from Allied authorities. From 1951 until his arrest and extradition in 1967 he lived quietly in Brazil with his wife and daughters.

Rudolph Hoess was another otherwise undistinguished but more ambitious SS officer who achieved notoriety as the commander of Auschwitz. It was his inspiration to bring mass murder to new levels of efficiency by employing a cyanide gas (zyklon B) instead of carbon monoxide.[30]

The cyanide compound had earlier been in wide use as a field sanitation disinfectant. Its convenient form—concentrated in crystals which vaporized upon exposure to air—made it particularly effective as a control measure against vermin carriers of epidemic diseases. Testifying at Nuremberg, the former commandant of Auschwitz said that the idea of using zyklon B on humans came to him after he saw it employed to fumigate prisoner quarters during a typhus epidemic. And it has been noted by several writers that the idea of killing Jews with a fumigating agent neatly fitted into Nazi anti-Semitic themes describing Jews as lice.

In September 1941, Hoess tested the new technique by packing six hundred Russian prisoners into a cellar at Auschwitz. After having the windows sealed with earth, he ordered the gas crystals thrown in as the door was barred. It worked well enough to justify an immediate start on construction of underground gas chambers holding up to two thousand persons each.[31] Records show that by the end of 1942, over nine tons of zyklon B had been delivered to Auschwitz.[32] The efficiency of the new killing method was such that body disposal became a serious problem, so in August 1942, plans were drawn for a huge crematorium to be installed near the gas chambers.

Auschwitz quickly became such an impressive model of efficient killing that the Wirth-designed carbon monoxide camps were recognized as obsolete. After rebellions occurred at Sobibor and Treblinka in the fall of 1943, these camps were closed and, along with most of his "expert" staff, Wirth was transferred to the Adriatic area, where he is supposed to have been killed by partisans in 1944.

Although killings continued through the end of the war, it is clear that the basic methodology for the Holocaust was established in Russia and Poland during 1941–1942 by a relatively small number of SS officers assigned to implement the "final solution."

At the end of 1942, the total strength of the SS stood at approximately 250,000 men. They were widely distributed in many, different units and departments. Even if all of the killing operations are taken together, it would seem that at most, only about twenty or thirty thousand SS men could have had direct experience or firsthand knowledge of the genocide program. Considering that their victims could be numbered in the millions by this time, the estimated number of SS men involved seems quite small. But the character of the organization could not fail to be influenced when approximately one out of every ten men in it must have known about murder programs extending beyond all traditions of warfare or social revolution. Combined with the constant flow of Himmler-inspired propaganda about the unique quality of the SS as an institutional "order" dedicated to promulgation of Germanic ideals, knowledge of the extermination programs tended to seal off SS men psychologically from other institutions in Germany. Memoirs and other personal statements from SS officers indicate that they felt on many occasions a greater psychological kinship with Soviet secret police than with their own Wehrmacht or Nazi party colleagues.

This awful and awesome secret of genocide, hardly even discussed among themselves except in a special language of euphemism, was shared by all of the higher-ranking leaders and a good many of the rank and file. It permeated the organization and influenced its reputation to such an extent that by 1944–1945, when a whispered knowledge of the death camps was current throughout Germany, SS recruiters discovered that the parents of many young men would not permit them to enlist.

Another important source of resistance to service in the SS was undoubtedly knowledge of the high casualty rates suffered by its combat units; yet the constant rumors of unspeakable SS atrocities committed both inside and outide the camps were also significant. These unimaginable tales, often the constant rumors of unspeakable SS atrocities committed both inside and outside the camps were also significant. These unimaginable tales, often including sadomasochistic imagery, were later documented ad nauseum in testimony by former prisoners, and help account for the universal fear of the SS in other Germans as well as the later stereotyping of SS camp personnel as psychopathic monsters.

At the same time, however, it is known that (1) the vast majority of victims were killed quickly and impersonally shortly after reaching the death camps; (2) Himmler explicitly warned that men who used their positions to torture or abuse prisoners simply for the pleasure of doing so were "degenerates," unworthy of the high calling of "racial purification"; (3) at various war criminal trials there have frequently been ex-prisoners willing to testify that the accused had shown them a kindness or even saved their lives.

The apparent paradox of SS behavior has been a matter of controversy for many years, and may never be resolved except on a case by case basis. Some useful explanations may be suggested, however, when relevant material is examined from the perspective of contemporary psychiatric knowledge concerning so-called senseless or other paradoxical forms of violence. Such violence is comparatively rare, and perhaps for this reason makes an exaggerated impression, being perceived today, for example, as much more frequent and intense than it really is. This may have occurred to some extent in the camps. According to one qualified medical observer—a physician imprisoned in Auschwitz—by conventional clinical criteria no more than 10 percent of the SS could be considered "abnormal."[33] This observation fits the general trend of testimony by survivors indicating that in most of the camps, there was usually only one, or at most a few, SS men known for their intense outbursts of sadistic cruelty. The others were not always decent persons, but their behavior was at least considered comprehensible by the prisoners.

The accumulating contemporary knowledge of child abuse can also be useful here, because prisoners in the camps were generally reduced to the status of weak, helpless children who remained, nevertheless, a profound source of frustration, anxiety, and guilt for their seemingly all-powerful SS guards.[34] Considering that child battering, gross sexual abuse, severe neglect, and cases of outright child or infant torture persist in our society despite strong negative sanctions, it is not so difficult to conceive how the extreme SS atrocities could have occurred. Psychodynamically, there appears to be a close parallel to child beating, in which the helplessness of the victim provokes more rather than less cruelty. Furthermore, the fact that the SS were free to "prove" the inferiority of their prisoners without any fear of reprisal, knowing that the prisoners were soon to be killed anyway, must have provided a nearly irresistible incentive for those so inclined to release their sadistic impulses in ways that now defy normal imagination.

Clearly, this analysis is not definitive, but it offers some insight into the paradox of SS behavior. If the psychosocial circumstances of child battering can be brought to intelligent interpretation, so too, perhaps, can the actions of the SS. Ironically, there are many more stories of SS kindness to children in the camps than there are of special cruelties, and there is no doubt that most SS would have viewed the cases of child abuse reported in our daily newspapers as utterly scandalous and degenerate.

The death camp killings tapered off somewhat during the last two years of the war, apparently because of a shift in policy advocated by the SS department of economic affairs. Arguing that concentration camp prisoners and the remaining Jews should not be immediately destroyed but rather could be put to use in SS-owned factories or rented out to other industrial enterprises as slave labor, SS economic planners persuaded Himmler to slow down the killing. It was never completely halted, however, because rival leaders in the internal security department kept pressing for completion of the "final solution."

Consequently, by 1945, the genocide program had become chaotic: some elements in the SS wanted to finish off the remaining Jews; others wanted them working in war industries; and still others thought that they might be used as bargaining tokens with the Allied powers. Eichmann testified that he encountered all sorts of obstructions when trying to ship additional Jews to death camps in 1945.

## The Military Role of the SS

The Waffen SS seems to be totally removed from the SS killing operations. From 1941 onward, despite the German manpower shortage, Himmler steadily added men to the SS army by enlisting racial Germans and other Nordic types, mainly volunteers from Holland, Norway, Belgium, and France. More men were found by soliciting volunteers from the SA, transferring concentration camp personnel and ordinary police and replacing them with over-age reservists, and even by forming a special unit (later known as the Dirlewanger Brigade) of convicted criminals.[35]

The overall performance of the SS combat units in Russia was spectacular; they even received public praise from regular army generals. Expansion accelerated accordingly, and by January 1943 there were eleven SS divisions organized into corps with their own headquarters staffs. From its inception, moreover, the Waffen SS was serviced by its own quartermaster and supply organization. This supply infrastructure grew with the proliferation of new field divisions until it constituted a substantial bureaucracy in its own right, with close ties to the SS economics department. The latter organization had gradually obtained direct or indirect control over various armament production facilities and was in a good position to fill the requirements of the burgeoning field units. Therefore, with the birth of corps headquarters and then of army headquarters staffs, the Waffen SS became virtually an independent fighting force.

Himmler managed to continually justify the growth of the Waffen SS throughout the war. At first, with the quick victories over Poland and France, he claimed the necessity for additional troops to control the conquered territories. Later, when military setbacks occurred during the first winter in Russia, he pointed out the excellent performance of his troops. And so, in principle at least, the growth of the SS would seem to have been all but unstoppable, because either victory or defeat offered plausible rationales for further growth.

By 1944, the position of the Wehrmacht vis-à-vis the SS had been sharply eroded. From the field came the voices of hard-pressed army commanders who were glad to have the elite SS divisions assigned to them and were willing to say so in public. At home, the traditional army training and supply branches were no match for the SS when it came to acquiring new war materials. And by this time Hitler had begun to rely upon several of the best SS armored divisions as a strategic "fire brigade," kept in reserve under his orders until he decided where they were most needed.

Along with the rapid material growth of the Waffen SS, there were also profound psychosocial changes. The early units (1940) had been composed of a select, ideologically indoctrinated rank and file led by military zealots such as Felix Steiner and Paul Hausser. Like other unconventional fighting leaders of this century (Orde Windgate, Billy Mitchell, T. E. Lawrence, Otto Skorzeny), these men inspired genuine enthusiasm among their followers, but invariably went against the norms of regular army life. Consequently, the innovative, improvisational atmosphere of the SS was well suited to their talents.

Another important factor making the Waffen SS attractive to both senior and junior officers was the absence of the traditional social class prejudices of the German army officer corps. In the army, a man's name and family origins typically determined the quality of his assignments, the character of his social life after duty hours, and his opportunities for promotion. By contrast, the revolutionary-elite thinking permeating the SS was not only a model of egalitarianism but also neatly matched the ideas of soldiers seeking to organize revolutionary military units.

Finally, the demand for personal loyalty to Hitler did not seem severe to officers who compared it with the hypocrisies of the regular army. If one was, indeed, relatively apolitical, then the Hitler loyalty was easy enough to accept and simulate; and if, like so many of the younger men, one did really believe in National Socialism, then personal loyalty to Hitler seemed quite appropriate.

But because of rapid growth and exposure to heavy combat, all of these conditions began to change drastically by 1943. Casualties took their toll from the hard core of experienced veterans, and the need for cadres in newly formed divisions spread the remainder more and more thinly through the field units.

There was also a change in the men who were moving up to influential officer and NCO positions. After two years in Russia or fighting partisans elsewhere, these men bore little resemblance to the enthusiasts of 1940. The old blood oaths and campfire mysteries were no longer very impressive to them. And despite all the racist indoctrination emphasized by Reichsführer Heinrich Himmler (now often called "Reichsheinie") the veterans were sufficiently impressed by the fighting qualities of Russian troops to abandon doctrinaire racist beliefs. (This development is quite similar to the experience of American soldiers in Vietnam who gained increasing respect for the North Vietnamese after fighting them.) Furthermore, after the disaster at Stalingrad, it was difficult to maintain blind faith in Hitler as an infallible war chief.

The most profound psychological change in the Waffen SS, however, grew out of its reputation as a superior fighting force. Together with an increasing internationalist ideology fostered by the presence of many foreign volunteers and auxiliaries (25 percent of the Waffen force was "racial German" by 1943), their superior military image led many Waffen men to think of themselves as a new Roman legion: a special breed with a special mystique transcending narrow national boundaries and their own parent organization.

Among the higher-ranking leaders, contempt for Himmler increased as the pressures of field duty brought them into a closer, mutually satisfying relationship with Wehrmacht generals. The latter, of course, were also not quite the same as they had been before, and the common experiences of war they shared with the Waffen commanders gradually brought both groups into a new harmony.

In general, therefore, primarily because of its success in the field and its rapid growth, the psychology of the Waffen SS changed drastically from what it had been in 1940. by 1944–1945 the organization had gained a strong ego of its own and a very real measure of autonomy which was maintained and enlarged through the exercise of simple political tactics. If Waffen leaders felt a threat of domination by the army, Himmler could be counted upon to support them; if Himmler threatened to wield his authority too heavily, then the army could provide countervailing support. The fact that Hitler paid special attention to the needs and deployment of key Waffen SS formations made it all the more convenient for the Waffen leadership to extend its independence.

During the last year of the war, friction between the Waffen SS leaders and Himmler and Hitler steadily increased. General Steiner, for example, refused to use the Hitler salute, referred to Himmler as a "sleazy romantic," and publicly criticized Hitler's strategic decisions and racial policies. Himmler was outraged, but aside from writing threatening letters and appealing to Steiner's sense of loyalty, he did nothing. Generals Hausser and Bittrich apparently knew of Rommel's plan to depose Hitler and were at least mildly sympathetic to it. And after the failure of the bomb plot against Hitler's life in 1944, General Dietrich is credited with using his influence to save the life of Hans Speidel, Rommel's chief of staff, who had been correctly identified as an important conspirator and had been arrested by the Gestapo.

Furthermore, although he had the longest and most intensive history of personal loyalty to Hitler, it was Dietrich who committed the ultimate symbolic act of repudiation. Ordered by Hitler to lead the old elite SS divisions against the Russian forces surrounding Budapest in March 1945, Dietrich's attack failed and quickly became a retreat. The retreat continued despite direct orders from Hitler to stand fast. This so enraged Hitler that he ordered the SS divisions, including the *Leibstandarte* Adolf Hitler, to remove their identifying sleeve bands. But Dietrich demonstrated greater loyalty to the men he commanded than to his Führer. He allowed the retreat to continue so that his forces would be able to surrender to the Americans instead of the Russians, and he simply ignored the sleeveband order. According to various sources, after a heavy drinking bout and a visit with his division commanders, he packed up all the decorations he had received from Hitler and returned them.

## Death and Afterlife

Summing up the status of the SS during the final days of the war, Höhne suggests that it had become fragmented into five different factions, three of which actively worked against Hitler.[36] These included, first, the Waffen SS generals (Steiner, Hausser, Dietrich, Bittrich, and others) who were mainly interested in preserving their military reputations and saving their remaining men from the Russians. Second, there was a group centering on Arthur Nebe of the criminal police department that worked with the July bomb-plot conspirators. Third was a group in the SD dominated by Walter Schellenberg, who thought that a negotiated peace might be accomplished if Himmler could be persuaded to remove Hitler. A fourth faction included men like Ohlendorf and Best. Knowing the war was lost, disillusioned with Hitler and Himmler, they waited for the end and tried to salvage their reputations by careful acts of independence or disobedience. A great many middle-rank SS men fit this category and, as one survivor of the extermination camps has remarked, after the war it was almost impossible to find an SS man who could not point out some Jew whose life he had saved.

Finally, there was a fifth group which maintained loyalty to Hitler until the very end. It included such men as Kaltenbrunner, Heinrich Müller, and Eichmann, who were so deeply and directly involved in various murder programs that they had no option except to hope for a last-minute miracle that would keep the Nazi state intact.

It is tempting to speak of this period as the time of the "final solution" for the SS, but this would be false because its apparent death at the end of the war was followed by a strange afterlife. When the Nuremberg tribunal condemned the SS as a criminal organization and serious efforts were made to charge individual SS members with war crimes, the SS veterans developed an escape organization called ODESSA. According to information compiled by Simon Wiesenthal, this acronym stood for *Organisation der SS-Angehörigen* ("organization of SS members"). It was controlled by former SS leaders who financed the escape operations with loot obtained during the war. It is evocative of the Wonderland principle that at the same time (1946–1948) as former SS men were trying to escape from Europe, many Jewish survivors of the SS-run camps were also using undercover methods to escape from Europe to Israel. Wiesenthal was quite sure that their respective escape routes overlapped: "Sometimes the two organizations [ODESSA and Bricha, the Jewish escape apparatus] used the same facilities at the same time. I know a small inn near Merano, in the Italian Tyrol, and another place near the Reschenpass between Austria and Italy, where illegal Nazi transports and illegal Jewish transports sometimes spent the night without knowing of each other's presence."[37]

The SS also achieved legal status in June 1951, with the founding of the veterans organizations called *Hilfsgemeinschaft auf Gegenseitigkeit* (HIAG; Mutual Aid Association). This organization was formed under the auspices of

Otto Kumm, who had commanded the *Leibstandarte* Adolf Hitler division in 1945. The apparent purpose of HIAG was literally mutual aid; since the Waffen SS had been declared criminal along with the other SS branches, neither the surviving veterans nor the dependents of those who died in action or in Russian POW camps (where many Waffen SS prisoners were held for five or more years) could receive pensions or other financial aid which the West German government was providing for Wehrmacht veterans [38]

In general then, instead of going to a final *Gotterdämmerung* in 1945, the SS continued to exist in a dormant state with life breathed into it by killers in hiding (ODESSA) and aggrieved Waffen SS veterans (HIAG). Any analytical summary of the SS must take this postwar afterlife into account because it further emphasizes the tenacious psychosocial vitality of the organization. Whether one looks back to its earliest days as an elite bodyguard, or to its halcyon days as a "state within a state," or even to more contemporary events such as the imitation of SS styles in the dress and behavior of American motorcycle gangs,[39] one sees a species of élan vital which seemingly defies rational explanation.

Perhaps the ultimate psychohistorical truth about the meaning of the SS is this: it was a genuine expression of certain aspects of modern industrial civilization. The fact that it performed actions so atrocious as to dwarf the imagination and intimidate efforts toward understanding has obscured the essential legitimacy of the SS, but it must be recognized as an "authentic" social phenomenon in the same way that R. D. Laing and other psychiatric writers have come to recognize schizophrenia as an authentic individual phenomenon.

It is no contradiction in terms, moreover, to recognize that an organization centered on death can be as existentially authentic as any other. Cancer may be terrible, but it is a genuine aspect of the human condition, and the same may be said of the SS. The organization grew, prospered, and attained an institutional status because it was a viable instrument for actualizing the ideological policies of a modern industrial state.

Psychohistorical analysis of the SS shows that it had much in common with other paramilitary and unconventional military formations of the twentieth century: the British Black and Tans used in Ireland; the French paratroop units used in Algeria; the American Green Beret and CIA units used in Vietnam; the various secret police organizations of the Soviet Union; and sundry smaller "illegals," such as the Palestine Liberation Organization and the Japanese Red Army. Such comparisons have only heuristic value, because the SS far exceeded all the others in size and magnitude of atrocities. But the fact that so many other modern states have had to create their own particular versions of the SS—albeit pale miniatures for the most part—when they have followed policies of severe mass repression offers clear evidence that the SS was not merely an aberration of the Nazi system.

The comparison to other forces organized to carry out repressive policies thought to be beyond the capacity of regular armies or police is also instructive when it comes to the question of personnel. There is apparently no shortage anywhere of men willing to volunteer to serve in special formations with distinctive uniforms and a self-proclaimed elite rationale. Even more important, however, there is an increasing accumulation of social, psychological, and historical evidence indicating that when ordered to do so, otherwise average soldiers, including draftees, will brutalize or kill defenseless people. It bears repetition that the SS *Einsatzgruppen* were not composed of men specially selected for personality traits predisposing them to brutal behavior, any more than were the American infantry soldiers who slaughtered the inhabitants of My Lai in Vietnam.

Speaking more generally, all of the available evidence shows that the psychology of the vast majority of SS men was not characterized by any symptoms of gross pathology. It was apparently based instead upon a personality structure emphasizing obedience in service to heroic ideals and intense loyalty to the group and group leaders embodying these ideals. It should be made clear immediately that the absence of manifest pathology does not mean that the typical SS man was indistinguishable from the average man on the street, only that he was not in any normative psychiatric sense perverted, paranoid, or psychotic. Our judgment is that the overwhelming majority of SS men, leaders as well as rank and file, would have easily passed all the psychiatric tests ordinarily given to American army recruits or Kansas City policemen.

There is no comprehensive file of psychological test data on SS men, yet the indirect evidence shows that their personalities were sufficiently stable and integrated for them to endure situations of normal and even abnormal stress without serious impairment or breakdown. For example, Henry Dicks describes detailed psychiatric interviews he conducted with eight former SS men convicted of atrocious crimes.[40] Not one of these men showed behavior that would ordinarily be deemed sufficient for them to be kept in a mental institution. Moreover, these and many other wanted SS men who have either never been apprehended or else have already served sentences and been released all seem able to function without drawing special attention to themselves in anonymous social circumstances.

Eichmann lived a quiet family life in Argentina for some years prior to his capture by Israeli agents. Franz Stangl did the same in Brazil. And while in command at Auschwitz, Rudolf Hoess traveled back and forth to his family in much the same way as any business commuter. These men all had loving wives and were good to their children. Himmler himself was not only kind to his wife and family but also to his mistress.

The psychiatric paradox emerging from what can be understood about individual personality among SS men—how can "normal" people perform terrible horrors?—is matched by an equivalent sociological paradox concerning the organizational character of the SS. According to all accepted principles of modern organizational sociology and psychology, the inconsistencies, conspiracies, and internal violence of the SS should have yielded stagnation and inefficiency rather than innovative growth. But the SS was not a business or bureaucracy of the type comprehended by contemporary social science. Instead, it was something of a multilevel conglomerate held together by a shared, superordinate ideology. Conventional social science demonstrates that every enduring organization builds up an ethos in the form of an identity and related habit patterns that have to do with self-maintenance apart from efficient functioning. Because of its unique history of rapid growth and personal loyalty to Hitler, however, this type of organizational inertia did not occur within the SS until almost the end of the war. As an organization which required total loyalty from its members, even to the point of demanding formal renunciation of all religion, the SS could operate without the internal inhibitions that are usually present in conventional organizations. There were no serious conflicts of conscience to contend with; no Colonel Blimps cluttering up the administrative machinery; and no time-servers mainly worried about their tenure and pension rights.

In the face of such paradoxical issues—indeed, a whole organizational case history filled with apparent contradictions tending to negate most conventional psychiatric and sociological principles—what conclusions can be drawn from study of the SS? It is, first of all, abundantly clear that ordinary people may be organized to carry out the most ferociously destructive activities human intelligence can contrive. Second, it is clear that apart from a few exceptional efforts to conceptualize organized human destructiveness without appealing to what Thomas Szasz calls "the myth of mental illness," little is known about this subject.[41] Hannah Arendt has discussed the problem of violence at the societal level, but her work is primarily oriented to issues of social policy formulation, authority systems, and reactions to social protest.[42] Frantz Fanon has explored the meaning of personal violence as therapeutic in connection with revolutionary movements, but the material he provides is more appropriate to analysis of individual resistance fighters than to state organizations such as the SS.[43]

Working at the level of group psychology, however, Herbert Kelman has analyzed the modern phenomenon of sanctioned massacres in a way that seems directly relevant to the SS.[44] He argues that moral inhibitions against atrocious violence will be eroded when the violence is authorized (by official orders and highly placed leaders); routinized (by institutional practices and role specifications); and when the victims of the violence are dehumanized (by ideological definitions and indoctrination). Kelman suggests that these three conditions can be recognized as psychosocial processes permitting extreme violence to become a normal or at least normative activity for a group or institution, and scrutiny of the SS appears to confirm this view, although it is obviously limited to the surface description of established SS killing programs. Many other important matters, including the dynamics of SS growth, its extraordinary flexibility, and the energetic dedication of its membership, all of which helped to make it such an effective instrument of mass destruction, remain beyond reach of Kelman's discussion.

Indeed, as a final conclusion or judgmental perspective on the SS it must be said that despite detailed empirical study and theoretical analysis, the organization still stands as something of a modern historical enigma, for there is as yet no better way to epitomize the SS than in romantic, Faustian terms as an organization of men who traded their souls for power, glamour, and a mystique of transcendental superiority. Its organizational life history is so consistently filled with surprises and contradictions to conventional intelligence that the ultimate effect is to push scholarly judgment back toward preenlightenment categories of thought. One begins to see the SS, then, as a technical-industrial embodiment of pure evil, an evil made doubly potent by the fact that its human instruments were not conspicuously different from other men.

# Chapter IV

# *Victims: The Fallacy of Innocence*

Jews have been the preeminent historical victims of Western civilization. It is a striking and brutally simple fact that wherever one looks in the larger sweep of European history, there one will find either a waxing or waning persecution of Jews.[1] This historical continuity is so singular that a sufficiently distant and emotionally detached observer might easily conclude that along with warfare and the domination of nature, the general purpose of Western civilization must have included persecution of the Jews.[2] In this connection, the Holocaust is exemplary, showing that it was left to the scientifically most advanced Western nation to attempt the total destruction of the Jews.

So far as the Nazis are concerned, the only contradiction to the general thesis of Jewish victimization is the fact that vast numbers of non-Jews were also deliberately killed. But this contradiction may be partially if not entirely resolved when it is understood that according to Nazi ideology, the undesirable qualities carried genetically by the Jews could also occur by other means in other groups who were for all practical purposes definable as virtually equivalent to Jews. Therefore, we have made no important distinctions between the Jew *qua* victim and the victim *qua* Jew.

The word victim is derived from the Latin *victima*, "a living being sacrificed to some deity, or in the performance of a religious rite." This primary definition is particularly appropriate because it stands in sharp contrast to the more general, secondary meanings indicated when the word is used to describe experiences with random misfortune such as a train wreck, earthquake, or flood.

The Jews in Nazi-dominated Europe in the 1940s were chosen for death. If the frequently voiced explanation of Nazism as a secularized religion is accepted, then in that context the Jews were the embodiment of darkness and evil. In Nazi theology their destruction was necessary if goodness was to triumph. Contrary to Christian myth—in which Satan must coexist eternally with God—National Socialism expected that it could within one generation destroy these forces of evil and achieve the utopia of a racially pure Europe.

The destruction of the Jews became one of the central good works required of the committed National Socialist. Just as the devoted adherent of any conventional religion must validate his commitment by acting out a certain behavior (rituals or good works), the committed SS man also had to perform validating actions. These have rightly been described by Leo Alexander as a strong "blood cement" binding members of the Nazi elite to one another.[3] The sacrificing of Jews—not least because of its antiutilitarian aspect—was the Nazi equivalent of a religious act of faith.

More generally, it should be recognized that when people seriously embrace any abstract ideal or deity, be it metaphysical, political, or intellectual, they must always offer proofs by making sacrifice to it. The sacrifice may be no more than a ritualized act of bearing witness, as in the case of certification procedures accompanying entrance to a learned profession. Or it may involve deadly human costs, such as the duty of a dedicated Muslim to sacrifice others and himself in a jehad or holy war. Similarly, it was the duty of dedicated Nazis to sacrifice the Jews even, if need be, at the price of their own life or well-being.

This theme of human sacrifice should not be difficult to comprehend because it follows directly from the Nazi ideals discussed in previous chapters. Moreover, the Nazi metaphysical imperative leading toward genocide of the Jews would hardly require any further mention here were it not that the underlying sacrificial quality inherent in the Jews' status as historical victims is so often overlooked. And being overlooked, the tendency on the part of victims and observers alike is to perceive the victim simply as the innocent target of an aberrant force in nature or society.

Understandable as it is in terms of the commonsense psychology of social behavior, this tendency to ignore the sacrificial status of the innocent victim demands special emphasis because it generates false and complacent attitudes based on the logic or, more precisely, the "psycho-logic" of innocence.

### The Fallacy of Innocence

If individuals or groups cast in the role of victim are aware of being innocent—that is, that there is no rational basis for their status as victims— there follows an almost inevitable and fallacious conclusion. They can only assume that their oppression proceeds from a mistaken judgment or a momentary lapse of rationality by their oppressor. In this case, the cause of their predicament must lie in the oppressor. It then follows that if this cause or fault in the oppressor can be understood ("Why do you mistake me for something I am not?") it can be corrected, or at least moderated.

Thus, when Sartre wrote his brilliant essay on anti-Semitism, he began by addressing himself primarily to the mind of the anti-Semite.[4] And among the many volumes of social science research on prejudice, the focus has generally been upon the etiology of relevant thoughts and actions by those identified as prejudiced. In short, when a victim is manifestly innocent, commonsense logic immediately leads to scrutiny of the oppressor who is the cause of the situation and who presumably has the power to correct it. Such forms of commonsense thinking are epitomized in the contemporary American truism that white racism is a white problem. But if one accepts that this truism and others like it are in fact true, where is the fallacy?

Concretely, it is very simple: white racism is also a deadly serious black problem, and no amount of logic-chopping causal analysis can alter this existential truth. More abstractly, the fallacy of innocence lies in the historical and psychological fact that logically correct conclusions may yield drastically incorrect actions. Hence, if the fault is in the oppressor, it would seem that victims need only guard their innocence while efforts are made to correct the fault. Victims who accept such plausible and seductively straightforward definitions of their situation are accepting the historical-psychological fallacy of ignoring their status as victims. By focusing upon their innocence, victims inevitably fail to pay sufficient attention to their state of being as a victim per se.

Psychic innocence tends, therefore, to play an extraordinary trick upon the consciousness of victims, leading them to deny the blatant existential reality of their situation. Denying the justice and logic of their victimhood, as it were, and bending every effort toward correction or redefinition of their case, they may ignore what it means to be a victim: "a living being sacrificed to some deity." Consequently, the questions that require consideration if one is to survive in the role of victim—innocent or not—may not be raised. Therefore, the fact that one is innocent, in the sense of not being guilty of the oppressor's accusations, clearly works against adoption of effective action because of fear that such action may contaminate or discredit one's primary claim to innocence. The psycho-logic is very strong here: where there is resistance even in thought there must be some guilt, if only the guilt of resistance.

Considered from this standpoint, the surprising success of the Nazi actions against the Jews—and it was a surprise to the Nazis themselves—can be understood as largely due to the brute fact of Jewish innocence. Quite apart from the traditionally passive Jewish response to persecution, which historically had served them as a more-or-less effective defensive technique, their manifest innocence of all the Nazis' accusations blocked them from clear awareness of an unprecedented threat and the need for a new mode of response. Being innocent victims, the vast majority of Jews were unaware of the simple truths known almost reflexively to guilty victims, namely, that to be a victim is first and most importantly to be a nonperson, one who has no acknowledged right to be treated as a person. At least a part of this argument concerning the fallacy of innocence was anticipated in Elie Cohen's remarks about the behavior of concentration camp prisoners. Describing the condition of Jews in Buchenwald, who spoke of their imprisonment as being due to a "birth defect," Cohen observed: "Hence for the majority, there was not the slightest occasion to regard themselves as criminals. This feeling of being innocent and yet having to suffer all this misery aroused self-pity and *weakened the energy that was essential for survival.*"[5] (Italics added.)

More generally, the prototype of the victim or nonperson of the twentieth century is the individual without direct or indirect power to secure fair treatment by appeal to either force or an effective body of law. In accord with this proposition, whether one speaks of the Jews, the Armenians, the stateless people produced by World War I and the Russian Revolution, the Asians in many nations of Africa, the Bengalis slaughtered during the revolt against Pakistan, the blacks of South Africa, or the Vietnamese "boat people," all of the principal victims of the twentieth century have had in common a status as nonpersons: they were unable to avail themselves of the protection of a national state.

There were such victims, to be sure, in earlier times. But their proliferation in this century relates to a changing sociocultural dynamic whereby individuals maintain their status as persons deserving of humane treatment. Throughout the eighteenth and nineteenth centuries prevailing religious values supported the view that people, particularly Europeans, were endowed with "natural" rights. With the rise of modern nationalism, however, the trend has been for individuals to derive their rights as persons—to personhood, as it were—from the state. It is the state which endows its people (only those considered to be citizens of the state) with human rights (only those rights the state deems reasonable). Civil rights have replaced natural rights.

Moreover, it is the state that enforces observation of its citizens' rights through its monopoly of the legal means of violence. When a state will not or cannot use its forces in defense of these rights (protection from outlaws, adjudication of disputes, enforcement of equal access to public institutions, and so on), the citizen does not have them. Indeed, if the state denies individuals the essential rights of citizenship, the denial transforms them into nonpersons: objects vulnerable to arbitrary manipulation and control. This is a main theme in the works of Franz Kafka; in *The Trial* the protagonist is arbitrarily arrested, judged guilty without ever knowing his crime or his accusers, sentenced by judges he never sees, and finally executed, dying, in his own words, "like a dog." Reality has caught up with the nightmarish imagination of Kafka. Nor should this situation be taken as exceptional, limited to the confines of Kafka's central Europe. The Japanese-Americans who were deprived of their rights and interned in concentration camps ("relocation centers") during World War II were placed in exactly the same position as nonpersons. Roger Daniels reports the case of one such individual who only in 1971 realized that his citizenship rights had been restored.[6]

In this connection, what makes the twentieth-century right to personhood so distinctive is the fact that it depends upon satisfying the demands of socioeconomic, political, and racial criteria as well as simple nationalist strictures. Thus, with the rise of ideological justifications for governments, individuals may find nonnegotiable ideological barriers blocking their way to fair treatment as persons. In some emerging nations of Black Africa, for instance, to be anything but black is, ipso facto, to be in contradiction of ideology. Similarly, in South Africa today, and in the United States not so long ago, to be anything but white was equally definitive of either de facto or de jure nonperson status.

The ubiquitous ideological exploitation of racism, however, should not obscure an analogous use of economic, political, or social class factors. Those identified as kulaks in the Soviet Union and communists in the United States, for instance, have at one time or another also been deprived of their status as persons. Therefore, up to 1940–1941, the situation of Jews under the Nazis was not categorically unique; what made it unique afterward was the ferocious intensity and extent of the Nazi genocide program.

If it is objected that this analysis is arbitrary, that the nonperson interpretation of victimization is an unsupported assertion, a brief consideration of relevant evidence may be useful. At the most concrete level, virtually all of the retrospective accounts produced by victims emphasize the reality of their nonperson experience. Bettelheim has described this phenomenon as a feeling of depersonalization, in which the individual's self-concept seems literally detached from immediate events.[7] Reviewing several other first-person accounts of concentration camp survivors, Hilde Bluhm identified a common theme in which individuals initially cannot assimilate the reality of their situation ("It cannot be true—such things don't happen") and later retreat into a self-protective psychological shell allowing them to live more as an object than a person ("You must not see or hear . . . you must go through this like a stone").[8]

Other evidence suggests that the guards themselves were not immune to feelings of unreality. Wiesenthal reports a conversation with an SS man at the end of the war who remarked that after all he had seen in the camps, he still could not believe that it had actually happened.[9] It is significant that on certain occasions guards felt impelled to demonstrate the inhumanity of their prisoners by arranging unimaginably cruel situations which forced prisoners to behave like beasts. Such behavior was then taken as proof that the prisoners were, indeed, subhumans.

Such self-serving attitudes of innate superiority to their victims seem to be quite universal among all oppressors. If the victims lack proper sanitary facilities, they are described as enjoying filth; if they are prevented from finding dignified work, they are called lazy; and if, under the weight of their oppression, they struggle among themselves and betray one another, this may be taken as proof of their violent, irresponsible nature. After observing these processes at work in colonialized areas of Africa, Fanon concluded that native victims who had come to accept the inferior, nonperson status imposed upon them had no recourse except bloody revolt, because they could only regain their sense of equal humanity by literally cutting Europeans down to size.[10]

The ultimate formal statement defining victims as nonpersons occurred in early nineteenth-century America, when it was stipulated in law that slaves were objects of property. The fact that the Dred Scott decision could become law in a state with a constitution, a Bill of Rights, and traditions supporting revolt in the cause of freedom offers ample testimony to the ingenious psycho-logic of oppression: if persons are endowed with inalienable human rights, then those deliberately stripped of these rights cannot be persons.

Finally, the nonperson thesis is supported by survivor reports emphasizing that in both German and Russian concentration camps, common criminals were typically given better treatment than those imprisoned for political or racial reasons. The psycho-logic here seems quite obvious. Criminals have a legally recognized, "official" role as lawbreaking citizens; they are persons to whom the state has given a specific, limited punishment for a specific criminal act. Hence petty privileges and authority will more easily be delegated to them than to others whose "crime" is that they exist contrary to the ideology of the state and for whom punishment has no limits because they have no official status as socially recognizable persons.

Given these general considerations, how is the situation of the Jews to be understood? Even if it is accepted, first, that they were the traditional internal victims of Western civilization, with a long history of nonperson status, and, second, that their inability to avoid destruction at the hands of the Nazis was due at least in part to the "fallacy of innocence," their unique torment in the Holocaust is not explained. To understand their situation, it is necessary to examine the Nazi racial policies that created it.

## Development of the "Final Solution"

As noted earlier, historians are generally divided over whether the geno-cide program should be viewed as an event in the continuous historical tradition of Jewish victimization, or as a massive aberration produced by criminal minds momentarily in control of a modern state. The evidence now available suggests that while it was both these things—"normal" history and aberration—it was most specifically a social policy that emerged from a complex pattern of psychological, political, military, and economic problems.

At the level of formal analysis, the genocide program appears analogous to other extreme national policies that have also arisen from complex historical and psychological patterns. Thus, psychological, military, political, and economic factors were all relevant to the decisions leading to incarceration of Japanese-Americans during World War II and more recently to the Ameri-can policy of bombing the North Vietnamese into acceptance of a peace settlement. For the Nazis, however, the eventual policy followed with respect to their self-created Jewish problem was far more bizarre than any other analogous national policy, because they carried it out in a fashion so extreme as to negate many of the factors which initially inspired the policy.

Scholarly research studies have made the evolving pattern of Jewish oppression under the Nazis very clear.[11] After the Nazis came to power in

January 1933, their first major action against the Jews was a nationwide boycott of all Jewish-owned or Jewish-operated businesses, beginning on April 1, 1933. This turned out to be a dismal failure for several reasons. Many Germans went out of their way to patronize Jewish shops despite the presence of SA pickets; the SA acted in character by taking the boycott as an occasion for street brawls and looting; foreign press reports of lawless disorder hurt the credibility of the new Nazi government; and, to top off the confusion, some Gentile financial backers of the party objected because they had money invested in Jewish-operated firms. In one striking instance, it turned out that a large department store chain under apparent Jewish ownership was really on the verge of bankruptcy and virtually in the hands of Gentile creditors.

As Schleunes observes of this period, apart from their own extreme rhetoric, the Nazi leaders had no coherent Jewish policy prior to 1933 and after this time they were forced to improvise action simply in order to pacify the radical anti-Jewish sentiments they had encouraged earlier.

The second major effort against the Jews took the form of laws promulgated in spring 1933 which (1) provided for dismissal of Jews from civil service positions; (2) prohibited Jews from entering the legal profession; (3) restricted the number of Jewish students allowed to enter German schools; and (4) disallowed national health insurance payments to persons visiting Jewish physicians.

Jewish immigrants to Germany were attacked through laws passed in July 1933 and March 1934 allowing the government to denaturalize those who had become citizens after the end of World War I. There were also new legal restrictions prohibiting Jews from owning farm land (September 1933) and from doing work in all the mass media, particularly journalism (September and October 1933). In 1935, a military conscription law restricted military service to those of Aryan birth.

The high point of legal action occurred in September 1935, when Hitler announced a Law for the Protection of German Blood at a major Nazi rally in Nuremberg. Later known as the "Nuremberg laws," the measures quickly approved by Hitler's Reichstag outlawed marriage between Jews and Gentiles, made extramarital sex relations between them a prison offense, and specified that no Jew could employ a Gentile housemaid who was under forty-five years old. This last touch was presumably added because for many years, anti-Semitic propaganda had emphasized despoliation of innocent Aryan maidens at the hands of their lecherous Jewish employers.

Following promulgation of the Nuremberg laws many observers, including both Jews and high Nazi officials, thought the Jewish question was more or less closed. Indeed, one answer to those who—after the fact—have questioned the intelligence if not the sanity of German Jews for not seeing the catastrophe looming before them is that there was no certain catastrophe to be seen. In 1935–1938 none of the many legal or extralegal restrictions placed upon the Jews were, historically speaking, notably cruel or unusual. Intermarriage had always been difficult, and many Jews were as opposed to it as the Nazis. And how many people care about their legal right to sexual relations with housemaids? Restrictions on professional activities and school attendance created more serious problems, but there were always private schools available; and disbarred professionals might find alternative means of support much more easily by remaining in a society where they had connections and recognized skills than by going elsewhere to start again from scratch.

Most important of all, however, was the general idea that as German citizens (some of whom could even point to exceptional war service), Jews felt they could live with the Nazi oppression which, in any case, was not likely to go on forever. In the fall of 1935, for example, the head of a national organization of German Jews stated an intention to accept all the existing legal restrictions as the basis for a "tolerable arrangement" with the Nazi state.[12] Nazi leaders themselves made statements indicating that they planned no further actions so long as the Jews did not cause trouble. Furthermore, orders to tone down their anti-Semitic activities were issued to lower party and SA echelons—apparently out of a desire to reduce foreign press criticism during the Olympic Games scheduled for Germany in 1936.

Although serious harassment of Jews was never brought to a complete standstill, especially in business where many Jewish firms were being nominally bought out or otherwise liquidated through connivance between Gentile entrepreneurs and Nazi officials, the situation remained relatively calm until November 1938. By that time most of the moderating factors that had curtailed the scope of Nazi actions were no longer present. Germany was economically and militarily stronger than it had been for twenty years; Hitler held the initiative in foreign affairs, having reoccupied the Rhineland, annexed Austria, and taken the Sudetenland from the Czechs; internal threats to his regime had largely been eliminated; and Hjalmar Schacht, economic minister who had steadily warned against the consequences of an extreme Jewish policy, had resigned from Hitler's cabinet.

All of these conditions meant that at the level of internal party-government politics, rabid anti-Jewish forces were freer than ever before. Moreover, after having been in power for five years without making important progress against the Jews, all of the higher Nazis including Hitler felt that new action was required; this seemed to be the time to push harder for their vision of a totally Aryan Germany.

At the street level, dramatic attacks on Jews were unleashed when on November 7, 1938, the third secretary of the German embassy in Paris was assassinated by a young German-Jewish student living in France. Goebbels' propaganda ministry used this event to inflame anti-Semitic action, and on the night of November 9, SA units were turned loose throughout Germany to lead plundering terror attacks. During that night and the next morning hundreds of synagogues were burned, at least thirty-five Jews were killed, and twenty-five thousand were rounded up into concentration camps. Property damage was so widespread—always first signaled by the sound of breaking windows—that the attack quickly became known as *Kristallnacht* (literally, "crystal-night").[13]

In general, however, the results did not satisfy the Nazi leaders. Himmler viewed Goebbels' initiative as a challenge to his own authority and his own more systematic anti-Jewish program. His SS men had to be called upon to prevent the SA from continuing their socially and commercially disruptive street attacks. In addition, the Jewish forced-emigration program operating under Himmler's authority was upset because certain key Jewish figures were beaten or arrested. And Göring, by this time in charge of the new German economic development plan, also felt that *Kristallnacht* was both a needless disruption and a challenge to his status in the Nazi hierarchy.

Hitler decided to end the squabbling once and for all by placing Göring in full charge of the "Jewish question." Göring's first move was to call a large conference of all interested party and government officials where it was announced that henceforward, the Nazi effort to Aryanize Germany would be conducted in a stable, systematic fashion. Instead of disorganized street action, drastic new legal measures were planned: Jews would be forbidden to operate any business and forced emigration would be accelerated. These measures went into effect on January 1, 1939, and then more were added. A fine of one billion marks was levied on German Jews as indemnity for the Paris assassination; all Jewish organizations and newspapers were proscribed; Jews were even forbidden to use railroad dining and sleeping cars. Forced emigration was stepped up with the aim of getting every Jew out of Germany as soon as possible.

The emigration program was essentially a very harsh confiscation plan. Allowed to keep only the minimal amounts of cash required by receiving countries, Jews had to turn over all the rest of their goods and property to the state. Adolf Eichmann had first attained prominence in the SS by streamlining the emigration legal work into a mass production operation used against the Jews of Austria. He was now placed in charge of a similar program in Germany.

By the spring of 1939, therefore, actions fitting the "normal" tradition of Jewish persecution had reached their peak. Nazi policy had developed to the outer limits defined by law and custom, and the Jews of Germany were left with only one choice: either to get out as paupers or to remain, hoping for some miraculous end to the Nazi regime. In the event, almost half chose migration. Out of a total German Jewish population of 503,000 in 1933, over 200,000 left Germany before wartime conditions made travel impossible. Those remaining were later to face the Holocaust.

No evidence of plans for a massive killing program can be found at any point in the Nazi history up through 1939. In fact, much of the evidence suggests something very different—one does not bother with endlessly complex race laws and emigration programs if one really plans murder. Furthermore, various sources show that as late as 1940–1941, SS functionaries were working on plans to deport Jews to a special reserve in Madagascar. Nor did the killing program suddenly spring into being later on. After 1939, the campaigns against Poland and France so preoccupied the Nazi leaders that anti-Jewish activity languished in the hands of lower-echelon officials.

On the other hand, by the middle of 1941 there is unmistakable evidence that the Nazi leaders were committed to a mass killing policy. Consequently, the problem is to understand how this unprecedented policy emerged and why, after an initially very tentative and secret trial-and-error period, the policy could be implemented so effectively as to decimate the European Jews.

Several factors converged in 1941 to form what logicians might call an immediate "context of plausibility" for the final solution. There were, first of all, sheer numbers. Approximately three and a half million Jews were living in Poland alone, and there were large numbers in other occupied countries. It should also be kept in mind that as the Nazis planned their move into Russia, they had not yet succeeded in their efforts to remove the two hundred thousand-odd Jews still remaining in Germany; what could they possibly do about millions more?

In a more rational setting the answer would have been either to forget about them while getting on with the war, or to exploit their labor in some war-related activities. Indeed, most of the SS policy planners suggested both these alternatives. Having failed to bring off any of their grandiose emigration schemes, and having already imposed race laws designed to assure segregation, exploitation, and oppression of Jews, there seemed to be no other possible actions in a war situation. Yet this state of affairs did not last long because of a second important factor, namely, Hitler's obsessive association of the Jews with the war.

Years earlier he had made public statements threatening that if any general conflict broke out in Europe, he would know whom to blame and he would destroy them. In the event of war, he said on November 12, 1938, "the first thing we Germans would obviously think of would be our final reckoning with the Jews." On January 30, 1939, he said: "If the Jewish international financiers . . . succeed in involving the nations in another war, the result will not be world bolshevism and therefore a victory for Judaism; it will be the end of the Jews in Europe."[14]

The fact that Hitler maintained a deeply psychotic vision of Jews which he projected in political terms is well documented in the psychobiographical studies discussed above. Thus, as Hitler prepared for the Russian campaign it is not surprising that he ordered (March 1941) immediate execution for captured Soviet political commissars and other "undesirables" such as Jews and Gypsies. But orders are only orders—especially top-secret directives of this type; they become real only when appropriate tools are available for their implementation.

In this instance, implementation was left to Heydrich, who arranged an organizational structure for killing that can be identified as a third major contributing factor. After seeing to the training of four battalion-sized SS *Einsatzgruppen* and verbally instructing their commanders just prior to the attack on Russia, he later described the essence of the killing policy in a written memorandum distributed to other high SS security chiefs serving in Russia. Dated July 2, 1941, the memo reiterated Hitler's March 1941 order for executions and added that anti-Jewish groups in the conquered population should be discreetly encouraged to carry out actions against Jews. A few weeks after this, Heydrich's work was formally encouraged in a directive from Göring requesting him to prepare "a master plan for carrying out the final solution of the Jewish problem." Other documents, including operational orders and reports from the *Einsatzgruppen* in the field, show that by the fall of 1941 mass shootings of Jews were in full swing in Russia. Therefore, it is apparent that in the several months intervening between Hitler's order to execute "undesirables" and the Wehrmacht advance deep into Russia, the SS under Heydrich had accomplished the steps needed to make genocide a reality.

The reality was still comparatively small, however, because it was limited by the uncertainties prevailing in the war zone as well as the shortage of manpower available for *Einsatzgruppen* service. The latter problem was solved in a few months by recruitment of an "anti-partisan army" from among the anti-Semitic peasantry. Organized as auxiliaries under SS command, the antipartisan units operated in conjunction with *Einsatzgruppen* on the premise that Jews were all latent partisans or partisan supporters.

Meanwhile, Heydrich occupied himself with the wider mandate he had received from Göring. At a meeting of various concerned officials in January 1942 (the "Wannsee Conference"), he announced formal termination of the emigration program. Hereafter, all Jews remaining in Germany and living in other parts of occupied Europe would be forcibly deported to Poland. Those fit for work would be put to manual labor, and although the fate of the others was not specifically noted in the conference minutes, later testimony from participants, including Adolf Eichmann, states that it was clearly understood that the others would be killed.[15] Similarly, those who did not perish during the labor experience would also have to be eliminated.

Only one significant objection to Heydrich's plans was raised at the conference, and this had to do with difficult conditions already existing in Poland. Speaking on behalf of Hans Frank, the Nazi governor general of Poland, one of the conferees noted that outbreaks of epidemic diseases had already begun to occur in the overcrowded, unsanitary Jewish ghettos. He went on to suggest that the Polish Jewish situation should be given priority over the German Jewish situation if only because uncontrollable epidemic disease might spread to the larger population and frustrate plans for the exploitation of Poland.

Aside from being duly noted, there was no significant reaction to this statement before the conference ended. But in his own Polish domain, Hans Frank had meanwhile concluded that he simply could not cope with the millions of Jews already on his hands, let alone with the prospect of receiving more. Thereafter, at a staff conference of his own he argued that all feelings of pity must be conquered and the Jews must be dealt with in the only way possible:

> I ask nothing of the Jews except that they should disappear.... We must destroy the Jews wherever we meet them and whenever opportunity offers so that we can maintain the whole structure of the Reich here.... We can't shoot these 3.5 million Jews, and we can't poison them, but we can take steps which, one way or another, will lead to extermination, in conjunction with the large scale measures under discussion in the Reich. The Government General must be as free of Jews as the Reich itself.[16]

The tone of all this bureaucratic byplay indicates how the final solution policy was shaped during the winter of 1941–1942. Thus, in addition to the general factors already mentioned—the large numbers of Jews in conquered territories, which seemed to nag for action in the Nazi consciousness; Hitler's obsession, leading to the killing program in Russia; and Heydrich's success in organizing special SS units for this purpose—a further contributing factor was the felt need to drastically reduce the large Jewish ghettos in Poland. Moreover, there is a critically important psychological condition conveyed by most of the material on Nazi thinking about their Jewish problem in 1941–1942: a promethean quality, a sense that with total war going on and an extraordinary string of quick victories validating the mystique of their movement, anything was possible. The die seemed irrevocably cast and as a result they felt able to do things that would have been unthinkable only a few years before.

What, after all, were the Jews, or conventional moral feelings, for that matter, to Faustian men who had lifted themselves from obscurity in a few brief years to control the principal areas of Western Europe? Following all the years of anti-Semitic rhetoric, could not the Jews now indeed seem little more than a pernicious form of subhuman vermin, a species of crabgrass infesting the Nazi estate? There is, of course, much to be said for deeper analytical perspectives suggesting that in their wartime haste to destroy the Jews, key Nazi figures were trying to destroy threatening instinctive qualities projected from their own psyches, particularly in the case of Hitler himself.

But while it may be acknowledged that such interpretations offer plausible explanations for traditional forms of anti-Semitism or racism, it is vital to emphasize the historical realities that ultimately gave impetus to the Holocaust. If Poland had not fallen so quickly in 1939, and France in 1940, or if the German armies had been stalled or thrown back in Russia during the summer of 1941, the final solution would have been virtually impossible. Extermination could not have been carried out in the face of serious military reversals or uncertainties, because too many logistical, political, and psychological difficulties would have blocked the way. Preoccupation with the Jewish problem did not go forward to extreme lengths until the Nazi leaders felt themselves to be securely in power and confirmed in this power by their remarkable military successes. Nor could the SS have become an effective instrument for extermination if the Nazi mystique had been compromised early in the war.

Briefly, our thesis is that while a number of specific factors all contributed significantly to the development of the final solution, it is the credibility of the Nazi regime in 1941–1942 that stands out as the most fundamental enabling factor. The policy itself evolved quickly from a secret and relatively specific Hitler directive in the spring of 1941 to a broad-spectrum program by January 1942. No such rapid development could have occurred if the party and SS leadership had not been swept along in the current of their success.

Subsequent growth of the extermination program has already been described. During 1942, as the SS specialists perfected their mass production gassing-cremation techniques, Eichmann and his colleagues in the Gestapo evacuation and transportation department were perfecting deportation procedures for application to Jews throughout Europe. And so the Holocaust went into full operation.

## Reactions of the Victims

In *The Destruction of the European Jews* Raul Hilberg observed that there were only four courses of behavior logically available to the victims: resistance, evasion, paralysis, or compliance.[17] During the first phase of Nazi oppression in 1933–1939, there was virtually no resistance, and although efforts at evasion were substantial, the general norm was paralysis and compliance. This judgment is neither an insult to the Jews nor a tribute to the Nazis, for it is clear that until 1939, the oppression was tolerable.

Moreover, insofar as the German Jews existed in coherent groups, they were divided into factions in ways that prevented organized resistance. Among more conservative, tradition-bound elements, the normative reaction was transcendental endurance. Orthodox Jewish teachings emphasized that as God's chosen people, they might expect to suffer persecution and they might properly construe this to be a test of their faith or their worthiness of the covenant with God. Some Jews would have accepted Hitler enthusiastically if he had dropped anti-Semitism. The Ansbacher rabbi, Elie Munk, spoke for many of them when he stated publicly: "I reject the teachings of Marxism from a Jewish standpoint and commit myself to National Socialism without its anti-Semitic components. Without anti-Semitism National Socialism would find in the tradition-bound Jews its most loyal followers."[18]

At another extreme stood conservative and socialist Zionist groups who typically disagreed with one another (and continue to do so today in Israel) but were united in the belief that Jews should have their own homeland. In some respects, Zionism was based upon the same mixture of romanticism, genetics, and social Darwinist philosophy that appealed to the more intellectual Nazis, namely, that a people could only fulfill its destiny when it became a racially pure nation rooted in its own soil. If traditional orthodoxy led many older Jews to feel primarily responsible for keeping a metaphysical covenant with God, Zionism led many of the younger people to feel primarily responsible for redemption of the age-old pledge "next year in Jerusalem." Neither position contained within itself any important elements suggesting militant resistance to Nazi oppression. And while the Zionists might deplore excesses of gutter anti-Semitism, they could also see the persecutions as a spur toward emigration, and perceive that they shared a fundamental premise with the Nazis. A statement issued by the Zionist Union for Germany, 1933, declared: "Zionism believes that a rebirth of true national life as it has developed in Germany through the union of Christian and national values should also develop in Jewish national life."[19]

Falling between the "metaphysical-passive" and "Zionist-active" extremes, two additional prototypical reactions can be identified. Those who were members of Marxist socialist or communist organizations fought the Nazis in what amounted to a nonsectarian political context. Whether this resistance should be construed as being "Jewish" must remain a debatable issue. However, it is certainly true that some Jewish workers and intellectuals were attracted to Marxism because it promised an end to anti-Semitism. Among the rabid Nazis who maintained "Jewish bolshevism" as a key phrase in their political vocabulary, there was never any doubt that leftist opposition had a Jewish base—what was Karl Marx, after all, if not a Jew? Yet any general scan of the available evidence on this period demonstrates that socialist and communist resistance to Hitler was largely dictated by ideological considerations which gave no special priority to the Jewish situation in Germany.

Finally, there were a great many Jews who were quite well assimilated to German society and not very religious but who still kept their primary identity as Jews. Composed most significantly of middle class and upper middle class professionals and businessmen, with a few exceptions this group reacted to Nazi oppression by making a deliberate effort to avoid provocation. "Don't make waves" was the attitude, and the justification was simply that if public disturbances or confrontations could be minimized, this would deprive the Nazis of excuses for further anti-Jewish action.

Such an attitude is a perfect representation of the fallacy of innocence; yet it should be recognized as no retreat into the passivity of indifference. Instead, it reflected an idea widely shared by Jews and non-Jews alike that by holding to an unswerving posture of dignity and restraint, Jews could outlast and even discredit momentary anti-Semitic passions. Indeed, by this process they might demonstrate themselves to be good German citizens worthy of respect.

In general, therefore, prior to 1939 there existed no firm organizational or ideological basis for Jewish resistance, and no clearly recognized threat of destruction that could make resistance imperative. Between 1939 and 1941, the various Jewish organizations in Germany were broken up, and those outside Germany put all their energies into efforts to cope with hardships created by the Nazi forced-emigration policy. Consequently, when the genocide program emerged in an atmosphere of high secrecy and wartime confusion in 1941–1942, it is not difficult to understand why the Jews were totally unprepared. And if this conclusion is valid for the situation in Germany, it is doubly so for the situation of Jews in Eastern Europe.

In Poland, where millions of Jews had lived for many generations as a repressed underclass, the polarity between ideas of metaphysical endurance and Zionist activism was much greater than in Germany. The same condition prevailed in Russia, where Jews dispersed in countless rural slums (shtetls) were traditionally hard-pressed to maintain themselves and had little inclination to form effective organizations. Moreover, to the extent that Polish or Russian Jewish youth became discontented with the status quo, emigration became the typical solution.

Ironically, the organization problem was epitomized after the war by SS General von dem Bach-Zelewski, who testified that the lack of effective organization among the Jews was a key factor in the success of the genocide operations: "Contrary to the opinion of the National Socialists that the Jews were a highly organized group, the appalling fact was that they had no organization whatsoever. . . . If they had some sort of organization these people could have been saved by the millions; but instead they were taken completely by surprise."[20]

## Destruction and Survival

The SS death campaign against the European Jews involved four general steps or phases: concentration, deportation, selection, and death. During the concentration phase, SS officials working with local authorities arranged for Jews to be gathered together or concentrated in limited areas such as ghettos, relocation centers, or work camps. It was in this phase that the attitudes of local authorities often played a critical role determining the fate of "their" Jews.

In the next phase, deportation, victims were systematically removed from concentration areas to death camps. This would be done either slowly or rapidly depending upon such factors as the availability of rail transport facilities, and the need of local SS units for the Jews for slave labor. The deportations were typically conducted under the pretext of relocation. Until 1943–1944, when firm knowledge of the "final solution" had leaked out to large numbers of Jews and Germans alike, many Jews accepted the relocation story as legitimate. In this connection, the sheer implausibility of massive killing as an official German policy worked to the advantage of the SS because ordinary people could not believe it. It was partly for this reason that the Jewish councils of elders who were made responsible for keeping order in many of the concentration areas were usually willing to cooperate when the SS demanded that certain numbers of Jews be presented for "resettlement."

Upon arrival at a death camp, the victims were paraded for "selection" past SS medical officers who would casually separate those who seemed able-bodied enough for work from those who were to be immediately killed. The severity of these selections varied with local conditions. In camps set up entirely for the purpose of killing (Sobibor, Treblinka), only a few of the victims might find themselves saved to work as part of the killing machinery. But in Auschwitz and other camps where prisoners might be used in nearby industrial enterprises, a larger number were usually spared for slave labor. These people were also ticketed for death (it has been calculated that the average slave laborer only lasted for about three months, but some survived for much longer periods).

In the face of such a pitiless destruction process, what chances did the victims have for survival? This question must be approached on at least two different levels, because answers depend upon two different categories of particulars. Most generally, escape from the death process depended upon what country one was in and at what point in the war one had become a target of the SS. And on a more specific, personal level, once individuals were caught up in the death machinery, survival depended upon their particular situation and whether or not they possessed certain qualities allowing them to cope with extraordinary stress. Before examining these matters any further, however, it is useful to consider once more the question of resistance, if only because this question is inevitably raised about the victims.

It has been shown that no important organizational basis for resistance existed prior to the start of the genocide program. Once the program began to operate, events moved quickly and with enough secrecy so that by the time significant numbers of Jews became genuinely convinced of what was happening, there was little chance for them to do anything about it. The only real choice for the vast majority was whether to accept a relatively quick death or, by an act of resistance, to be killed in an exceptionally brutal, painful fashion. As is described below, many groups of Jews did carry out armed resistance actions, the best known being the Warsaw ghetto revolt. But these actions were all more or less improvised affairs that usually only delayed SS operations for a period of days. More important in the present context, examination of records and accounts of resistance actions make it quite clear that with some few exceptions, open resistance did not increase chances for survival. Therefore, whatever else may be said about the resistance question—and the subject has been a matter of bitter controversy among both scholars and survivors—it can be said that open resistance was not an appreciable factor influencing survival. It might indeed have been otherwise if Jewish resistance had been organized more thoroughly and been supported with arms and leaders from the outside; but this did not occur, and resistance efforts never became an important barrier to death.

Instead, survival depended more than anything else upon government power in the occupied countries. The following table gives a breakdown of the percentages of the prewar Jewish population killed, which shows that the proportions varied immensely in different areas of Europe. This variability was no mere matter of geography or logistics; it related directly to the degree of autonomy existing in each country.[21] With a few exceptions, in those countries whose governments retained significant control over their own internal security by means of an independent army or police force or both, Jews had the greatest chance of survival. The data for Germany and Austria are a special case because many Jews were able to emigrate before the killing policy was adopted. In Czechoslovakia, local authorities that had initially cooperated in the concentration and deportation of Jews for "resettlement" began to oppose this policy when they learned the true nature of the program in the fall of 1942.

### Estimated Percentages of Prewar Jewish Populations Killed in Germany and the Occupied Countries

| Countries (prewar borders): | Lestchinsky | Hilberg |
| --- | --- | --- |
| Poland | 88 | 98 |
| Greece | 80 | 84 |
| Yugoslavia | 73 | 84 |
| Hungary | 50 | 50 |
| Holland | 70 | 86 |
| Belgium | 44 | 55 |
| Luxembourg, Danzig | 33 | 33 |
| Romania | 50 | 46 |
| Czechoslovakia | 76 | 86 |
| Germany | 57 | 67 |
| Austria | 50 | 88 |
| USSR (Percent of total Jewish population in the Nazi-occupied territories) | 71 | 21 |
| France | 30 | 26 |
| Italy | 26 | 34 |
| Bulgaria | 14 | 6 |
| Lithuania | 86 | — |
| Latvia | 84 | — |
| Norway | — | 50 |
| Denmark | — | 15 |

SOURCE NOTE: The percentages are calculated from statistics summarized by Jacob Lestchinsky, as revised in 1955 and published in *Yad Vashem Bulletin* (April 1961) and from statistics given by Raul Hilberg in *Destruction of the European Jews*, p. 670. Both are reproduced in the appendix to Nora Levin, *The Holocaust: The Destruction of European Jewry, 1933–1945*. Although Lestchinsky and Hilberg are both reliable scholarly sources, the discrepancies between their estimates underscore the fact that no final, perfect death count exists.

The Vichy government of France retained considerable autonomy, and although it was sympathetic to anti-Semitic policies and collaborated with the Germans by turning over many foreign Jews and stateless persons, there was strong opposition to wholesale deportations of French Jews.

In Italy, neither the civil nor the military authorities were inclined to support strong anti-Semitic measures suggested by their German ally, let alone deportations later in the war, following the Nazi occupation. The Italian army protected Jews in southern France and in Greece during the period it had control of these areas. The Greek Jews were decimated by deportation only after Germany took over full control and no countervailing authority existed.

Looking beyond the apparent general relationship between Jewish survival and national government autonomy, the pattern of destruction and survival occurring in every country appears unique. The Jews of Denmark and Bulgaria fared better than any others in Europe, yet apart from the relative independence of both governments concerned, the two situations were very different. In September 1943, when the Germans gave orders to round up the 6,500 Danish Jews for deportation, local government officials were able to act quickly, and with the energetic cooperation of a friendly population were able to arrange a mass escape for the Jews to neutral Sweden. This dramatic rescue occurred partly because Georg Duckwitz, a high German official in Denmark, warned the Danish authorities and then delayed implementation of the deportation order. It also appears that the civilized Danes had been able to "corrupt" their lower-echelon German occupiers to a significant degree.[22]

The Bulgarian Jews were also saved, but their good luck might best be attributed to the fortunes of war. In April 1943, when the SS killing apparatus turned to Bulgaria, it was already clear to this German ally that the war could not be won, and so, rather than collaborate further with a dubious Nazi enterprise, the government simply refused to accept the deportation demand.

Yet another, more complex set of events occurred in Romania, where approximately one half of the Jews survived. The Romanian government was dominated by passionate anti-Semites who had on their own, early in the war, conducted a vicious persecution campaign. By the time SS professionals decided to move in, however, Romanian Jews were aware of their danger and were able to bribe or subvert enough local officials to frustrate plans for large-scale deportations.

In general, as the war began to go against Germany in 1943, the extermination program began to slow down. Local collaborators lost their enthusiasm; the real character of the final solution became more widely known and provoked second thoughts even among high Nazi officials; and the economic section of the SS made stronger efforts to save able-bodied Jews for slave labor. A major tragic exception to this trend was the fate of the Hungarian Jews late in 1944. Although they had escaped serious harm up to this time, their fate was indirectly determined by Hungarian plans for a unilateral surrender. When Hitler learned of this Hungarian intention, he moved quickly to crush their government and placed the country under total SS control.

Consequently at a time when most of the Nazi party and SS hierarchy knew that further killings were pointless, Eichmann and his group in the deportation department went fanatically ahead to murder the Hungarian Jews, chiefly because they were available.

Aside from the degree of government autonomy, another general factor requiring careful consideration is anti-Semitism in various native populations. Although native anti-Semitism was clearly an important element influencing the chances of Jewish survival, as shown in a detailed quantitative study by Helen Fein,[23] it was not nearly as important as Nazi control. Popular misunderstanding of this issue is perhaps traceable to the impact of vivid anti-Semitic material from Poland, where a great deal of evidence demonstrates that the mass of the population was either indifferent to or actively pleased by the genocide program. Organized Polish resistance groups reflected this attitude by ignoring Jewish pleas for aid and by occasionally killing Jews who escaped from the ghettos. One Jewish survivor from Poland recorded his bitter comments: "For years the Poles have been dreaming of getting rid of the Jews and now at last Hitler does it for them ... at bottom they are delighted, however horrified by the inhuman cruelty. The Krauts devouring the Kikes: what could be sweeter."[24]

To support the claim that native anti-Semitism was a major causal factor, the situation in Poland has been compared with that in Denmark, where a friendly population apparently saved their Jews. Plausible as this idea may seem, however, it cannot be accepted. Individual Jews undoubtedly benefited in important ways occasionally if they lived in the midst of a friendly population, but in general, survival had little connection with the attitudes of common people. The Danish Jews were saved because the local government had the capacity to act, had enough advance warning to plan action, and because nearby Sweden offered itself as a safe haven. The attitude of the population in and of itself seems relatively incidental in comparison with these facts. An important demonstration of this proposition may be seen in the fact that large numbers of Jews living in Holland were killed despite the presence of a friendly native population. The Dutch authorities had virtually no discretionary power because the Nazis imposed extremely harsh occupation policies and backed them up with substantial troop garrisons. When the SS initiated deportations, there was no practical way for the Dutch to interfere.

Some evidence also indicates that in certain areas of Western Europe and Italy, German army generals commanding occupation forces went out of their way to oppose SS deportation operations. In Belgium, for instance, the army would not cooperate with SS activities and many Jews were saved who would otherwise have been killed. But this was an idiosyncratic affair dependent upon the character of particular officers. In general, the argument that Jewish survival was heavily determined by whether the local population was anti-Semitic cannot be accepted because throughout most of occupied Europe the unorganized mass of the population had no power to offer significant interference.

Indirect confirmation of this analysis can be seen in the policies of the

Polish government-in-exile based in England. Their directives to the resistance organization specifically prohibited any important collaboration or aid to the Jews. Acting on their own initiative, some resistance units did provide help during the Warsaw ghetto uprising but it was relatively small. If, however, despite indigenous anti-Semitism, the exile government had ordered direct cooperation and the recruitment of Jews into partisan groups, it is very likely that a considerably greater number would have survived. Furthermore, it takes no great strength of the imagination to suggest that if the British and American governments had put pressure on the Polish leaders to order significant action, they would have complied.

This point leads to a more general aspect of the victims' situation: the official indifference of the British, American, and Soviet governments. Throughout the war, even after the genocide program had been amply documented (initially, the British and Americans discounted reports of the killings as exaggerated, and the Russians either did not care or were too preoccupied with their own survival), none of the allied powers made any significant effort to interfere with it. On the one hand, they responded to pleas for action with a military argument: winning the war comes first and will, in any case, take care of everything. On the other, when specific suggestions or demands for actions were made they were dismissed with official explanations that such activity would impede the war effort. For the most part, the allied governments even tended to ignore the Holocaust in their war propaganda. A recent review of American newspapers and magazines published during the war shows that on the few occasions when relevant news stories appeared, they were usually brief and buried on inside pages.

Some of the facts concerning allied indifference have been well established. Thus, when a representative of the Warsaw Jews, Artur Ziegelbeim, escaped to England and sought aid for the ghetto revolt, he received only official statements of sympathy instead of the parachute drops of arms requested. In despair, Ziegelbeim committed suicide. In another instance, the Palestinian Zionists represented by Chaim Weizmann requested that British planes bomb the railroad facilities servicing Auschwitz. Churchill forwarded the request to his air ministry with a favorable comment, but the reply was that planes could not be spared from the military bombing campaign. And when the Zionist Joel Brand approached the British government with a scheme to save Hungarian Jews in exchange for goods, a British senior officer replied: "What on earth are you thinking of, Mr. Brand? What shall I do with those million Jews? Where shall I put them?"[25] This remark stands as a fairly accurate epitome of allied attitudes, and seems to offer a confirmation of the official Nazi view: "All we want to do is to get rid of our Jews. The difficulty is that no country wishes to receive them."[26]

If Jews were saved, it was either because local authorities had the inclination and power to obstruct SS deportation plans, or because of individual attributes which allowed some Jews to survive following deportation. The latter issue is very difficult, because experiences in the death camps were extraordinary and must be approached cautiously, with due regard for the warnings survivors have posted against outsiders presuming to trespass. Elie Wiesel, for one, has been eloquent on this point: "As for the scholars and philosophers of every genre who have had the opportunity to observe the tragedy, they will—if they are capable of sincerity and humility—withdraw without daring to enter into the heart of the matter; and if they are not, well, who cares about their grandiloquent conclusions? Auschwitz, by definition, is beyond their vocabulary."[27]

Wiesel cannot be gainsaid, and we are concerned below not with the meaning of the survivors' experiences per se, but with the accounts they have tried to pass on to future generations, and with the construction of meanings these accounts require from those who must live with the history of Auschwitz.

### Experience in the Camps

The term that has become accepted usage—Holocaust—reflects the special status reserved for destruction of the innocent millions. There is little dignity or dramatics implied by the word "extermination," for it refers to a process usually associated with rats and roaches. A holocaust, however, is something outsized and significant; to be immolated in a holocaust implies, at the very least, an unusual and perhaps an epic fate. Hence the metaphoric language employed with reference to the victims of the Nazis is sometimes taken to be an indicator of political or moral values.

In a critique of Bettelheim's writings on this subject, for example, Jacob Robinson complained that by not referring to the murder of the Jews in terms such as "holocaust" or "catastrophe," Bettelheim showed his failure to comprehend the event as a "unique and unprecedented murder of an entire people."[28] Yet Robinson himself does not offer any substantial justification for his preferred metaphor, only indignation against those who seem to be insensitive to the special meaning of Jewish victimization.

This insistence upon a special meaning is shared by a number of writers, the most prominent of whom is Elie Wiesel. One reason for the insistence is the sheer mind-boggling impact of the Jewish situation as distinguished from that of other Nazi victims. The Israeli author Amos Elon offers a brief but eloquent explanation: "But if others were struck by Nazi barbarism, the Jews nevertheless seem different—and not merely in their own eyes—because of all, they alone were singled out for extermination as a people. They were singled out, not because of what they did, or refrained from doing, and not because of faith or politics, but simply because they were there, they existed."[29]

Another closely related reason for the special status given to the Jewish victims is the age-old human tendency to attach metaphysical meanings to large events. And the more atrocious the events—note the critical importance of sacrifice and martyrdom for Christianity—the more significant they are assumed to be. For Jews in particular, with their almost unbroken record of persecution extending back to the covenant marking them as God's chosen people, the Nazi genocide stimulates a powerful psycho-logic expressing itself through reverential treatment of the Holocaust.

There are, furthermore, the survivors themselves, who carry a literally unspeakable burden of experienced horrors. In various psychiatric writings, Robert Lifton has indicated that those who live through extraordinary horror will resent dispassionate analysis by outsiders because of what he calls their "survivor complex,"[30] that is, a justifiable but nevertheless neurotic defense mechanism arising from unconscious guilt feelings at having remained alive when so many others died. Whatever validity one assigns to Lifton's survivor-complex formulation (he has discussed it in relation to American Vietnam veterans and Japanese survivors of nuclear bombing, as well as Jewish victims of the Nazis), it deserves mention as a relevant attempt to understand the personal long-term effects of extraordinary experience. Similarly, and in the same general context, psychological research following from Leon Festinger's theory of cognitive dissonance suggests that the more painful or difficult an experience has been, the more the inclination to think of that experience as important.[31]

It is not difficult, therefore, to see why virtually all writing on the Holocaust becomes controversial; whatever is done is liable to give offense to one party or another working from the standpoint of religion, history, psychology, or personal experience. The purpose of the discussion below is to offer a relatively dispassionate review of the social-emotional qualities allowing some persons to survive when caught up in a ferocious death machinery. This is not a purpose that can be served by obscurantist mysticism, however helpful that may be for some individual survivors. If the death camps are transformed from a series of human acts to a transcendental vision of extreme evil, then human accountability and responsibility are denied, scrutiny of what actually happened is prevented, and future generations will only be informed through myth.

Enough memoirs and histories are now available so that two general conditions governing the survival chances of deported Jews may be identified. First, the "object-qualities" of individuals—age, sex, health, profession—were frequently decisive. Wherever the arriving victims were sorted out for forced labor, healthy males between the ages of sixteen and fifty were most likely to be spared from immediate death. Medical professionals of either sex were also typically selected to work in dispensaries or camp hospitals; these were not very significant facilities, since few medical supplies were available, but the SS was always concerned to keep up the appearance of a well-ordered military facility.

The second condition determining survival was the type of camp to which one was sent. The chances were best for those (mainly German Jews) who were in concentration camps set up prior to the start of the war, particularly if they were able to live through the brutal initial "reception period." It was also generally true that if Jews were imprisoned for some specific reason other than their Jewishness, they stood a better chance of survival, because they might then be kept alive as a "case" instead of being eliminated as an "undesirable." Thus, the Jewish assassin of von Rath lived through the entire war in a German jail. No major mass killing centers were established on traditional German *(Altreich)* soil. The reasons for this were ideological ("We do not want German soil contaminated by the remains of inferior beings") and practical: tighter security could be maintained in conquered areas. Many deaths did occur in the older concentration camps, but they resulted from brutality, malnutrition, and random sadism rather than a deliberate, large-scale killing policy.

The death camps in Poland—Belzec, Chelmno, Sobibor, and Treblinka— were specifically designed for mass murder. To be sent to one of these camps was to face certain death because every arriving trainload of victims was killed in a matter of hours. The only exceptions were those few men who were selected to work in service of the killing operation itself, and even these *Sonderkommando* prisoners were scheduled for death when the camps closed down.

In terms of chances for survival, Auschwitz stood roughly between the older concentration camps in Germany and the full-blown extermination camps in Poland. The difficulty in categorizing Auschwitz arises from the fact that it was a complex of facilities including industrial plants, a slave labor barracks, and the largest mass production killing apparatus that has ever existed.[32] Arrivals at Auschwitz judged unfit for labor were sent immediately to the gas chambers. Among those remaining, the probability of survival varied depending upon the type of work they were assigned (indoor or outdoor; heavy or light), and the brutality of the prisoner-overseer (Kapo) who had immediate power over them. If prisoners became unable to work because of physical exhaustion or disease, or if they displeased their Kapo, they would be killed. Therefore, those selected for slave labor at Auschwitz and elsewhere found themselves in an extraordinary nightmare world of uncertainty and death. It is no wonder that Wiesel and other survivors have said that they themselves could hardly believe it was real.

It should be emphasized again that the immediate fate of deportation victims was almost entirely a matter of chance. Life or death depended upon the type of camp to which they were sent, and how they appeared to the eyes of SS slave labor selectors. It was only after passing through the vagaries of deportation and selection that the individual qualities of the victims became significant.

The most general statement that can be made in this respect seems at first glance a tautology: survival depended upon the individual's will to survive. Yet the evidence supporting this is very firm. Those in the camps who made desperate efforts to live often succeeded, and those who could not keep up an unceasing struggle for life went under rather quickly. Emphasis upon a strong, irrational will to live appears in almost every personal memoir of camp

. Moreover, it became a truism among the prisoners that they could
the signs of impending death in those of their fellow prisoners who
the struggle. In Auschwitz, such persons would show gross signs
ological withdrawal and were referred to as "Musselmen."

Apart from the direct testimony of survivors, other sources confirm that the
will to live cannot be taken for granted as fundamental in every human being
under all conditions. Quite the contrary. Social psychology studies have
begun to reveal that when atrocious experiences make life seem unbearable,
people tend to cut off their emotional engagement with immediate environ-
mental realities, and this detachment leads quickly to death. The process was
noted by Edgar Schein in his retrospective analysis of American POWs held
during the Korean War.[33] More detailed material is also showing up in studies
of death among the elderly. After carefully examining events preceding the
death of hospitalized elderly patients, Weisman and Kastenbaum reported a
surprisingly large number of instances in which death occurred shortly after
the patient suffered a serious loss of morale.[34] In one typical case, for
example, an elderly man who accidentally urinated near his bed announced
that no one should live this way and died shortly afterward without showing
any particular change in his physical condition.

Obviously, a strong determination to live was not in itself sufficient to
insure survival in the Nazi camps. Such determination had to be translated
into effective forms of action under conditions in which any action was liable
to be extremely hazardous. The prisoner who broke a rule or accidentally
irritated a guard or Kapo could be killed on the spot. By all accounts,
therefore, survival required both obsessive sensitivity to the mood of the
guards and constant alertness to take every relatively safe opportunity for
gaining extra food or a better work assignment.

The means by which different individuals found it possible to live varied
immensely. There are enough reports of dark episodes involving thefts of
rations from weaker prisoners, collaborations with guards, and even hints of
cannibalism, to indicate that conventional morality had little place in the
camps. On the other hand, some of the more experienced prisoners with better
work situations or influence (typically doctors or work-crew leaders) occasionally took serious risks to help newcomers. More surprising, there are a
number of survivors who mention small acts of spontaneous kindness or
charity from SS guards which sometimes made the difference between life and
death. Wiesenthal describes SS men who helped him and other prisoners and
who remained decent throughout the war.[35] But contacts with guards were
usually very dangerous, because many who showed kindness at one moment
might revert to extreme cruelty at another.

The first several weeks in the camps were the most difficult, for it was
during this time that people were particularly vulnerable to emotional despair
as well as the impact of malnutrition and overwork. Those who came through
this period because of their stamina and good luck learned the routines and
subtle cues allowing them to identify dangerous situations. They were then
better able to take steps associated with survival.

One of the more essential steps involved finding an indoor work assignment that did not drain off energy as rapidly as outdoor work. Another related factor involved the establishment of friendly contacts with older prisoners. Many survivor accounts state that death would have been certain without aid from a friend or acquaintance among the older prisoners. The longer people were in a camp, the more people they were likely to know, and the greater became their chances of gaining important help.

Generally, therefore, those who did not perish during their first few weeks were likely to live for several months. But then the chances of death increased again. The reason for this is not entirely clear, although it was apparently due to either the long-term effects of malnutrition or an accumulated burden of terrible experience that eroded the will to go on struggling. As the war dragged on, persons who were isolated in the camps and whose existence was virtually unknown to any outsider found it more and more difficult to maintain their hopes for freedom. Some were sustained by deeply rooted belief systems. Jehovah's Witnesses are usually mentioned in this connection because of their strong religious convictions; communists often felt confident of eventual vindication; some Zionists and social democrats had equally strong ideological beliefs; and there were others who simply lived in hopes of getting revenge.

Yet these were the exceptions rather than the rule. For the majority of prisoners, hope died as their vitality slowly ebbed away. The ego defense mechanisms of the prisoners—sublimation, rationalization, regression, identification with the aggressor—could not be maintained as their sources of psychic energy were depleted. If the allied governments had made significant real or symbolic efforts offering direct encouragement to the prisoners, their capacity to survive would undoubtedly have been enhanced. Almost every survivor account contains descriptions of persons who gave up the struggle for life because they lost all hope of rescue. A few propaganda broadcasts or leaflet raids directed at the camps might have made a great difference, for if there is anything more crushing than the burden of an atrocious captivity, it is the sense of being forgotten in that captivity.

Individual survival may be seen in general, therefore, as an issue which was essentially a matter of both good luck and persistent determination to stay alive. An individual's will to live is an elusive quality that has only recently become a subject for serious psychological study. Survivors who themselves embody this quality have for the most part been unable to provide more than simple descriptions emphasizing their refusal to give up. Cohen, for instance, said that he and most of his fellow survivors are unable to analyze their experience in greater depth because their sufferings were too intense: "ourselves to a certain extent victims, we lack in ourselves the vibrations essential for a true and deep penetration."[36] One exception is Bruno Bettelheim, who has argued from his relatively short-term concentration camp experience that the essential requisite for individual survival was an "autonomous ego": a sense of self-respect, inner dignity, and meaning. He suggests that many of the victims might have survived if they had been able to see beyond their everyday material concerns and appreciate their situation in time either to flee from the

Nazis or organize resistance. Once in the camps, he says, many died because, lacking ego autonomy, they lacked the inner strength to persevere.[37]

Viktor Frankl is another psychoanalytic writer with much more extensive experience in the camps than Bettelheim. His reflections on survival center on the prisoner's "will to meaning."[38] Somewhat similar to Bettelheim's, his perception was that life and death in the camps depended upon whether persons could find a deep conviction about the meaning of their lives. Those who could were much better able to cope with the hardships. Frankl's system of psychotherapy (logotherapy) is directly geared to individual values, and thus stands as a closely related outcome of his camp experience.

These prominent psychological perspectives stand as an obvious counterpart to more widely descriptive material showing that deep commitments to political or religious values were an important aid to survival. The will to live, which appears to be so clearly at issue when people have been brutalized to a point where death may seem the only way out of further suffering, must be strong enough to counterbalance the burden of suffering. Some persons were able to find such a counterbalancing force via their beliefs in externally organized metaphysical values. Others, as emphasized by Bettelheim and Frankl, were able to find sustaining forces within themselves, through internal dynamics associated with a state of ego autonomy or will to meaning.

What emerges from this inquiry, finally, is the picture of a concrete, personal struggle against the ultimate result of depersonalization: destruction of the will to live. In the last analysis, the will to live in the camps can best be grasped as a defiant, perhaps transcendental resistance against reduction of the self to an object of sacrifice.

Examined retrospectively and from the standpoint of its victims, the Holocaust appears as a sequence of depersonalizing events that culminated in mass-production death. Every major thread in the Nazi genocide pattern may be traced backward from the deaths themselves through identifiable stages of depersonalization: the selections, the deportations, the concentrations, the collaboration of various European authorities, and the relative indifference of the allied powers—all contributed to deprive the victims of their humanity.

Victims in the mass are not born; they are made through a convergent blend of historical and psychological circumstances allowing political bureaucracies to determine criteria for the right to life. Once categories of people are defined and perceived as nonpersons, they can readily be disposed of with minimal guilt feelings arising in their oppressors, for then the situation is such that "not the murderer but the murdered is guilty."[39]

# Chapter V

# *Resistance: The Idea and the Action*

If one backs away from particulars to view the destruction of the European Jews as a unitary event, the perception gained is inevitably suffused with a primitive feeling of mystery. Psychologically, this feeling is understandable, a basic human reaction to that which cannot be comprehended according to familiar standards of meaning. The extraordinary killings of millions are thus frequently described in a language of mystery and treated as such in Israel today, where monuments and museums variously convey it as a massive, dark horror, almost impossible to verbalize and then only in a whisper.

Yet among all the important elements composing this mystery, one that has remained more obscure than any other involves the efforts of Jews to forcibly resist destruction. These efforts have remained something of a mystery even for those who participated in them, and not merely for the scholars and writers who have come later seeking explanations. Why?

To ponder this question while immersed in relevant documents and commentaries is to gradually learn that a fundamental part of the answer has to do with conceptual ambiguities surrounding the idea of resistance. The difficult first truth one gradually discovers is that "resistance" has no clear historical, psychological, or political meaning. Contemporary usage of the term was promulgated during World War II as part of a moralistic propaganda campaign (resistance good; collaboration bad) denying the legitimacy of Nazi authority in conquered territories. Furthermore, ever since World War II, the term resistance, or derivatives such as "freedom fighters," has been claimed as a form of semantic legitimization by every sort of national and international movement, particularly those involving violence. This is the kind of conceptual confusion George Orwell discussed more than thirty years ago in his essay "Politics and the English Language."[1] It should, therefore, be apparent that any study of resistance may easily become an exercise in immediate political expediency or word magic unless analysis begins with a firm construal of what resistance means. Accordingly, while remaining primarily concerned with Jewish resistance to the Holocaust, in order to place this resistance in a meaningful context it is first necessary to seek a general definition for all forms of struggle against powerful political authority systems.

## The Idea of Resistance

There is no single, generally convenient path toward discussion of either the idea or the act of resistance except for situations in which it is considered under the heading of revolution. Yet resistance is not revolution and need not invariably seek revolution. Many forceful acts against a prevailing authority system or power group are aimed only at self-preservation or reform, not overthrow. Moreover, revolutions are overt affairs involving public statements of purpose, shadow governments, flags, and other symbols, whereas resistance may be covert and quite disorganized.

It would also be a mistake to classify resistance under the heading of dissent. Both terms refer to opposition against authority, but dissent is better used when describing opposition that is tolerated by authority. In this connection, it seems appropriate for heuristic purposes to describe the quality of opposition to existing authority on a continuum, with dissent at the mild end, revolution at the most intense end, and resistance somewhere in between.

On such a scale or continuum of opposition, dissent includes all legal and mildly illegal expressions of disagreement or protest. Those who dissent may well risk various forms of punishment officially or unofficially sanctioned by authority, but both the risk and the punishment are quite small. This assertion may seem absurd in view of examples that could be cited to demonstrate the contrary, yet insofar as dissent does carry the risk of severe punishment—exile, imprisonment, death—it becomes resistance. In many practical situations, therefore, it must be recognized that acts of opposition can only be judged after the fact, by the quality of the reaction they provoke.

Most actions against the Vietnam war in this country were clearly matters of dissent because they were either entirely legal (for example, signing petitions), or only mildly illegal (parading without a permit). But such acts as refusal to serve when drafted or destruction of government records were acts of resistance because of the severe penalties involved. The main point is that meaningful distinctions between dissent and resistance can only be made in situations where significant opposition remains essentially legal. Where there is no scope for dissent, all opposition is resistance.

Apart from the reactions of authority, another basis for separating dissent from resistance has to do with purpose: if the purpose of opposition is simply a change in policy and the legitimate right of authority to carry out its chosen policy is not challenged, then it is in the "loyal opposition" tradition of dissent. If such dissent is ineffective, or repressed without being crushed, however, it may ripen into an attack on the legitimacy of authority and thus be transformed into resistance. Opposition challenging the intrinsic right of authority to select and implement policy ("no taxation without representation") is the nucleus of resistance.

Recent American history provides many good examples of this in events of the past generation. The Black Panther organization represented a move toward resistance from dissent against racism; draft board raids and Weatherman bombings of public buildings signified resistance emerging from dissent against the Vietnam war. Neither of these efforts were able to maintain themselves against the harsh reactions of authority, and their failure demonstrates the difficulty of conducting significant resistance action in a society allowing substantial opposition to be expressed as dissent. Indeed, everything known about modern resistance movements shows that no amount of passion, charismatic leadership, or ideological agitation can long succeed in maintaining resistance action when the core premises for the action can be expressed legally and with some apparent (if not genuine) prospect of effecting change.

However, the considerations noted above reflect only surface contingencies influencing the genesis of resistance. To go deeper, it is necessary to analyze resistance at its own level, beginning with the complex of sociopolitical factors endowing forceful opposition to authority with its concrete meaning.

From the family to the tribe to the modern industrial state, all organized human groups are characterized by some form of sociopolitical authority system. The system must inevitably include two essential components: values defining right and wrong behavior, and social processes enforcing these values through institutions such as law and religion.

Obedience to the authority system is typically rooted in tradition as a historical norm, which, through the workings of institutions, is acted out in the immediate present in sociopolitical terms. Furthermore, as Freudian theory takes great pains to explain, obedience to authority is most basically an individual psychological attribute understandable as a dynamic aspect of personality, the superego, which provokes guilt feelings in the individual who may think of going against the authority system.

Authority systems are, therefore, not easily challenged in a significant way because they are so deeply woven into the social-psychological fabric of group life. It is for this reason that all paths of analysis lead toward one major thesis: resistance requires an existential leap, a going beyond the existing pattern and structure of obedience. To resist an authority system, no matter how oppressive and corrupt it may manifestly be, is to leap over the boundary lines defining conventional experience. In so doing, one must necessarily defy the conserving, stabilizing forces that regularize social life and provide the basis for feelings of security within the community.

Setting physical risk aside for the moment, it may be said that every act of resistance contains contradictory short-term and long-term psychological effects. The short-term effect is an immediate release of the emotional tension that has led up to the act of resistance. Abstractly, and for the purpose of formal analysis only, there is no fundamental difference between the emotions of an adolescent who feels an immediate, heady sense of liberation when going against his parents and the emotions of an adult who experiences catharsis on finally taking action against a political authority system.

The longer-term psychological effect of resistance, however, is to generate new forms of tension. Significant acts of resistance carry the actors beyond the frontiers of shared behavior norms. Once they have breached the conventional pattern of obedience in their society, important behavior standards can no longer be taken for granted. The immediate result is that questions of trust become paramount issues of concern, constantly being raised, debated and reevaluated. And no resistance group heroes or leaders of today can ever rest easy in such circumstances, for they may well emerge as the traitors of tomorrow. Over and above physical risk, this is the true peril constraining resistance. Acts of serious disobedience open a Pandora's box of anarchy. Obedience norms are terribly strong because they keep the lid down on the chaos and distrust Freud correctly understood to be the concomitants of unleashed instinct.

On the other hand, it is striking that despite the strong forces combining to maintain obedience, much of Western history is nothing if not a record of disobedience, of violent resistance and revolution impelled by the promise of significant change. Moreover, the record consists of either revolutions aimed at the overthrow of authority systems per se, or, in the case of nonrevolutionary resistance, of demands for fundamental alterations in the obedience norms serving an authority system. And these two purposes have frequently been coterminous.

Very broadly, therefore, the idea of resistance emerges as both an abstract and a literal paradox. Little wonder that it has occupied a central position in the works of modern existentialist, Marxist, and psychoanalytic thinkers; for if the resistance paradox must ultimately remain a gross unknown suspended in the phrase "human nature," it also remains a primary challenge to all serious social philosophies. Dealing with either the impulse toward resistance or the action itself, contemporary philosophical discussions have been influenced by, and have in turn exerted influence upon, the whole spectrum of social science and whatever remains of religion and of law that is not social science. The net result that can be drawn out of all this—apart from confusion— seemingly comes down to three separate but related criteria appropriate for evaluating the authenticity of resistance. However different their particular views of society may be, serious writers from Mao to Marcuse to Arendt tend to agree that resistance efforts depend upon the following three considerations.

1. The probability of success: How likely is it that resistance will succeed in achieving its purpose? Judgments here require analysis of the relative strengths and weaknesses of both the established authority and the resistance. To be authentic, the resistance must be geared to plausible goals and must offer a practical route toward their attainment.

2. The intensity of oppression: How severe is the pain or suffering imposed by the established authority? Those physical and psychological perils of resistance discussed above will hardly be risked unless obedience to the status quo is accompanied by a significant feeling of oppression. In situations where oppression is only latent, or is present but not experienced as such by its victims, some

form of consciousness raising is necessary before authentic resistance can be set in motion.

3. The presence of an alternative authority system: To what extent is the resistance effort supported or justified by values and norms contradicting the authority system in force? In common revolutionary parlance, this question is ordinarily understood to involve the ideological basis for denying the legitimacy of established authority. It is *not* ordinarily understood that the ideological basis for resistance is itself a real or nascent authority system; yet no resistance can be genuine if it is not guided by alternative values and norms.

None of these three criteria is completely free of ambiguity. On the contrary, each could easily be treated as a proposition to be debated, elaborated, and greatly enlarged upon. But such discussion is more properly the business of scholars of revolution; our immediate aim is to emphasize that residual ambiguities notwithstanding, resistance can be evaluated for its authenticity according to rational and relatively straightforward standards. Taken together, these standards may in principle be arranged to serve as a formal "resistance equation." Thus, authentic resistance would be a function of (1) the probability of success, (2) the intensity of oppression, and (3) the presence of an alternative authority system.

In many respects, this hypothetical formulation can serve as the basic equation defining effective resistance, for it suggests an orderly, relativistic framework describing the fundamental dimensions of action against authority. Much of the confusion in revolutionary literature is reduced when it becomes clear that prominent writings in this field tend to focus upon different factors in the equation. Marcuse has been roundly criticized, for example, because his work stimulates awareness of oppression and indicates a Marxist-Freudian basis for alternative authority systems without offering programmatic statements on how change may best be accomplished. He is, therefore, seemingly unconcerned with what we have called the probability of success.

Similarly, writers such as Che Guevara and Regis Debré, who focus primarily upon organizational matters tied to the probability of success, are often criticized for not giving enough attention to alternative authority systems and the awareness of oppression. The circumstances of Guevara's death appear to further confirm this judgment. Camus, finally, in his classic work *Resistance, Rebellion, and Death* devotes himself almost entirely to the problem of oppression and how it may reach sufficient intensity to generate resistance. His existentialist outlook apparently led him away from concerns with both the probability of success and alternative authority systems. The latter factor is almost ignored in a way that seems naive today because it only enters when Camus pleads for "justice" as the alternative to oppression.

Beyond the clarification it can bring to general discussions of resistance action, the foregoing analysis also has value as a tool for historical interpretation. Even a brief review of celebrated World War II resistance movements reveals that they could not have been sustained without the alternative authority system and probability of success provided by the allied powers. In

France, Greece, Yugoslavia, Italy, and Norway, for instance, intensities of German oppression varied immensely, but resistance action increased as the viability of allied support increased.

A somewhat contrary situation characterized the anticolonial movements following World War II. In Algeria, Vietnam, Indonesia, and other places, resistance went forward with relatively little outside support, depending mainly upon the recalcitrance and venal clumsiness of the colonialist authorities to increase awareness of oppression among the native populations. It is noteworthy that although resistance primarily based on the oppression factor can be as potent and as genuine as any other kind, available knowledge of such movements suggests that they are also the most difficult to maintain. So long as a powerful, established authority remains determined to impose its will and is not seriously distracted by other internal or external conditions, the resistance tends to have a low probability of success.

Jewish resistance was a perfect example of this condition because it developed almost entirely as a desperate response to the Nazi mass murder program. The extraordinary oppression factor was unsupported, however, by any significant possibility of success or alternative authority system offering substantial material or moral support. Success could only be conceived in terms of delaying SS operations and demonstrating to the world that Jews could fight. A further impediment to Jewish resistance was the absence of any unitary alternative authority system. The mixed ideals of various Jewish fighting groups in Eastern Europe ranged from personal revenge to left and right-wing Zionism and socialism. Some West European Jews fought out of nationalistic loyalty to their home country. Consequently, apart from shared horror at the Nazi oppression, there was no single ideology or affirmative goal that could provide a cohesive force for the disparate Jewish resistance groups.

Useful as it is for discussing the sociopolitical logic of resistance, however, the three-factor equation fails to capture an essential psychological element: the individual will to resist. That is, like so many other formulations based on a rationalized, "scientific" mode of analysis, the resistance equation serves well enough as a tool for reductionistic description but offers little insight into the dynamics of personal causality. How is it possible for individuals to make the existential leap over the boundaries of established obedience norms? And what qualities of their experience can carry oppressed persons forward to forceful resistance despite utterly hopeless odds? Questions of this type cannot be properly addressed through the exercise of formal, objective logic. Instead, they require a more subjective, phenomenological examination of experience.

### From Victim to Resister

The transition from victim to resister is never accomplished without the reality or threat of violence. Frantz Fanon developed the psychological aspects of this thesis in relation to the struggles of colonial populations to achieve independence, but it fits all serious resistance efforts.

Writing from a dual perspective—his professional background in psychiatry and his experience of the Algerian revolt against France—Fanon identified the existential moment of resistance as occurring when the victim is able to act with the same violence as the oppressor. Such violence is the means whereby persons oppressed to the point of internalizing a subservient, inferior self-image may throw off their role as victims. The direct action against their oppressors is therapeutic, enabling them to gain a new consciousness of self.[2]

Tied as it is to the horrors most of us associate with violence, this view of resistance is at first difficult to accept. Violence as a necessary component of revolt? Yes. But violence as therapeutic? Bizarre. Yet the evidence supporting it is too strong to be ignored. Consider the testimony of Zivia Lubetkin describing one of the first violent acts of resistance against the Germans in the Warsaw ghetto during January 1943. Hiding with a group of forty young people who had resolved to fight back with a few smuggled revolvers, she tells of the successful ambush and pursuit of a German search party: "We were overjoyed; all the suffering seemed worthwhile. With our own eyes we had seen scared Germans, we had seen them turn to run; and we had pursued them. German soldiers who thought they were conquerors of the world were being chased by Jewish boys."[3] Later that same day, while hiding out in another building, Lubetkin saw German parties moving through the ghetto cautiously and showing fear, whereas earlier they had always acted with absolute confidence. Her reaction was a perfect illustration of the psychological generalizations Fanon would develop some twenty years later: "Our spirits rose. No more did we feel the worry, the anguish of the days that had gone before. We felt redeemed—we felt our lives were again useful. What we were doing would be recompense for the murders, and our own deaths, which seemed inevitable, would not be in vain—would make sense. Beyond that, a spark of hope remained: perhaps we might live."[4]

This type of statement appears over and over again in the writings of victims who were finally able to resist. Their reflections invariably convey a sense of intense euphoria at the discovery that their oppressors were, after all, human and could be fought. There is, for example, the testimony of a Jewish partisan who operated in Russia. He was very frightened during his first combat action, yet at the same time elated: "But our joy was greater than our fear. For the first time we had fought the German soldiers face to face! We had proved that it was possible to do so and that it was possible to kill them."[5] Even in less extreme circumstances than those created by the Nazis, the resistance euphoria inevitably appears. It can be found in such diverse sources as Norman Mailer's self-reported feelings while taking part in an antiwar march; in the correspondence of the Berrigan brothers' group as they planned war resistance activities; and even in the remark attributed to an American B-52 pilot who refused to fly missions in Indochina: "This is the first time in my life that I have been able to feel really happy and good, because I have made the right decision."[6]

Placed in a more general psychological context, the euphoria we have identified as characterizing the transition from victim to resister might seem to be of dubious importance. Why should any special meaning be attributed to the elation of resisters when in fact others—including oppressors—have also reported euphoric "highs" following successful combat? Indeed, civilians who have had a close brush with accidental death may also feel elated to find themselves alive. What is so special about resistance euphoria?

The answer is that unlike most soldiers or accident victims, the resister is usually someone who has deliberately chosen to step beyond the boundaries of everyday life as it is defined by prevailing authority systems. By making the decision to resist (the "existential leap" described above), the resister not only accepts physical risks, but also enters a very new psychological situation. The general meaning of resistance euphoria cannot be reduced to the emotions accompanying any straightforward experience of severe risk or danger. To oppose oneself to a powerful, deadly authority system is not equivalent to making a parachute jump or volunteering for a dangerous military mission, for in these latter situations the individual does not necessarily undergo profound psychological change. The conception of self and of others may be changed quantitatively as a result of daring action—enhanced ego strength might follow from demonstrated bravery, perhaps—but this is not the same as the qualitative changes that follow from resistance.

The essence of the euphoria characterizing serious resistance is that it signals the experience of a new world view. Once engaged, action against that which has been avoided, feared, and repressed works a sudden and deeply pervasive change on the individual. This is the therapeutic that Fanon indicated in his discussions of anticolonialist revolts. The release of pent-up energy allows the victim to feel suddenly different, healed of internal conflicts and relieved of the burden of tension and guilt that has accumulated in consequence of being victimized. In more general terms, the resister is one who has "taken arms against a sea of troubles" and ended them, if need be at the cost of life itself.

Yet, like Hamlet's decision to oppose his stepfather, the individual's decision to go against powerful authority does not come easily. In Europe under the Nazis, and in many other situations as well, the general rule seems to be that so long as most people are allowed to maintain themselves in some kind of minimally bearable condition, they are unwilling to take the risk of forceful resistance. As noted above, such an attitude can be justified by an appeal to religious values, traditional norms, and the brutal considerations of *Realpolitik:* to resist might be to provoke a further repression worse than the one at hand.

No responsible person can ignore such arguments. Every threatened community of Jews in Europe contained respected leaders who made precisely this point. In the Warsaw Ghetto in 1941–1943, for example, the question of resistance was steadily debated by various leaders prior to the eventual revolt. As described by Izhak Zuckerman, one argument made by a well-known Jewish historian was that "if we declared war we would only destroy that which it was possible to save." Another position repeated by a religious spokesman was simply "The Lord giveth and the Lord taketh away. . . . we could not raise a hand against the Germans, and so bring about the murder of hundreds of thousands of Jews." And there were still others who believed that no action should be taken except in collaboration with the Polish underground organization: "Let us fight when the Poles fight!"[7]

Several of the more militant groups, mainly Zionist youth and some with communist connections, eventually formed a united front toward the end of 1942 and began to train for revolt while accumulating smuggled and home-made weapons. But it is noteworthy that no formal, collective decision to begin fighting was ever made. Instead, when the Nazis brought up forces to undertake a final liquidation of the ghetto in January 1943, the various combat groups that had been organized were taken by surprise. They began to fight on their own initiative with little or no coordination, in a series of sporadic actions against German patrols.

These unexpected firefights proved to be enough of a shock to the Germans, however, for them to halt their operations for several weeks until better trained troop units were available. The ghetto fighters used this respite to prepare for the extended final battle that was to begin in April. Along with some other surviving participants, Zuckerman stated later that if the combat groups had not spontaneously fought back in January, the revolt might never have occurred, because at that time the ghetto leaders were still undecided about plans for action.

The documents available on the ghetto revolt show how difficult it is to organize serious resistance when some hope of survival remains. This aspect of the Warsaw experience was repeated in many of the Jewish ghettos throughout Europe. When it is considered that in most of these same communities, people later gained reasonably sure knowledge of the mass killing program, the question then arises: what prevents open resistance once it is clear that there is no substantial basis of hope for survival? Logically, nothing; psychologically, a great deal.

During the earlier periods of Nazi domination, despite numerous arbitrary killings, the policy publicly announced and believed by Germans and Jews alike was that if the ghetto inhabitants followed orders and engaged productively in enterprises contributing to the German war effort, they would in effect be "earning their keep" and thus be safe. Even when news of systematic killings leaked out, people in the ghettos were encouraged by their Nazi supervisors to believe that their particular community or work group would be spared so long as it was productive. This rationalization was only abandoned in the last extreme moments when it was contradicted by events making effective resistance all but impossible. Moreover, since the habit of defensive rationalization seems hard to break, there were many who boarded the trains for Treblinka believing the Nazi cover story of transportation to a new work project.

In the town of Grodna, for instance, an eyewitness account states that when the deportation operation began, a few small groups of Jews tried to escape to the forest, but the majority were passive. "Everybody now knew that everyone taken out of the Ghetto was being shipped to Treblinka. Many rebelled. 'We shall not go! Let them rather shoot us here on the spot!' But their words fell on deaf ears. All of them went. They hoped that some miracle would occur on the train. They waited to be saved by a miracle—and they went to their death."[8]

A more complex but fundamentally similar pattern occurred in the Bialystok ghetto. A resistance group prepared to make a last-ditch fight against deportation with the understanding that none of the ghetto inhabitants would go voluntarily to the deportation assembly area. When the appointed time arrived, however, most of the people went quietly, ignoring the pleas of the young resistance fighters.

> Our messengers were speeding to every corner of the Ghetto, explaining, trying to persuade. Jews, don't go of your own will. This is not an evacuation to Lublin. Every time they take anyone from the Ghetto it means death. Don't go! Hide yourself! Fight with everything that comes to hand. Our colleagues turned from one group of Jews to another, exhorting, berating. But the wave was streaming into the streets, which were filled constantly with Jews.

Reflecting further on this scene, the writer was able to pinpoint the essential rationale of those who went to their deaths without struggling: "A family marched along in the sun. It was easier to die among many than to fight and suffer alone. As it looked, it was easier to die soon than to live a long, tortured life. Truly, living in a hole, in a cave, under a wall, in colonization sewers, in pits and cellars—*this was perhaps a curse to be weighed against a quick death that redeemed* (italics added)."[9]

This is the quintessential psychological and sociopolitical dilemma facing those who consider resistance: when the promise of survival seems strong, resistance will appear to be folly, a threat to the object it aims to preserve. And when there is little or no hope of survival, resistance would appear to be absurd, a guarantee only of further misery in addition to death.[10]

### Survival Is Not Enough

The transition from victim to resister does not grow primarily out of the desire to survive. Except in a few special cases, the hope of preserving one's own life stands as the least important personal factor in resistance efforts. More frequently than not, and despite popular views to the contrary, action against powerful authorities is undertaken on exactly opposite grounds. The first order of business for those planning acts of revolt usually involves the renunciation of personal concerns, including their own individual survival.

Such total commitment to resistance action is not accomplished easily and is virtually never shared by large numbers of people. Yet the history of this century provides a long list of relevant examples. From the fin de siècle Russian nihilists to present-day factions of the Palestinian guerrillas or the Irish Republican Army, it is not difficult to cite dramatic evidence of total commitment. Often revealing themselves only through terrorist acts, and dismissed as being merely rare fanatics or psychopaths, such persons define the leading, visible edge of ideologically inspired resistance action.

Although resistance efforts neither can nor should be defined according to their most extreme manifestations, the extremes do shed light on the processes that have nurtured them. Psychologically, the extraordinary acts of terrorists suggest the extraordinary motivating force of the ideological goals to which they are usually attached. Viewed in the broader context of contemporary history, moreover, there is no mistaking the evidence showing that ideology—not survival—is the chief inspiration for all serious resistance movements.

The ideology may be rooted either in a fully articulated world view such as Marxism or Catholicism, or it may involve only a simple belief in certain humanitarian values, but regardless of its roots, it must generate ideas powerful enough to overwhelm the desire for personal survival. Furthermore, a good deal of relevant evidence suggests that the abstract values inspiring resistance may gradually come to dominate the individual and literally compel dangerous action despite all contrary fears or rationalizations. The resistance ideation can take on a life of its own, and its logic may pervade other factors in the person's life to such a degree that living per se becomes meaningless unless the logic is acted out. Put in more precise psychological terms, it may be said that the person's ego or self-image becomes so enmeshed with the values at issue that nothing but direct action can maintain self-esteem.

Many examples of this process are described in Heimler's collection of essays on resistance. Sometimes the decision to act is sudden, as in the case of a journalist in Nazi-occupied Hungary who put up posters saying "National Socialism Is Death":

> The idea occurred to him while he was shaving one morning. He stood in front of the mirror, he said, and suddenly saw his face in a way in which he had never seen it before. He said it was the face of a traitor. The face asked him, "what are you going to do about the injustice that is on its way?" By the time he had finished shaving he was ready with the answer. When everyone had gone home that night he used his own paper's presses to print the posters and then went out and put them up himself.[11]

At another extreme are those for whom resistance is a style of life beginning in childhood. Heimler describes his own life in these terms, explaining that as the son of a dedicated socialist who was also a religious Jew and, therefore, twice damned in the atmosphere of prewar Hungary, he was aware of oppression and determined to fight against it even as a young boy: "Small as I was I determined never to give in, never to go under, and I decided that one day when I grew bigger I would stand up against oppression of any kind."[12]

A very powerful example of how resistance may develop in persons who are not themselves direct targets of oppression occurred in Munich in 1943. A small group of students acting entirely on their own produced and circulated leaflets attacking the Nazis. Known as the White Rose, the group was led by a twenty-four-year-old medical student named Hans Scholl. He had once idolized Hitler and been prominent in the local Hitler Youth group. Yet as he grew into a sensitive teenager who loved poetry and the woodland rambling that had been a part of the earlier, antiestablishment German Youth movement, brutal demands for conformity left him disillusioned. In this, Scholl was not different from many others of his background. What distinguished him was a particular set of circumstances that allowed him to work out his ideas and emotions in a way that led inevitably toward action.

Briefly, these circumstances included (1) a family that shared his feelings —his father saw Hitler as an antichrist; (2) a small circle of student friends who were also profoundly disturbed by their growing realization of what was happening in Germany; and (3) direct experience with the war and the Jewish liquidation program gained during a period of front-line service in Russia as a medical aid man. In this general context, Scholl moved from confused doubt to the conviction that the Nazi government was criminal, an evil force that was destroying the German people. It followed that an honest person had no recourse except to struggle against the criminal regime. Discussions in a group that included his younger sister Sophie, a fifty-year-old professor of philosophy named Kurt Huber, and three of his fellow students strengthened Scholl's beliefs. The group agreed that resistance was a duty they could not ignore: "We must do it for the sake of life itself—no one can absolve us of this responsibility."[13]

A few months later, after distributing leaflets calling upon Germans to understand their position under the Nazis and to engage in whatever forms of resistance might be possible, the group was caught by the Gestapo. They were beheaded for high treason in 1943.

The Scholl group exemplifies resistance in its purest form, originating as a matter of conscience and increasingly dominating the individual's ego until action becomes imperative, a duty that cannot be ignored.[14] Here too, one may see how conscience or moral thought translates into ideology, in the sense that it generates a rationale providing guidelines for action. Scholl's ideology was based on his belief in the innate integrity and continuity of the German people. He felt that leaflets speaking out against Nazi crimes would energize resistance by demonstrating that it was possible to protest, and in this way people could be awakened to their responsibilities. If the Nazi terror was so severe as to preclude open resistance, there still remained various forms of passive sabotage. And failing all else, if he and his colleagues were killed, they would at least have shown to future generations that the German people were not entirely without honor.

Such material might appear irrelevant to the Jews. Their peril was so concrete that resistance would seem to require no further justification in either conscience or ideology. But events reveal the contrary.

### Jewish Resistance Ideology

It is generally believed that organized Jewish resistance only occurred in Eastern Europe, most particularly in Poland and the Soviet Union. When Jews were active in resistance groups elsewhere, they participated in a nonsectarian, nationalist fashion, much as did any other citizen.[15]

This more-or-less standard historical view of Jewish resistance may be called into question, however, because of evidence showing that Jews in the West often conducted resistance in a deliberately obscured fashion. In France, for example, the Jewish poet David Knout organized a fighting group supported with Zionist funds. Consisting mainly of young people recruited from the prewar Jewish Scout organization, this underground group eventually fought with other French Maquisards in the South, but its Jewish identity was not widely known. The Jewish scouts themselves operated a clandestine escape and evasion network under pretense of working with the German-sponsored French Jewish Council. According to Poliakov, these scouts helped rescue more than four thousand persons from deportation. Poliakov also makes the point that Jews played a disproportionately large role in French national resistance organizations, but they often assumed Gentile names in order to avoid reprisals against their families.[16]

Qualitatively similar material can be found describing Jewish resistance in Italy, Holland, and other occupied countries. Greece in particular had substantial Jewish escape and fighting groups.[17] More generally, close study of the national resistance movements in Western Europe strongly suggests that Jews often constituted a kind of underground within the underground. And for this reason, perhaps, their activities have not received much attention.[18]

On the other hand, it remains quite true that Eastern Europe was the preeminent arena for visible Jewish resistance. Here, most Jews were cut off from native populations because of traditional anti-Semitism and the Nazi ghetto regulations. They could not follow the classic model for resistance action growing out of popular nationalistic feelings, and they received no significant external support: "As far as the Allies were concerned, they refused to aid the Jews as such; they would give assistance to Poles or Frenchmen, but not to some mythical Jewish nation; they missed many opportunities of saving groups of Jews from genocide."[19]

Added to these conditions of isolation, which were in themselves an immense barrier to organizing resistance, the Jewish population was also divided by religious and political differences. The conservative, semi-mystical religious sects withdrew into themselves to await a heavenly judgment, and the assimilationist groups of petit bourgeois were inclined toward accommodation if not outright collaboration. The socialist and secular Jewish Bund rejected Zionism as a solution to the Jewish problem and stood for a policy of recognition of Jewish national-cultural autonomy based on the Yiddish language. Zionists remained the largest organized portion of the Jewish population, but they were divided into at least four competing factions.

On the political right wing, the Zionist-Revisionist party stood as conservative nationalists. They favored immediate mass migration to Palestine and military action to establish the Jewish national homeland. Moderates were represented by the General Zionist party, which included a liberal social democratic element opposed to more conservative, business-oriented members. The left-wing Zionists were arrayed in several parties and youth groups based on moderate or extreme forms of socialism. Finally, there was also the Mizrachi party, composed of those who hoped for a Jewish homeland that would be organized entirely on the basis of religious law.[20]

Divided among themselves, isolated from the surrounding population, and unrecognized by the allied powers, the Polish Jews were in the worst possible position to generate serious resistance, and for almost two years there was very little. Conditions were much the same in the occupied territories of the Soviet Union. But there many Jews of military age were already serving as soldiers, and as the others were confronted by the Nazi murder units, many made their way into regular partisan units. In places where peasant anti-Semitism was so severe that Jews could not join the Russian partisans, they were able to form groups of their own. Yet since the Soviet military sponsored these groups, and since they operated according to regular partisan strategy and were often led by dedicated communists who were Jews in name only, the Russian Jewish partisan fighters cannot be said to constitute a true Jewish resistance.[21] Such resistance only occurred in Poland, where of necessity it developed in the ghettos as an authentic expression of Jewish identity.[22]

In 1941, approximately three million Polish Jews were concentrated in five major urban ghettos located in Warsaw, Vilna, Bialystok, Cracow and Lodz. They were administered by miniature Jewish governments set up by the Nazis. Known as the *Judenräte*, or Jewish community councils, these puppet authorities were charged with overseeing daily life in the ghettos and were responsible for arranging housing and sanitation, and maintaining order. For the latter purpose, the *Judenräte* administrators were permitted to maintain their own police forces, which soon became notorious as adjuncts of the Nazi control apparatus.[23]

At first, even Zionists and representatives of the socialist Jewish Bund participated in a considerable number of *Judenräte*. These councils included sincere assimilationists—some who ultimately took a stand in opposition to the Nazis, others who believed in following the tradition of survival through cooperation, and still others who were simply opportunists. Some distinctions may be made between the attitudes of the councils (the majority of whose chairmen eventually refused to hand over Jews for killing) and of the Jewish police (which generally collaborated much more willingly), but in general it appears that the conduct of the Jewish "self-governments" ultimately facilitated the genocide program.

Although the Zionist, socialist, and communist groups were later to initiate open resistance, until mid-1941 their activities were limited to propaganda and self-help projects designed to make ghetto life more bearable. Their most significant public action involved circulation of illegal newspapers that attacked the more blatant forms of collaboration and corruption of the *Judenräte*. Under the surface, however, these groups were preoccupied with organizational problems. Their older, better-known leaders had been imprisoned or executed immediately following the Nazi occupation. Younger people were quickly moved up to replace them, and while this forced a change to more youthful leadership that was to be an important contributing factor in the later development of open resistance, it initially created a good deal of confusion.

Organization was also hampered by poor communications between groups isolated in the different ghettos. The Nazis prohibited free travel and it took some time before a covert messenger system could be arranged. For obvious reasons, this system always remained relatively slow and unreliable.

The first reports of mass killings started to circulate in Warsaw and other ghettos during the summer of 1941. Most Jews, including the *Judenräte* authorities, dismissed these reports as mere rumors or exaggerations of isolated incidents. Systematic murder was unprecedented, unthinkable, and, therefore, unbelievable.[24] But the underground Zionist and left-wing political groups took the reports seriously enough to start further investigations, and as additional information was gathered by trusted party members it was established that large numbers of Jews were indeed being sent to killing centers under the pretense of relocation. In February of 1942, a comprehensive summary of the evidence given to underground political groups in Warsaw indicated that approximately half the prewar Jewish population had already been killed.

Key leaders were no longer in doubt about the killings; although there were a few who clung to the hope that only "unproductive" elements in the population were to be eliminated, the majority recognized that they were facing genocide. Reactions followed very much in accord with the ideological character of each group and the local conditions prevailing in each ghetto.

The Pioneer Youth components of the left-wing and right-wing Zionist organizations moved to form themselves into combat groups and began accumulating weapons. This was a natural outgrowth of their activist, paramilitary orientation toward the problem of resettlement in Palestine, only now the focus of struggle was shifted from emigration to defense. But if the decision to fight was clearly in line with prior ideology, the strategy to be followed posed a hard dilemma. Should the fighting youth act primarily to save themselves, or should they try to protect the remaining mass of Jews? The first alternative would entail a retreat to forest hideouts where partisan activity

would be aimed at self-preservation and maintenance of the Zionist movement. The second alternative seemed virtually suicidal, since it would require
direct attacks on the Nazi forces deployed against the ghettos. Yet the
emotional impact of the Nazi killing operations was so intense that most of the
young people could not tolerate the idea of letting it go unopposed.[25]

What emerged from this dilemma was a mixed situation that varied from
one ghetto to another. In Warsaw, debates among the leaders of different
factions continued until events reached the point (in autumn 1942) at which
only a last-ditch fight in the ghetto was feasible. In Bialystok, a compromise
was adopted, whereby all those who could manage it joined partisan units in
the forest, and others remaining in the city prepared to fight deportation. Here
there was armed resistance as early as spring 1942, but it was not until 1943
that all factions agreed to form an anti-Nazi coalition. Unified in a central
command structure and given substantial aid by Soviet partisan units, the
Bialystok fighters held off German forces for over a week in August 1943, and
after the ghetto was burned out, many managed to escape.

With only fifteen thousand Jews, the Cracow ghetto was too small to
sustain a sizable resistance force, but for this reason unity among the
underground groups came easily. The Zionists and communists pooled their
resources and supported effective urban guerrilla units as early as 1941.
These units operated to impede deportations for almost two years, and small
bands remained active even after the ghetto was substantially wiped out in
March 1943.

The Vilna ghetto held sixty thousand Jews and here too the Zionist,
Bundist and communist groups banded together for armed resistance early in
1942. Helped by good contacts with Soviet partisans, the Vilna combat units
were relatively well armed. When Nazi forces moved in to eliminate the
ghetto in September 1943, there was a general uprising as well as attacks on
the Nazi approach routes by partisan bands outside the ghetto. After a few
days of fighting the mass of the Jewish population was deported, but hundreds
were able to get away.

In Lodz, German domination was particularly severe and the *Judenrat*
collaborated very closely with their masters. These conditions prevented
formation of any sizable resistance organizations, but small bands of Zionist
youth conducted isolated raids and sabotage operations. There were also
strikes by Jewish workers in the German war factories. Deportations could
not be resisted with force, however, because of the strong German presence
and the danger of betrayals by collaborators.

The ideological basis for resistance is very clear in all the cases noted
above. It was founded on militant movements for Zionism, socialism, or
communism. These groups had always provided their members with both a
strong historical sense of struggle and an identification with group goals rather
than individual satisfaction. Politically, there were great differences between
them, but they were quite similar in terms of the psychological orientation required for resistance. And beyond their similar commitment to social

values offering a direct foundation for resistance ideology, these movements also shared much practical experience with underground organizational techniques.

## Resistance in the Camps

Resistance fighting was not limited to the ghettos. There were major rebellions in the death camps at Sobibor, Treblinka, and Auschwitz, and a number of small-scale fighting escapes from slave labor units. On the surface, these actions differ sharply from the ghetto fighting because they seem little more than last-minute attempts to avoid death. Yet, here again, the available evidence shows that personal survival was not the major factor underlying the rebellions. Indeed, most of the prisoners involved were so deeply immersed in a world of death that life had lost its conventional meaning.

Aside from occasional escapes attempted during transportation or while on casual labor parties, resistance in the camps was the work of "old" prisoners, those who had kept themselves alive under the most extreme conditions. The typical adaptation made by these people left them toughened to the point of seeming to be indifferent and even contemptuous toward the anguish surrounding them. It is impossible to exaggerate the psychological gulf separating old from new prisoners.[26]

The old prisoners' general attitude was described by Primo Levi, who survived eighteen months in Auschwitz:

> In history and in life one sometimes seems to glimpse a ferocious law which states: "To he that has, will be given; to he that has not, will be taken away." In the Lager, where man is alone and where the struggle for life is reduced to its primordial mechanism, this unjust law is openly in force, is recognized by all. With the adaptable, the strong and astute individuals, even the leaders willingly keep contact. . . . But with the mussulmans, the men in decay, it is not even worth speaking, because one knows already that they will complain and will speak about what they used to eat at home. . . . And in any case, one knows that they are only here on a visit, that in a few weeks nothing will remain of them but a handful of ashes in some nearby field and a crossed out number on a register.[27]

Resistance by new prisoners was all but impossible. They arrived in the camps exhausted and bewildered by their strange new surroundings. If they were not killed within the first several hours, they were placed in work groups among old prisoners indifferent to their distress. Suicide was not infrequent, and if there was any thought of attacking a guard or attempting escape, it was brutally discouraged by the constant reminder of extreme torture awaiting those who did not remain totally subservient.

Old prisoners were generally convinced that resistance was futile. Even if a revolt might allow some to escape, where would they go? In the absence of connections on the outside, the most immediate prospect was quick recapture and slow death by torture.

Consequently, direct resistance was rare. Yet in the three major instances where it occurred, old prisoners were responsible. Their familiarity with camp routines, personnel, and subtle weaknesses in the control system provided the basis for effective planning. More important, however, were the personal qualities of guile, toughness, and vicious determination developed in the course of their struggle to stay alive. While it is true that no formal ideological elements underlay any of the major rebellions, it is also true that in each case they were organized and carried out by persons who had been transformed by their camp experience.

Largely devoid of any commitments to particular ideological values, the old prisoners had nevertheless become converts to conspiracy and deception simply in order to live. In this sense, they were revolutionized psychologically and prepared for violent action because of their atrocious experience rather than an allegiance to abstract ideals. Almost by definition, therefore, no one could become an old prisoner without acquiring an informal ideology emphasizing desperate struggle against an incredible environment.[28] When on certain occasions groups of old prisoners learned that no such struggle could prevent death any longer, that they were all destined to be killed once their work assignments were completed, rebellion became the only alternative.

The revolt at Treblinka in August 1943 was of this nature. Maintained as a permanent slave labor force, several hundred Jews selected from among arriving trainloads had spent many months servicing the killing machinery. Gossip picked up from the guards and a new work pattern designed to destroy all evidence of the camp's existence made it plain that Treblinka was to be closed down and that they themselves would also be eliminated. A coordinated plan was developed to attack individual officers and guard posts with homemade weapons. After a core group of prisoners began the revolt, others joined in and succeeded in forcing several openings in the camp perimeter. Enough guards remained in action, however, to shoot down the majority of escaping prisoners. And of the one hundred fifty to two hundred who got out of the camp, only twelve ultimately survived.[29]

The Sobibor extermination camp had a work force of approximately six hundred prisoners, including among them a sizable number who had been captured while serving in the Soviet army. In concert with Polish Jews imprisoned for a much longer period, the Russian soldiers organized an uprising essentially similar to the one at Treblinka. Using hatchets and knives fashioned from their work tools, they killed several guards, took their guns, and used them to attack the main gate. According to the testimony of the Russian leader of the rebellion, the breakout itself was a success, but many of the prisoners were killed by mines and gunfire as they ran across an open area to reach shelter in a nearby forest. Here the various Russian, Polish, and West European Jews split into small groups, some heading East toward Russia and others moving off toward more familiar areas of Poland. Although no exact count has been made on the number of survivors, it is estimated that at least sixty men and women were able to link up with a Soviet partisan group.[30]

The third major revolt occurred at Auschwitz on September 6, 1944. This was chiefly the work of one hundred thirty-five Greek Jews who were assigned to the crematorium. Some of them had been active in the Greek resistance prior to being deported, and the group included three former officers of the Greek army. All the crematoria workers knew they were doomed, because it was common knowledge that these prisoners were periodically killed as a matter of SS policy. In order to slow down the mass killing, however, the Greeks resolved to blow up the body-disposal ovens. Acting with extraordinary skill and with aid from other underground groups in the sprawling work-death complex, the Greeks accumulated some guns and dynamite and were able to destroy two of the four ovens. A number of French and Hungarian Jews also working at the crematorium joined the action, but the SS response was very swift: within two hours the rebellion was crushed and all were killed except for a few wounded, who were later hanged in front of the other prisoners.[31]

Unlike the major prisoner risings that have become known through survivor statements or Nazi records, smaller-scale rebellions have remained relatively obscure. Judging from accounts that have gradually emerged during the past twenty-five years, these incidents of resistance were probably more frequent than has generally been known. In the Auschwitz complex, for example, Sim Kessel mentions a prisoner who dragged an SS guard with him as he leaped to his death in a mine shaft. Kessel himself, with four Polish prisoners, succeeded in escaping several miles away from Auschwitz before being recaptured.[32] Similar resistance actions occurred in the slave labor and extermination camps throughout Eastern Europe.

Leon Wells describes a fighting escape made by a party of prisoners assigned to burn bodies in a forest near Lvov. Knowing that they themselves would soon be killed, the hundred-odd men in the work group agreed that the strongest of them would attack several key guards and open a way to escape for the others. The plan worked well enough for most of them to get past the inner barbed wire fences, but then the aroused guard detachment killed the majority before they could scatter into the forest. Wells escaped by taking a different route.[33]

At a killing center named Punor, close to the city of Vilna, another party of about one hundred Jews were forced to destroy bodies. Here the work went on with the men hobbled in leg irons twenty-four hours a day; as an added security precaution, they were forced to sleep in an underground bunker surrounded by barbed wire and surmounted by guard posts. While constructing the bunker, however, two of the prisoners realized that it might be possible to tunnel their way out beyond the wire. The tunnel required eleven weeks of digging by more than a dozen men. After it was finished, they used homemade saws to remove their leg chains and broke out into the night. As the prisoners reached the outer fence, guards heard them and opened fire. Almost half the escapees were killed at this point; of the others who continued on, thirteen are known to have survived.[34]

In other places, prisoners who saw no hope of escape killed themselves rather than wait for a programmed death. One such case occurred at a slave camp called Konin, where a dozen men set fire to the buildings and hanged themselves. Resistance tantamount to suicide was also reported at Trabnik and Ponyatov in the Lublin area.[35] There is no way of knowing how many further cases of resistance have gone unrecorded either because there were no survivors or because the few who lived were unable to speak. Nazi reports of Jewish resistance are sometimes unreliable, and many of the lower-echelon records were lost or destroyed.

Taken together, all of the material available on resistance in the ghettos and camps reveals an impressive struggle by people facing hopeless odds. To fight back under such conditions was not simply a matter of personal courage or desperation, however. The ghetto fighters were sustained by formal ideological commitments, while those who revolted in the camps were moved by an informal but powerful existential ideology. This latter motivating force was by no means an automatic response to the threat of death. Prisoners in the camps could only organize resistance when they had passed beyond the normal boundaries of confusion and despair.

Where strong in-group discipline based on shared political convictions or on bitter camp experience was lacking, there was only chaos, fear, and resignation, not resistance. Kessel, for example, says that he might have escaped by breaking through the floor of the boxcar carrying him to Auschwitz but for the outcry of others in the car who were afraid they would be punished if he tried. He also described the hopeless atmosphere prevailing in a French camp holding Jews awaiting shipment to Auschwitz:

> Among this wretched mass of humanity, twenty jammed into a room, were individuals from every social level—millionaire bankers to penniless bums. All of them knew that, barring a miraculous change in the war situation, eventually and inevitably they were going to find themselves naked together awaiting death. . . . One might have thought that they would pool their resources, at least within the realm of possibility, to try to form a united front against their common misfortune. This never happened, or practically never. A few sensible people tried to preach wisdom, but they were preaching in the desert. . . . That famous racial solidarity so denounced by Nazi theoreticians as a peril to the world proved to be pure legend. It was every man for himself.[36]

Indeed, with the exception of those strongly committed to a militant ideology, the Jews in Nazi-dominated Europe were hardly capable of acting contrary to the principle of *sauve qui peut*. Raised in a subculture emphasizing individual achievements and primary responsibility to the family, and living in societies that permitted them few alternatives aside from competitive business enterprise, their immediate response to threat was to act in these terms. In most instances, this orientation led only to fruitless internal bickering and petty self-seeking behavior that hindered the organization of resistance activity but did not prevent it. Outright Jewish collaboration was rare, partly because fanatic SS enforcement of the extreme Nazi racial policies made it impossible. Yet no discussion of resistance can be complete without some mention of the other side of the coin.

## Collaboration

Collaboration with the Nazis went on throughout Europe for one or more of three reasons: genuine belief in National Socialist ideals; cynical opportunism aimed at personal aggrandizement; or the conviction that compromise with existing power was the only feasible course of action.

The first reason requires little elaboration. Every European state, including the Allies fighting against Germany, had its native fascist and neofascist elements sympathetic to Hitler. As the Nazis gained control over one country after another, their local sympathizers, such as Vidkun Quisling (Norway), Anton Pavelic (Yugoslavia), and Leon Degrelle (Belgium), quickly sought positions of power. These collaborators and many others like them typically saw themselves as patriots who would save their country from the corruption and inefficiency of democratic government. Needless to say, there could be no Jews in this category.[37]

It was, however, possible for Jews to engage in various forms of self-seeking collaboration. Every internment camp and killing center, for example, had its share of prisoners who would betray others to gain some small advantage. And some of those who managed to gain positions of power as work gang leaders or barrack chiefs were known to beat and torture in much the same fashion as non-Jews. But opportunistic collaboration was most serious in the ghettos, where many stories have been told of persons who attempted to profit from business deals with the Germans or by serving as informers.

One of the more extreme cases of collaboration centered on the activities of a rather mysterious character named Avram Gancewicz. Known only as a journalist and sometime Zionist, he appeared in the Warsaw ghetto as the director of a group called the Committee of Artists and Professionals. It was soon apparent that the committee funneled information directly to German authorities. Some of the Jewish agents for the committee operated openly with police powers, and because they worked from 13 Leszno Street, they became known in the ghetto as the "Thirteeners." Gancewicz also edited a Polish-language newspaper, the *Jewish Gazette*. It was sponsored by the Germans and circulated throughout Poland with news stories designed to conceal what was really happening to the Jews.[38]

Apart from such explicit but infrequent cases as Gancewicz, the ghetto *Judenräte* were notorious for corrupt practices and de facto collaboration. Officials were regularly accused of favoritism and bribe-taking in the underground press. It is clear, moreover, that some *Judenrat* officials believed that by working for the Nazis they could insure their own safety regardless of what happened to others. The Jewish police were the most obvious symbols and instruments of collaboration. Given full authority by the Germans, clothed in special uniforms, and provided with liberal food allowances along with opportunities to profit from black market enterprises, these police represented the most visible form of opportunistic collaboration. In some ghettos the police operated virtually as a law unto themselves, ignoring or bypassing directives from the *Judenrat* officials they were supposed to serve. So long as the police obeyed German orders to round up stated numbers and categories of other Jews for deportation and continued to enforce other regulations, they were given a free hand.

Probably the most significant fact about the Jewish police is the way they were gradually transformed from indirect to direct servants of SS policies. Beginning with conventional duties such as enforcement of rationing, housing, and sanitation regulations, the police were later used to assemble people for deportation. This was usually rationalized by *Judenrat* authorities with the argument that if they refused, the Germans would do it themselves in a far more brutal fashion. When deportation became known as a euphemism for extermination, some of the *Judenrat* leaders and police resigned or began to work with resistance groups, but the majority continued to follow German orders, claiming that by this means they could help save a larger number of people. A tragic illustration of the justification for such action appears in the diary of Zelig Kalmanovitch, who recorded his experiences in the Vilna area:

> Our policemen were sent there with passes to be distributed among the remaining workers, and to turn over the rest of the people, "the superfluous," to the hands of the authorities to do with them what is customary these days. The young took upon themselves this difficult task. They donned their official caps, with the "Star of David" upon them, went there and did what they were supposed to do. The result was that more than 400 people perished: the aged, the infirm, the sick, and retarded children. Thus 1500 women and children were saved. Had outsiders, God forbid, carried out this action, 2000 people would have perished. The commandant [of the Jewish police] said: "To be sure, our hands are stained with the blood of our brethren, but we had to take upon ourselves this dreadful task. We are clean before the bar of history."[39]

The situation in Vilna was not exceptional: Jewish police in other Polish ghettos performed similar service. According to the Kalmanovitch diary, collaboration reached its lowest point in Vilna when Jewish police arrested young people accumulating weapons for resistance. Writing in July 1943, Kalmanovitch saw the resisters not as heroes, but as extremists who were endangering what was left of the Jewish community.

> It cannot be that our extremists believe in the possibility of victory. . . . Then why make a useless uprising? The strength of the prisoner lies only in his continued existence. . . . In reality, when these people speak of the so-called "honor" which they defend they bring disgrace upon the tens of thousands that perished. These martyrs are in truth no less worthy than those who took to the sword. . . . Only cowards and confused people can think of bringing in arms here.[40]

Kalmanovitch himself believed that the only appropriate course of action was some form of compromise: by playing for time and yielding to German demands when necessary, the Jews might outlast the oppression or at least minimize its brutality. This compromise policy seemed plausible enough in view of the overwhelming German power, and it was especially appealing to

Jews with strong religious convictions. Unfortunately, as the war dragged on and killings increased, reluctant compromise became little more than a euphemism for reluctant collaboration.

Prominent Jews who accepted positions in the German-sponsored *Judenräte* found themselves being used more and more openly as tools of the SS. By aiding in registration and concentration of their people, they smoothed the way for deportation; by promulgating benign Nazi cover stories for deportation and denying warnings distributed by underground groups, they made deportation operations more efficient; and by harassing those who called for resistance, they hindered development of any counteraction. During his trial in Israel, Adolf Eichmann testified that the Jewish councils were so effective in these respects that German personnel could be released for other service.

A few of the *Judenräte* officials realized what was happening in time to resign or ally themselves with resistance groups. Others who made direct protests to the Germans were simply deported. For the most part, however, those who were appointed to the Jewish councils stayed on, often accused of using their positions to save themselves, but always maintaining that their actions were designed to save as many as could be saved. Under some conditions, of course, such rationalizations could not be maintained. In one dramatic instance, Adam Czerniakow, chairman of the Warsaw *Judenrat*, committed suicide in July 1942, after the first massive deportation of ghetto inhabitants had begun. Yet following his death, the *Judenrat* remained in operation under direction of the deputy chairman.

Collaboration originating from well-intentioned beliefs in compromise was not limited to Poland. The Jewish council appointed by the Germans in Holland also aided in the process of registration, concentration, and deportation. At Westerbork, where a large camp served as the way station to Auschwitz, the Jewish police—*Ordensdienst* (OD)—have been described as hardly different from their SS masters. Labeled by more than one camp prisoner as virtually a Jewish SS, the OD not only imposed a harsh order in the camp, but was occasionally used outside to help Dutch Nazis and SS with roundups of other Jews.

The two presidents of the Jewish council in Holland, Asscher and Cohen, went along with German orders and used their influence to protect "important" (that is, well-off) members of the Jewish community. Both men were investigated by secular authorities and a Jewish "court of honor" after the war because of the many accusations of collaboration made against them. In defense, Cohen cited the usual rationale that matters would have been worse if they had not worked with the Germans, and he compared himself with a general who is forced to sacrifice a company in order to save a division. Even during the war, such statements had been heard so often that they became the substance of a joke circulated among Dutch Jews in 1942: "Asscher and Cohen are the only Jews left, and the Germans demand the deportation of one of them. Says Cohen to Asscher: 'It had better be you, Abraham—lest worse befall the rest of us.' "[41]

Not all of the Jewish councils were invariably collaborationist. In France, working through the Vichy government, the Germans created a Jewish council, *Union Générale des Israelites de France* (UGIF). This organization actively opposed and subverted German policies to such an extent that several Jewish officials, including a president of the UGIF, were sent to Auschwitz. Along with several other more significant factors, the conduct of the UGIF helps to explain why approximately 70 percent of the French Jews were able to survive the war.[42]

## Romance and Reality

Resistance against Nazi oppression was enshrined early in the war as a romantic ideal by allied propaganda. The victorious Allies and liberated peoples have all of them, intellectuals and laymen alike, found their resistance martyrs and given them the special status of cultural heroes, mythic figures embodying the best qualities of their compatriots. This celebration of resistance is one of the few simplistic certainties of an earlier generation that has so far remained safe from the critical analyses of revisionist historians, for it is difficult to deny that the anti-Nazi struggle pitted the forces of light against darkness.

Yet the realities of resistance in general, and Jewish resistance in particular, were as far from the romantic ideal as any fresh battlefield is from the memorials that may later be erected upon it. Resistance is in no sense a categorical imperative arising spontaneously in heroic victims facing atrocious oppression. On the contrary, all of the available evidence shows that resistance emerges slowly in a gradual process that depends more on various situational factors than any unique personal qualities. The relevant evidence on this point is in fact so strong as to suggest that no claim for spontaneous resistance should ever be accepted at face value.

It is virtually axiomatic that the victims of powerful oppressive forces will be both psychologically and physically divided; otherwise they would not be victims. Hemmed in by the various situational constraints defining their condition, they are for the most part incapable of struggling against it. And the pathways awaiting those few who are capable of struggle are always ambiguous; although their struggle may ultimately lead toward heroic resistance, it may also lead toward collaboration. For the cruel dilemmas of survival do not present themselves complete with moral signposts indicating whether victims may best fight against their condition through forceful action, compromise, or a mixture of both.

Psychologically, compromise is always most appealing because it promises to bring some relief from oppression with a minimum of risk. This argument is extremely powerful among people facing great force, and little can stand against it at the popular mass level. Throughout this study it has been apparent that apart from scattered perceptions of compromise as a way station on the road to collaboration (a judgment that was easily discredited as adventurist, and which only seemed compelling after the fact), the only factor standing against compromise was ideology combined with organization. Ideological considerations set the boundary conditions for survival, the limits beyond which survival lost its meaning.

In much of Nazi-occupied Europe, however, and certainly among most of the Jews, there was initially no substantial organized, ideological opposition to compromise. Moreover, it must be acknowledged that contrary to the romantic aura surrounding resistance, many of those who staked their lives and honor on the possibilities of compromise acted with the same integrity and courage as those who are today honored in resistance memorials. At the level of practical politics there is no sure logic by which resistance can be set against compromise and the attendant dangers of collaboration, because these are not mutually exclusive categories of action. They stand instead as intervals on a continuum describing struggles for survival against oppression. This is not to say, of course, that all distinctions are meaningless. Those who could ignore the logical attractions of compromise in their existential leap toward resistance rightly deserve admiration. But to assume that such categories of action can be clearly perceived as a moral dichotomy during times of historical upheaval and extraordinary oppression is to expect more than the unaided human psyche can provide.

The situation of the Jews is terribly clear in this respect.[43] Although their resistance was slow to develop, and might indeed be judged as being too little and too late, the evidence is plain that they were perfectly able to fight in the ghettos, the forests, and the camps. What they lacked was neither skill nor courage, but an effective consensus and a morally authoritative leadership that could issue the call to arms. Unlike the other oppressed peoples of Europe, the Jews had no government in exile, no encouragement from the allied powers, and no strong nationalist tradition to serve as the basis for a coherent resistance program.

It is impossible to conclude whether or not a more extensive, forceful Jewish resistance movement could have disrupted the Holocaust machinery or saved many more lives. Our own retrospective view is biased toward a fighting resistance. However, perhaps the ultimate words on this subject were written by Emmanuel Ringelblum as he lay hidden in a Warsaw basement after the ghetto had been destroyed:

> A paradoxical situation arose. The older generation, with half a lifetime behind it, spoke, thought and concerned itself about surviving the war, dreamt about life. The youth—the best, the most beautiful, the finest that the Jewish people possessed—spoke and thought only about an honorable death. They did not think about surviving the war. They did not procure Aryan papers for themselves. They had no dwellings on the other side. Their only concern was to discover the most dignified and honorable death, befitting an ancient people with a history stretching back over several thousand years.[44]

Chapter VI

# The Holocaust and
# the Human Condition

When a universe of accepted meanings begins to go seriously out of joint, the result is fearful disorientation and paralysis of action. Human reactions to the unthinkable are invariably primitive and visceral: the hair rises on the back of the neck prior to a rational certainty that something is wrong. More concretely, people tend to perceive the onset of unthinkable events as a child perceives the transformation of humans into monsters in a horror film—with nervous, smiling disbelief and a rising fear that it may actually be true.

Just as an individual life crisis will be accompanied by feelings of chaos and fear that seem to accumulate without volition in the depths of the nervous system, so it is with major historical crises, and so it most certainly was for those caught up in the Holocaust. Nothing in the Nazi extermination program contributed more to its effectiveness than its shocking unbelievability. And apart from the testimony of survivors, nothing is so revealing of this truth as the way Holocaust material penetrates the ordinary psychosocial adjustment mechanisms supporting scholarly detachment. None of those who engage in serious study of these extraordinary happenings, including trained scholars, can escape without experiencing a deep personal crisis. In this sense, the enduring meaning of the Holocaust is profoundly rooted in the feelings it evokes.[1]

This is not a matter directly concerned with conventional standards of academic objectivity, for the emotional impact first occurs far back in the rear areas of awareness. This impact has no immediate connection with bias or distorted perception of facts, but operates instead in those dim reaches of the mind sheltering taken-for-granted beliefs about human nature and the basic requirements for all forms of social living.

Among serious scholars, the accumulated horrors of the Holocaust ultimately force recognition that these events defy both cognitive and emotional assimilation because they are off the scale of established human knowledge. There are, to be sure, intense feelings of disgust, rage, and frustration. It could hardly be otherwise, particularly during the early exploratory phase of study. But for those who persist, and it should be noted that there are many who cannot, these early or "preliminary" emotions eventually recede because they are too superficial; too variable, passionate, and "normal" for the material in hand. Rage and disgust can serve for a time to satisfy the transitory ego-defensive needs of tourists and dilettantes; such feelings are melted away from minds that are held in the fires of the Holocaust for prolonged periods.

What remains is a central, deadening sense of despair over the human species. Where can one find an affirmative meaning in life if human beings can do such things? Along with this despair there may also come a desperate new feeling of vulnerability attached to the fact that one *is* human. If one keeps at the Holocaust long enough, then sooner or later the ultimate personal truth begins to reveal itself: one knows, finally, that one might either do it, or be done to. If it could happen on such a massive scale elsewhere, then it can happen anywhere; it is all within the range of human possibility, and like it or not, Auschwitz expands the universe of consciousness no less than landings on the moon.

The tourists of the Holocaust, people with only casual or relatively stereo-typed knowledge of the events, do not understand this. They see the SS as monsters, not representative human beings; and they see the Jews as martyred innocents, flawed only by their failure to fight back against the primitive forces of destruction. Here, for example, is how a prominent literary critic has attempted to use the Holocaust to explicate the idea of tragedy: "The Holocaust is, among a thousand things, one immense story revealing precisely the major theme of traditional Tragedy: *the fragility of human culture before the state of nature.*"[2] Innocent and well-meaning as this statement may be, it is, nevertheless, a terribly offensive falsification because most serious students of the Holocaust know that what it reveals is the *fragility of nature* in the face of human agents operating with the technical and conceptual tools of "advanced" culture. As others have already noted: "There is more than a wholly fortuitous connection between the applied technology of the mass production line, with its vision of universal material abundance, and the applied technology of the concentration camp, with its vision of a profusion of death. We may wish to deny the connection, but Buchenwald was of our West as much as Detroit's River Rouge—we cannot deny Buchenwald as a casual aberration of a Western world essentially sane."[3]

In such matters, however, those deeply engaged in Holocaust studies usually find themselves alone, and they tend to work out their despairs in odd ways. The appropriate model here is the myth of Medusa: like the ancient Greeks who were turned to stone if they looked upon the serpent-crowned head, those who gaze deeply into the Holocaust may also find themselves, if not turned to stone, then at least profoundly changed.

This personal impact of the Holocaust upon people who have experienced it indirectly, through their efforts at historical reconstruction, is particularly noteworthy because it emphasizes a fundamental quality of all historical crises. That is, although they involve events that can be described in linear sequence, understood in terms of individual or group psychological processes, and even placed in some plausible context of historical development, their larger meaning nevertheless remains threatening and ambiguous, a subject of doubt and controversy as succeeding generations struggle for interpretations relevant to their immediate and remote historical circumstances. At the level of personal knowledge, therefore, historical crises are crises of knowing, knowing about events of such magnitude that their ultimate meaning appears unknowable.

The superficial illogic of this state of affairs does not preclude inquisitive discussion. Not only may one think about the unthinkable, but perhaps even more important, one may think about how people think about the unthinkable. And since it stands as the primary unthinkable crisis of our century, the Holocaust has inspired an abundance of relevant material. In this connection, the efforts of scholars may be temporarily set aside. Their special contribution as cultural sensor instruments "designed" for detection and recording of historical earth tremors has already been indicated. What remains of critical importance, however, is the thinking of survivors about their own experience.

This presents itself initially as chaotic and as diverse as the experiences and viewpoints that have inspired it. Yet the cutting edge of the question of knowing eventually reveals a simple truth: people who have experienced the Holocaust crisis tend to think of it mainly in accord with their dominant existential concerns.

Thus, for Jewish survivors and others primarily concerned with politics and matters of community, the Holocaust has come to serve as both the political and the moral foundation for the state of Israel. Having suffered unprecedented slaughter and persecution, Jews are not only entitled to their own place in the world, but must also maintain it at all costs lest they again become vulnerable to destruction. More generally, almost any form of political activity can now be justified by appealing to the Holocaust.

At the opposite extreme from the politically oriented, however, are those who understand their experience in metaphysical or quasi-religious terms. Survivor writings of this type emphasize a search for meanings that transcend all politics and practical affairs. The victimized Jews are seen here as instruments of a supernatural force guiding the destiny of humanity, and to the extent that their suffering in the Holocaust seems beyond human comprehension, this only strengthens the inclination toward a supernatural interpretation.

Lying between the two extremes are a wide variety of highly personal, individualized survivor accounts. What these works have in common is their projective-defensive quality: writers tend to project their own basic needs or tensions into their testimony. Thus, whereas some accounts constantly emphasize small acts of resistance as a saving factor, others note that any act of resistance was tantamount to suicide. And again, whereas some survivors rather proudly describe their ability to "organize" extra food or good work assignments, others describe such activities as contemptible. Occasionally, differences between personal views of the Holocaust surface with brutal clarity, as in this excerpt from Primo Levi's description of an incident immediately following an SS "selection" for the Auschwitz gas chambers: "Silence slowly prevails and then, from my bunk on the top row, I see and hear old Kuhn praying aloud, with his beret on his head, swaying backwards and forwards violently. Kuhn is thanking God because he has not been chosen. . . . If I was God, I would spit at Kuhn's prayer."[4]

This is not to say that survivor accounts are factually untrustworthy or that easy moral or psychiatric judgments can be made about them. It is, rather, to stress the general psychological principle that the more threatening and ambiguous any situation is, the more likely individuals are to react to it in accord with their own habitual pattern of social-emotional adjustment mechanisms. Prisoners in the unreal world of the Nazi camps could only construe their experience by looking inward to the ideas and values they had brought with them. Indeed, many have said that they only survived by retreating into an inwardly focused and self-centered shell which permitted them to ignore much of the surrounding horror.[5]

In the face of these limitations, it should be plain that no definitive understanding of the Holocaust can be drawn directly from the survivor literature. This literature may be the best source of the facts, but the facts do not interpret themselves. Where the viewpoints of survivors are not determined by doctrinaire secular or metaphysical considerations, they frequently reflect the relatively narrow personal concerns of individual authors.

Consequently, the general questions of meaning that are provoked by the Holocaust are no more likely to be resolved by survivors bearing witness through their direct experience than by scholars with indirect experience. It is arguable that the former have been so close to the events that they cannot put them into a broader historical or psychological context, and that the latter work upon the events from a distance that only allows them either to assimilate the Holocaust into conventional history by ignoring its uniqueness, or to languish in numb despair at this spectacle of human degradation.

In part, it is this very impenetrability of the Holocaust, its persistent resistance to any straightforward analysis, that requires it to be recognized as an historical crisis. Those who search deeply into the events of the Holocaust probing for meanings find themselves overcome by the dark enigmas that accompany historical crisis. Nor should this be surprising, for historical crises break the preexisting social consensus and shared values. In more formal terms, historical crises involve events that shatter the credibility of preexisting epistemologies. In *The Structure of Scientific Revolutions,* T. S. Kuhn suggests that this occurs in science when a dominant paradigm for theory and research is overturned by new ways of thinking about scientific phenomena. It is being suggested here that an analogous process occurs in history when real events outstrip the conceptual structures of historians, philosophers, and laymen alike.

Yet the Holocaust may be hard to grasp as a historical crisis because the breakdowns of consensus and culturally defined meanings consequent to it are not easily perceived. There were no great changes in ideas concerning government and political power, for example, because the Holocaust was not a revolution. Economic systems and practices were not influenced, for it was not a financial or economic collapse. Furthermore, the Holocaust itself led to no startling changes in national boundaries; it did not generate any sweeping new religious forms or views of human nature; and it had no discernible impact on modern science.

In fact, if there is any approximate analogy to be found between the effects of the Holocaust and other historical crisis events, it is to the Black Plague, which also left in its wake uncountable millions of dead bodies. Yet even this analogy is very unsatisfactory, because the plague was an unselective, natural phenomenon that profoundly disrupted the major communities of Europe. The Holocaust, by contrast, for the most part stripped only the Jews from communities, which were otherwise intact and able to conduct business as usual. The enduring psychosocial effects of the Holocaust, therefore, are not easily perceived, and may conveniently be denied or ignored, because once the bodies are out of the way nothing remains of it except mental images. Yet these images persist and grow and have steadily spread out into the moral foundations of Western society.[6] Morality, of course, is also invisible, intangible. And, as we do with other intangibles supporting our human existence, most of us ignore morality until something happens to compel attention.

Because it lies deeply within the fabric of society, morality, including all standards of ethics and value judgments, only becomes conspicuous when it dramatically fails, as in the case of senseless crimes or other sharp violations of accepted social practices. Furthermore, when questions of morality do surface, they are typically engaged by legal or religious institutions. The former provides approved technical procedures for handling transgressions, and the latter provides metaphysical discussions and rationales aimed at giving everyday meaning to the events at issue. Supported in practice by the efforts of culture agents such as parents and teachers, the primary institutions of law and religion maintain the historical norms in matters of justice, equity, and the sundries of everyday conduct.

The Holocaust stands as a crucial moral crisis because within the Nazi state, and in most of the territory it eventually came to control, neither traditional law or religion could prevent or comprehend the massive killings. Moreover, those nations allied against the Nazis in the name of law and religion not only failed to act effectively against the Holocaust, but tried for a time to maintain an official unawareness that it existed.

The explanations ordinarily given for this state of affairs emphasize the difficulties of resisting Nazi power and the inability of both peoples and governments to realize that such crimes were possible. Such explanations may be true enough, but they also disguise a more fundamental and threatening truth: that the legal and religious structures of morality were simply inadequate to confront an unprecedented form of organized evil supported by tne authority of a modern state.

In Germany and the occupied countries, most of the major social institutions made no special effort to oppose the Holocaust, and those persons who attempted to do so acting as individuals or in small groups were easily brushed aside and eliminated. If anything, the drastic punishments meted out to such people served to further intimidate others who might have followed their example. It is also a fact that the fate of the Jews under German control was not an important concern of any of the allied governments fighting Germany. It has been well established, furthermore, that the Christian churches generally did not take a firm institutional stand against Nazism and the Holocaust despite persistent efforts toward this end by some individual members of the clergy. There is even material available suggesting that the leaders of various Jewish communities in Europe, America, and Palestine did not use all the resources at their disposal to act against the Holocaust.[7]

Given these facts, the conclusion seems inescapable that the existing moral structures failed. The basic explanation for this failure is, at least in principle, not hard to discover. Insofar as Western concepts of morality have evolved in connection with the rise of secular nation-states, these concepts and practices have gradually come to derive their authority from the state rather than any higher force. Both the institutional actions and the traditional values of law and religion are for all practical purposes only allowed to operate in whatever framework is made available to them by the state. By one means or another, the salient interests of the state must be served by law and religion. If these interests are not served, then legal and religious institutions will be threatened or intimidated until they either conform to state policies, or state policies change. Frequently, however, the state will ally itself with one of these institutions in order to isolate and intimidate the other, which usually then retreats to a compromise position allowing its continued existence.

There is nothing particularly new about the foregoing analysis, but when taken in conjunction with the Holocaust, it leads to stark conclusions: within certain limits set by political and military power considerations, the modern state may do anything it wishes to those under its control. There is no moral-ethical limit which the state cannot transcend if it wishes to do so, because there is no moral-ethical power higher than the state. Moreover, it seems apparent that no modern state will ever seriously interfere with the internal activities of another solely for moral-ethical reasons. Consequently, in matters of ethics and morality, the situation of the individual in the modern state is in principle roughly equivalent to the situation of the prisoner in Auschwitz: either act in accord with the prevailing standards of conduct enforced by those in authority, or risk whatever consequences they may wish to impose. Just as there was no higher moral authority outside Auschwitz to which the prisoner could appeal, there is no such authority available to citizens of the modern state. If they are critical of the dominant ethos, they can only express this criticism within the limits permitted by the state.

Exceptional persons, such as Solzhenitsyn and Sakharov in the Soviet Union, and the Berrigan brothers in the United States, may test the limits for moral-ethical criticism, in effect pitting their personal will to meaning against the power of the state. People with such heroic qualities are rare, however, and when they act in accord with their moral convictions it is usually necessary for them to go beyond the established boundaries of law and religion. But the survival of such persons is always uncertain, and the practical effect of their heroic action always remains questionable. Like the occasional heroism shown by prisoners in Auschwitz, such actions seem to provide moments of moral inspiration precisely because they are so far beyond the capacity of most people. Put otherwise, it may be said that whereas many can be inspired by the life of Jesus, there are few indeed who can be carried by their inspiration to the point of risking crucifixion. The fact that certain exceptional people may set themselves against injustice, therefore, does not materially alter our view of the Holocaust as a historical crisis revealing that the conventional moral structures of law and religion have little or no meaning when set against the authority of the state.

This conclusion may seem obvious or even trivial when it is given in the language of sociology and confined to implications about the credibility of social institutions. Indeed, as George Steiner, Thomas Szasz, and other thinkers have argued, the language of social science can hardly do anything but trivialize human experience by turning it into an alien and mystifying subject matter.[8]

Psychologically, however, the profound impact of the Holocaust is that it leaves the individual stripped of moral authority and moral security. If millions of innocents could be systematically murdered at the very center of modern European civilization, then that civilization can provide no firm sense of moral security to its inhabitants. Prior to the Holocaust, Western ethics and moral values that had gradually been accumulated and codified in the institutions of law and religion were generally thought to be virtually immut able—a basic element in the makeup of Western humanity. Centered in cultural ideals represented by such figures as Goethe, Newton, Tolstoy, and Beethoven, the modern European might have acknowledged the presence of exploitation and injustice, but direct, extensive human slaughter was simply unthinkable except as it might occur among relatively uncivilized peoples such as "the Turks."

The strength of this belief was indicated by the reactions of those caught up in the Holocaust as victims, perpetrators, or spectators. Yet this question of "how such things are possible," which springs so spontaneously from the revealed impotence of the moral-ethical values that had been taken for granted in the modern West contains within it the ultimate psychological demonstration supporting our conclusion. That is, since the Holocaust *was* possible, prior cultural values supposed to make it impossible were manifestly false, and a moral crisis is imposed upon the whole fabric of the culture.

What the Holocaust forces upon us, therefore, is recognition of nothing less than a moral equivalent of the Copernican revolution. Western European culture is not an orderly, ethical center for our social universe, and the historical development of its moral instrumentalities—law and religion—was a failure ending in Auschwitz. But to accept this conclusion as a justifiable psychohistorical or philosophical statement is only to make a small step toward understanding the sociocultural significance of the Holocaust. Without careful consideration of how the process for killing millions could work, the crisis posed by the Holocaust will remain as hardly more than a basis for the proliferation of questionable alternative moral value systems.

Those who see no further origins for the Holocaust other than simple failures of the legal and religious institutions that should have prevented it reveal the limits of their understanding by arguing for reform or extension of these institutions. Exponents of Western law, for example, look toward development of an enforceable international system of jurisprudence, a world court that can override the authority of any nation state. Implicitly, at least, such views are in agreement with the premise that no national legal system can prevail against the power system of which it is a part. Yet insofar as there seems little possibility for the development of supranational law—if anything, the steadily declining status of the United Nations makes this prospect look dimmer than ever—the credibility of law as a primary vehicle for Western morality is no greater today or in the forseeable future than it was in 1942. Actually, a good case could be made for the argument that the moral credibility and potential of law has been steadily shrinking as the power of modern nation-states has expanded.[9]

Religion seems to be an equally empty alternative, and for much the same reason, namely, that no Western religious institution has been able to stand successfully in clear opposition to the power of the modern state. Thus, despite calls for morality in government and appeals to a higher moral law against killing, torture, and all of the other forms of political repression that have become so familiar in this century, there is no evidence to suggest that religious institutions have any greater capacity to influence national policies today than they had in Hitler's Germany. Dissident clergy today may still be routinely arrested, harassed, or otherwise discredited wherever they attempt forceful opposition to secular authorities.

The Holocaust has made it clear that the two traditional pillars of Western morality, law and religion, are inadequate to the task of protecting human beings. However well these institutions may have served in the past to prevent masses of people from thinking or doing the unthinkable, they have been rendered impotent by modern political power systems and the bureaucratic structures these systems have created. Traditional Western religions are hard put to confront problems of "authorized" mass murder or lesser wrongdoings, because they have in practice identified sin or evil with motives of either passion or profit. The idea that it might indeed be fundamentally sinful to carry out orders issued by established state institutions weighs little in the balance against centuries of church teachings to the contrary.

As the only new Western moral-philosophical movement to have emerged strongly during the second half of this century, existentialism undoubtedly became popular because it addressed the moral emptiness revealed by the Holocaust. Existentialism rests on the assumption that human beings are alone. The existential view follows from realization that neither law, religion, nor science can provide compelling satisfactory answers to the questions, "Why not commit murder? Why not commit suicide?" And in the face of the Holocaust, the existentialist response has been to explore these questions with the suggestion that morality can only be understood as an act of will. That is, if one does not commit suicide or murder it is because one chooses not to do so, rather than because of any fear that retribution will eventually follow. Alone, therefore, persons hold their lives in their own hands and existence itself is hardly more than a construct of consciousness. It cannot be derived from any exterior metaphysical or scientific principle, nor even from culturally determined aspects of consciousness, for if the culture can be recognized as being flawed or fraudulent, then culturally dictated aspects of mind cannot be accepted as a foundation for morality.

In this connection, the popularity of existentialism in all the diverse forms it has assumed over the past thirty-odd years may be attributed as much to the institutional failure of science as to religion or law. The science and technology which had been increasingly celebrated for almost a century as the bastion of Western rationality and had become synonymous with liberal-progressive thought turned out to be a major factor contributing to the feasibility of the Holocaust.

## The Failure of Science

It is not particularly difficult to grasp the arguments for the failure of law and religion; both are primarily institutions oriented to matters of morality and the maintenance of civilized behavior, and the fact that the Holocaust could happen is prima facie evidence for their failure. It is much more difficult to grasp arguments pointing toward the failure of science, because science is still generally thought to be amoral, a value-free enterprise devoted solely to the accumulation of knowledge. Furthermore, although it is clear that applied science provided the technology that made the mass killing possible, it is also true that applied science provided means to fight against the killing. In short, the prevalent view is that science is neutral, a method of gaining knowledge leading to control over the physical and social environment, and evil only insofar as evil people may use it badly.

Our view is different. In a number of ways, the evidence surrounding the Holocaust suggests emphatically that from its dim origins in the concentration camps and the euthanasia program to its final large-scale industrial actualization in Auschwitz, the scientific mode of thought and the methodology attached to it were intrinsic to the mass killings. Quite apart from the technology, the mentality of modern science is what made the Holocaust possible.

At a fairly superficial level, it is quite obvious that the rational-abstract forms of conceptual thought required and promulgated by science provided the basis for systematic and efficient identification of people by race, transportation of large numbers to concentration points, killing, and body disposal. But the more central role of science as a mentality was in providing the inspiration and justification for these technical activities. The abstract, categorical thinking encouraged by the culture of science paves the way for acceptance of categorical racist ideas.

In present-day American psychology, for example, the argument is all too widely made and all too frequently accepted that scientific studies of intelligence test scores reveal intelligence to be about 80 percent genetically determined and that because of their genetic structure black Americans are on the average well behind whites in their intellectual achievements. Once it is accepted that such abstractions as genes distributed in populations are, so to speak, "real facts" instead of theoretical constructs, the way is opened toward instituting and justifying social policies based on these "facts."

The point at issue here has nothing to do with whether or not there can be some merit or utility in the accumulation of evidence leading to scientific generalizations about people; it is that in a scientifically oriented culture, people will accept generalities produced by science as fact, particularly when the generalities fit other culturally determined predispositions or biases. Thus, a detailed study of the history of European racism shows that with the rise of science during the Enlightenment, preexisting mythic racist traditions were not truly repudiated but simply assimilated into the new context of "reason." Instead of justifying racism by appealing to interpretations of the Bible, for example, reasonable people began to justify it by appealing to morphological data and the specimens of native humanity encountered in Africa and the Americas.[10]

It was Hitler's political genius and an intrinsic aspect of his psychopathology as well, to shape his racist ideas in such a way as to meld both the scientific mentality allowing theories to be reified into concrete thought patterns and the more primitive emotional feelings which have traditionally energized racist beliefs.[11]

The scientific orientation in Western civilization also encourages and even forces people to detach their emotions from the rational intellect. Education is virtually synonymous with the ability to be dispassionate and detached. This is not to say that ignorant, brutish people with no education and no ability to detach emotions from intellect are not capable of performing horrible actions. The camps had a full share of brutal guards recruited from the Ukrainian peasantry, in addition to some sadistic Kapos (inmate "trusties") and SS men. Moreover, it could hardly matter to victims whether they were killed by a blow from an excited brute or a calm and detached SS officer with a master's degree in biology. But there is a difference in the scale of the killing. Ferociously anti-Semitic peasants might organize vicious attacks on Jews, and might even kill a sizable number during a rampage, but they are not capable of killing millions by designing an efficient system of death camps. The latter is only possible as a manifestation of detached technical expertise grounded on a scientific rationale or *logos,* and only in a relatively small degree supported by emotionality or passion.

Recent studies suggest that Hitler's inspiration in exterminating the Jews had diverse sources in traditional Austrian anti-Semitism, the social Darwinism promulgated through Haeckel's Monist League, and assorted mystical-political ideas—all of which became an integral part of his psychosocial adjustment following his experience as a soldier in World War I. What is most striking, however, is his success in attaining power by playing his own special pathology in harmony with the deep psychic traumas of defeated German society. Yet the genocide program succeeded only because the middle- and low-ranking organization men directing its day-to-day operation could reduce massive killings to a routinely efficient industrial operation.

Insofar as SS leaders realized that emotional reactions might interfere with efficient operation of the death camps, they took rational precautions. Men who objected to death or concentration camp assignments (there were not many) were either transferred or coerced into participation. Special training was given to members of the branch of the SS charged with running the camps, the *Totenkopf*, under the direction of Theodore Eicke. The attempt, which seemed to be successful enough, was to teach men to keep emotional interference down to the minimum by encouraging practices that tended to define Jews as inferior organisms, not really human beings. The splitting process involved is roughly analogous to the way some animal research scientists come to view their rats or monkeys without any trace of empathy. (Undergraduates, who—perhaps with good reason—often show spontaneous feelings of empathy with caged laboratory animals are traditionally seen as poor lab assistants because of their inability to maintain a proper scientific detachment.)

It should be clear that the mental splitting which separates emotionality from rationality is deliberately inculcated by science-oriented Western culture in order that people may repress or suspend reflexive emotions that might block achievement of abstract, distant goals. The ability to categorize objects, to then perform mental (imaginary) operations upon these objects, and thus transform the meaning of the objects into something other than what one started with is fundamental to all science. Indeed, it is precisely this ability that has come to be accepted as our definition of intelligence in accord with the cognitive development theory of Jean Piaget and the empirical efforts of intelligence testers. Yet this capacity for scientific-intellectual functioning in Western culture is what can make extraordinary horrors possible. By exercising this capacity, we can make judgments that some people are better than others, and, ultimately, that some people are not even people at all. So it is that the scientific mode of thinking—the mode of thinking required and promulgated by science—allows us to perform promethean acts that transform the world.[12]

Philosophers and historians of science who have studied the underpinnings of scientific activities typically point out that the issues here involve the language of science. That is, the abstract and abstracting thought patterns associated with science are distinct from more reflexive forms of thinking, and cannot be attained without the use of special language systems. These systems may be entirely symbolic and empty of all content, as in the various algebras and geometries, or they may involve ordinary words used only according to certain agreed-upon rules of meaning.

Analysis of the general implications of the special language system essential to scientific thinking became the life work of Ludwig Wittgenstein. He recognized the dangers inherent in the amoral language of science and based his work on the tradition of moral philosophy established by Schopenhauer and Kierkegaard. The former had argued against Kant's idea of equating morality with rationality based on the assumption of a "categorical imperative" moral law. For both Schopenhauer and Kierkegaard, morality was clearly independent of rationality or intellect. They argued that the ultimate source of moral thoughts, feelings, and actions could not be rationality. Instead, the immediate transfer or communication of emotions between people must be recognized as the touchstone for all genuine passion, moral or otherwise. We all experience this in limited ways as adults, and more generally as children, when the sight of another child being punished evokes immediate fear and sadness, or when seeing another person hit their thumb with a hammer makes us cringe at the vicarious experience of pain. Just where this reflexive, empathic aspect of human nature comes from and how it is to be explained remains an open question, but the fact that it exists, and that it has nothing whatever to do with intellect or rational calculation, is indisputable.

Wittgenstein's contribution begins here. Unlike Kierkegaard and Schopenhauer, he was very much a man of the twentieth century, raised in upper-class fin de siècle Viennese society, decorated for bravery under fire in World War I, and for almost ten years a professor at Cambridge prior to his death in 1951. As it was for so many philosophers and intellectuals of his generation, the great challenge to Wittgenstein concerned the meaning of science, its theories, methods, and implications.

He saw this problem in terms of the special language of science, and his early work elaborating upon the denotative validity of scientific language was interpreted as a powerful justification for the view that scientists should eliminate all speculative, ambiguous, and evaluative elements from their language—from the substance of their work. The closing line of his famous first book, *Tractatus Logico-Philosophicus,* was "Whereof one cannot speak, thereof one must be silent." It was generally understood to mean that speculative, discursive language had no place in science, or in any other disciplined human enterprise; language could only be useful when its terms were tied down to empirical evidence or operations. In any other case, one had best be silent. But this was not what Wittgenstein meant at all. Instead, as his students and biographers later pointed out, he wanted to suggest that precise scientific language did not allow one to speak of the really important matters in life, matters of morality and values. One could use precise language in a positivistic fashion to "do" the sciences well enough, but that was all. As his friend Paul Englemann explained: "Positivism holds—and this is its essence —that what we can speak about is all that matters in life. Whereas Wittgenstein passionately believes that all that really matters in human life is precisely what, in his view, we must be silent about."[13]

Later on, Wittgenstein's work changed, and he began to see that language was not only the means by which people could create certain realities (as in science) and assert certain values (as in religion), but that it is more generally the means by which all human affairs are connected to physical or social realities. This change in Wittgenstein's ideas has been epitomized by H. Stuart Hughes: "[Earlier] he had maintained that language proceeded from reality— that the structure of the real world determined the structure of speech. Now he had come to believe that the reverse was the case: language, as the vehicle for understanding reality determined the way in which people saw it."[14]

From this standpoint, science and the special use of language allowing the conduct of science is irrelevant to questions of morality or value, which stand at the center of the human condition. Science appears, consequently, as hardly more than a wonderfully complex and plastic plaything of the intellect, a toy that can be shaped in whatever forms clever intellects wish to shape it. It follows that science is totally amoral and terribly dangerous because its potent effects are ungoverned by any intrinsic human limits. We see it ever more clearly these days, of course: the weapons, nuclear plants, food additives, pollutants, etc., that cumulatively, as the result of science, threaten the future existence of our species and determine the conditions under which we exist.

Where then was morality to be found? Having "seen through" science via analysis of language, toward the end of his career Wittgenstein began to echo, somewhat, the ideas of earlier humanist philosophers, and some of his ideas also had a Nietzschean tone: "It is the will, rather than the reason, that introduces value into the world: I call 'will' first and foremost the bearer of good and evil."[15] He argued rather concretely that the real purpose of philosophical analysis was to protect human reason from being "bewitched" by human language. Toward the end of his career, as recorded in the essays titled *Philosophical Investigations,* Wittgenstein's efforts were chiefly devoted to showing just how easily reason may be distorted or manipulated by language.

It should be plain enough, at this point, why the Wittgensteinian perspective on the connections between language, science, and morality is basic to any serious discussion of the Holocaust and the human condition. As the most powerful creation of Western civilization, science too stands revealed as completely ineffective and indifferent when it comes to preventing humanity from inflicting extraordinary horrors upon itself. More specifically, Wittgenstein's analysis of the language of science indicates that it is not only amoral, but that to an even greater extent than religion or law, science may be bent to any purpose—no matter how extreme or "unthinkable"—for it contains no internal mechanism to serve as a limiting factor. Instead, like any common weapon, science, and reason itself, may be picked up and used for whatever purposes can be justified by clever rhetoric.

The Holocaust provides such an overwhelming burden of evidence to this effect that perhaps people refuse to recognize it lest they be forced to acknowledge their own participation in horrors akin to those perpetrated by the Nazis. In connection with planning and implementation of the genocide program, for example, the capacity to think and act according to euphemistic language became a widespread and apparently effective form of individual psychological adjustment. Euphemisms such as "final solution," "relocation," and "shower bath" seemed to work nicely for the SS as a means of imposing a rationalized, business-as-usual emotional framework upon activities too atrocious to be contemplated in the raw. It was precisely in this same vein of word-magic-via-euphemism that the American forces in Vietnam conducted programs of "forced urbanization" (herding people into concentration camps) and "defoliation" (poisoning the natural ecology).

But in these and many other obvious examples of how euphemistic language facilitates the reification of atrocious activities into acceptable and routine "operations" that may then be implemented without a qualm by the corporate technicians of modern applied science, what one sees revealed is merely the tip of an iceberg. The deeper implications flowing from the falsification of language produced by political interests, on the one hand, and technical-scientific interests, on the other, ultimately involve the gradual disappearance of all authentic human experience. That is, fundamental elements of culture and civilization are slowly sinking out of sight in a mire of bureaucratic structures functioning in the name of humanity, against humanity. As Horkheimer and Adorno have noted: "There is no longer any available form of linguistic expression which has not tended toward accommodation to dominant currents of thought; *and what a devalued language does not do automatically is proficiently executed by societal mechanisms.*"[16]

If this discussion of language and the Holocaust seems excessive, it should be recalled that the history of this century is, manifestly, a record of the manipulation of reason by rhetoric. Not for nothing has this era been called the "age of ideology." It is entirely clear, furthermore, that the most massive human killings and horrors are closely associated with those societies in which ideologies have been most highly developed and pervasive in everyday life. People themselves are probably no more ferocious by nature in one place than in another. But ideologies, which blend linguistic rationalizations with political imperatives to the draconian actions made possible by modern science, have yielded such extraordinary horrors as the Holocaust. It is particularly noteworthy, in this connection, that American liberalism only became readily visible as an ideology in the 1960s, when it was perceived that the horrors of racism and the Vietnam war could be conveniently rationalized in the language of liberalism and carried out with the instruments of that same rigorously "objective" science that was, according to the values of liberalism, the foundation of human progress.

It is difficult to grasp the institutional significance of science in relation to ideology. Compared with science, for example, religion and law seem hardly more than primitive word structures. These institutions have no hardware or technology other than whatever crumbs may fall to them from the table of science. Religion and law have been effective governors of human action only where majorities of people have accepted the arbitrary assumptions these institutions are based upon: ideals of imminent justice, equity, retribution, life after death, revelation, and so on. None of these assumptions exists or can be demonstrated to exist in nature, except insofar as people impose them by collective acts of will. One can, for example, interpret the frenzied killing actions of a wolf or shark as either a terrifying judgment of God or a benign demonstration of ecological balancing processes. If one is persuaded of the value of ecological balance achieved in this fashion—a view which has become relatively popular only during the 1970s because of arguments created by biological science experts—well and good. But the key issue to see here is that one's view follows not from the phenomenon itself, but from a verbal interpretation of the phenomenon which may or may not satisfy prevailing criteria for the revealed word of God or the revealed facts of science.

This path of analysis is particularly difficult to follow because scientific thought has for more than three centuries been steadily discrediting and eroding the unverifiable assumptions underlying religion and law, substituting in their place the apparently verifiable, disinterested principles of reason, rationality, and empirical inquiry. The apparent disinterest of scientific thinking has, until recently, seemed to be a clearly superior value when compared with the vested interests built into the assumptions of law and religion. Yet as Wittgenstein saw, and as an increasing number of contemporary philosophers and scientists are beginning to see, placing trust in the rationalized assumptions and empirical methods of science is, fundamentally, just as much an arbitrary act of faith or "will" as trust in religion, or law, or voodoo witchcraft.[17]

Auschwitz and Hiroshima were as much enterprises of applied science (rationality armed with technology) as the Albigensian slaughter and the Inquisition were enterprises of applied religion (mystique armed with secular power). The chief difference between these two categories is only that the former destroyed more people in a far more impersonal but no less horrible way than the latter.

If anything, the Holocaust and other major horrors of this century must be laid more directly upon the doorstep of science than upon the doorstep of either religion or law. This is partly because science has been responsible for reducing the inhibitory "power" of religion and law. Thus, social science and biology have effectively wiped out most of the inhibitions prescribed by religion, whereas political science and sociology have revealed the arbitrary qualities of secular law. Science is far more deceptive than either religion or law, because the words describing the essence of science—reason, enlightenment, and son—are taken to indicate the core of civilization as opposed to barbarism.

Nevertheless, events of this century show such definitions of science to be an extraordinary semantic trick. One assumes, and is everywhere assured, that scientific thinking is antithetical to the ferocious passions that can unleash barbarism. Even to question this proposition seems "irrational." However, the fact is that our twentieth-century age of science is also, at least from 1914 onward, the age of both unparalleled mass human destruction and individualized human torture. How can the proposition that science is opposed to barbarism be reconciled to these plain facts? The proposition must in some way be wrong or misleading. The inescapable conclusion, it seems, is that whereas scientific thought is indeed antithetical to the wild passions of barbarism, it is not at all antithetical to efficient, dispassionate destruction, slaughter, and torture. The equation that fits the historical data is this: As the quality of thinking grows more rational, the quantity of destruction increases. In our time, for example, terrorism and torture are no longer primarily instruments of passion; they have become instruments of political rationality. Governments adopt them dispassionately, as policies aimed at discouraging revolution; revolutionaries adopt them dispassionately, as methods to intimidate governments and the apolitical masses. Furthermore, the empirical rationality of terrorism and torture has become so apparent that to question their use is to risk the accusation of irrationality.

Viewed against the fallacies and failures of law, religion, and science, it appears that those supposedly sadistic monsters of the Nazi SS, "Gestapo" Müller, "Hangman" Heydrich, "Papa" Eicke, "Reichsheinie" Himmler himself, and the many middle-management administrators of the death camps were perhaps no more insane than anyone else who has ever thought they were performing heroic actions for the sake of future generations. As noted earlier, there is little evidence to show that either the directors or the majority of the functionaries who participated in making the Holocaust took great pleasure in their work, although most took a certain pride in their ability to handle such a difficult assignment. On the contrary, there is considerable evidence showing that the majority of the killers found the substance of their work somewhat depressing and sometimes quite sickening. On the whole, it is in most instances true that they were "just following orders." What can this mean?

At the immediate individual level, for the killers themselves, it meant that their atrocious activities lost their "normal" meaning as atrocities. Authorized and encouraged by the state, organized to a high degree of industrial efficiency in accord with scientific technology, justified by the "political" imperatives of ideology, and verbalized in the abstract, euphemistic language of science, the routinized genocide program in our judgment influenced the mentality of the killers in much the same way as other repetitive, rationalized forms of industrial work influences the ordinary worker. That is, the activity becomes relatively meaningless and quite detached from the actor's sense of self. On an assembly-line job, one daydreams about vacations, plans how to get a new car, and is more concerned with how long it will be to the next break than with the quality of what one is doing. Moreover, the industrial worker does not identify himself as maker of automobiles or creator of refrigerators, but rather as an installer of radiators, a freezer-coil welder, a steam fitter, or some such. This is a definitive characteristic of alienated labor as Marx understood it: "the product of his labor confronts the worker as an alien (meaningless) object."

It become possible, finally, to comprehend those SS men who freely admitted mass killings when they were on trial, but indignantly refused to accept the idea that they could be called murderers. Their argument has logic. Would workers in the chemical plants that produced napalm accept responsibility for burned babies? Would such workers even be aware that others might reasonably think they were responsible? The analogy to alienated labor is far from perfect, of course, but it suggests why so many of the SS leaders and rank and file could not fully recognize their activity as murder. Caught up in the totally organized environment of the Holocaust, their general behavior seems directly in line with the idea that routinization and fractionization can reduce anything (violence, sex, torture, or whatever) to the status of alienated labor.

At the sociocultural level, the rationality of the Holocaust reveals that religion and law have no independent capacity to inhibit atrocious behavior because both institutions are subordinate to the state. The moral principles codified in these institutions can only be enforced at the discretion of secular political leaders. Moreover, these principles have steadily lost their intrinsic force under the impact of Enlightenment philosophy and science.

The idea of evil is a relevant case in point. All the major traditions of morality in our civilization have specified that evil actions are primarily those that serve selfish interests. Evil has traditionally been identified and defined by the emotional or material satisfactions it brings: wrongdoing has occurred when an emotional thrill, sensory pleasure, or material profit is gained. The whole structure of Western morality conveyed by the institutions of religion and law is based on this premise, and the Judeo-Christian tradition of wrongdoing is utterly clear on this point: sin is unauthorized pleasure. It is also very clear that hardly anywhere in this tradition is there any story or statement to the effect that "thou shalt not obey legal orders from superiors if they seem atrocious to you." Abraham, who was prepared to obey the directive to murder his son Isaac as a demonstration of his faith in the superior being of Jaweh, is not condemned for his blind obedience, but rather held up as exemplary. The Protestant tradition of individualism and the direct confrontation of the individual to God has emphasized that individual conscience applies almost exclusively to *private* rather than *public* acts. Luther's own position on war and the peasant revolts is significant in the origins of this tradition. By traditional religious standards, therefore, it is difficult to identify the Holocaust as evil because of its rationality as a program implemented in obedience to higher orders, and without any substantial motives toward achieving pleasures of the flesh or the pocketbook.

The intrinsic irrelevance of the Western legal tradition of morality can be epitomized easily enough by the various contingencies it provides for killing people. If you kill people by accident, it is not murder; it is manslaughter. If you kill people in order to protect your person or property against serious transgression, it is not manslaughter, it is justifiable homicide or self-defense. If you wear a uniform and kill people named as enemies of the state that gave you the uniform, in accord with legal orders, it is not self-defense, it is patriotic duty. As Wittgenstein might have argued, depending on how killing is categorized in language, religion may condemn you or bless you, and you will be either punished or honored by lawmakers. Once the moral essence of the Holocaust is seen to lie in obedience to constituted authority, then the failure and irrelevance of religion and law become apparent, for insofar as both institutions have construed obedience to constituted authority to be the cornerstone of morality, they are impotent before situations in which that authority has been corrupted.

Added to this state of affairs is the unique contribution of science, which, apart from devaluing the premises of religion and law for their unverifiability, also makes possible the organization and control of massive human enterprises to such an extent that horrors may be perpetrated as a form of alienated labor. Taking all these considerations together, it may be suggested finally what the Holocaust reveals about the human condition: none of the chief achievements of our civilization offer protection against infernal horrors. By virtue of the Holocaust it is clear that religion and law, and science in particular, not only have failed to ennoble humanity or prevent inhumanity, but have contributed to its degradation. Much of what has been taken for granted as defining the "ascent of man," may be seen as equally defining a descent toward self-destruction.[18]

Apart from its substantive horrors, the terrible fascination exerted by the Holocaust resides in its bloodless rationality, and in what this rationality shows us about ourselves and our culture. Nothing we have created in the way of religion, law, or science can be taken at the face value our language provides. In proportion as these creations furnish the good things of modern life, they also make possible the horrors. The prevailing rationality functions to celebrate the former and conceal the latter. In the Holocaust, however, one may see what lies beneath the mask called civilization. There is no morality per se, because there is no immutable religious or legal standard for human behavior. Insofar as morality exists, even as a concept, it does so as an act of an all-too-fallible human will.

There is no scientific progress in the naive sense of the phrase, there is only an ever-increasing supply of technology, virtually all of which has as much potential for destroying life as for enhancing it. There is, indeed, no normality, for the madness or amorality of one generation or one culture may be the required norm for another. And there is, finally, no special sacredness, purpose, or minimal dignity to human life—except insofar as these values can be created and sustained against all the forces that tend to traduce them.

The ultimate fact staring all of us in the face is that starting with nothing except personal determination, Hitler could mobilize enough of the elements of modern civilization subsumed under the headings religion, law, and science to create a human inferno, a hell on earth. Since the institutions supposed to prevent this sort of thing could not do so, and since these institutions are today, with the possible exception of science, no stronger than they were in Hitler's day, the truth of our human condition is that existence now is more and more recognizably in accord with the principles that governed life and death in Auschwitz.

Like the prisoners who struggled to survive by banding together in little fraternities of desperation, people today appear everywhere clinging together in groups devoted to their special interests. Living immersed in an atmosphere of power and bluff, of the frequent threat and occasional reality of violence; distrusting others and often ourselves, we yet realize that the tensions and struggles for life security, if not prosperity, are taking their steady toll. In Auschwitz, the prisoner population was culled by SS physicians who seemed virtually a force in nature; in contemporary society, we are culled by forces in nature (heart disease, cancer) which seem as inevitable as SS physicians. And, in the ground and under the seas, there are the instant mobile crematoria: nuclear missiles carefully crafted by master scientists to be always ready to burn us en masse if some unknown person should make a mistaken calculation or decide, perhaps rationally, that life on earth requires drastic alteration.

Of course, the world is not literally an Auschwitz, and we merely live under the shadow of nuclear holocaust. But the Nazi Holocaust did happen; and now the only visions of the world that can be taken seriously are those that come through the irrevocably ash-darkened prisms of post-Holocaust sense and sensibility.

# Notes

## Chapter I

1.  The nature of the events precludes a precise estimate of the number killed. Nora Levin, *The Holocaust: The Destruction of European Jewry 1933–1945* (New York: Thomas Y. Crowell, 1968) provides a summary from various sources estimating the numbers killed. Most place the figure at slightly below six million, a number first introduced at the Nuremberg trials. Nothing useful is served by discussion of the neo-Nazi literature such as A. R. Butz's *The Hoax of the Twentieth Century,* which denies the existence of mass killing. This issue has been considered in an important article by Bradley F. Smith, "Two Alibis for the Inhumanities: A. R. Butz, *The Hoax of the Twentieth Century* and David Irving, *Hitler's War,*" *German Studies Review,* 1:3 (October 1978), 327–335. Among the most important narrative accounts of the Holocaust in addition to the Levin work cited above are Leon Poliakov, *Harvest of Hate: The Nazi Program for the Destruction of the Jews in Europe* (Syracuse, N. Y.: Syracuse University Press, 1954); Gerald Reitlinger, *The Final Solution: The Attempt to Exterminate the Jews of Europe, 1939–1945* (London: Vallentine, Mitchell, 1953); Lucy Dawidowicz, *The War Against the Jews: 1933–1945* (New York: Holt, Rinehart and Winston, 1975); Raul Hilberg, *The Destruction of the European Jews* (Chicago: Quadrangle Books, 1961). The literature on racist ideology is substantial. See particularly George L. Mosse, *Toward the Final Solution: A History of European Racism* (New York: Howard Fertig, 1978).

2.  Robert G. L. Waite, in *The Psychopathic God: Adolf Hitler* (New York: Basic Books, 1977), p. xi, writes that "more will be written about Hitler than about anyone else in history with the exception of Jesus Christ." The best guides to the literature on the Holocaust are Jacob Robinson and Philip Friedman, *Guide to Jewish History under Nazi Impact* (New York and Jerusalem: Yad Washem Martyrs' and Heroes Memorial Authority and Yivo Institute for Jewish Research, 1960), and the catalogues of the Wiener Library.

3.  Dwight Macdonald, *Memoirs of a Revolutionist: Essays in Political Criticism* (New York: Farrar, Straus and Cudahy, 1957), pp. 33–44.

4.  Arthur Koestler, *The Yogi and the Commissar and Other Essays* (New York: Macmillan, 1945), p. 247.

5.  The development of Nazi anti-Semitic policies up to 1939 is described in detail by Karl A. Schleunes, *The Twisted Road to Auschwitz: Nazi Policy toward German Jews* (Urbana, Ill.: University of Illinois Press, 1970).

6.  David Rousset, *A World Apart* (London: Secker and Warburg, 1951), p. 109.

7.  The theological-mystical association is best expressed in the writings of Elie Wiesel, beginning with his autobiographical *Night* (New York: Avon, 1969). On Wiesel see particularly Irving Halperin, *Messengers from the Dead: Literature of the Holocaust* (Philadelphia: Westminster Press, 1970) and Lawrence L. Langer, *The Holocaust and the Literary Imagination* (New Haven, Conn.: Yale University Press, 1975). One of the earliest novels dealing with the Holocaust in these terms was André Schwarz-Bart, *The Last of the Just* (New York: Bantam Books, 1961; French edition published 1959). Emil Fackenheim argues that the Holocaust requires of Jews a reaffirmation of their Jewishness, so that Hitler's aim of the

destruction of Judaism should not succeed, and also a defense of Israel: "It is solely because of this connection of the events of May and June [the 1967 war] with Auschwitz that a Jew must both tremble and rejoice. He must tremble lest he permit any light after Auschwitz to relieve the darkness of Auschwitz. Rejoicing after Auschwitz, and because of Auschwitz, the Jew must be a Jew . . . a witness to the world, preparing a way for God," "Jewish Faith and the Holocaust: A Fragment," *Commentary,* 46:2 (August 1968) 30–36. See also Fackenheim's *God's Presence in History* (New York: New York University Press, 1970).

8.   Quoted in Helmut Krausnick et al., *Anatomy of the SS State* (New York: Walker and Co., 1968), p. 94.

9.   For a discussion of the eugenic-racist basis for the genocide program see, inter alia, Leon Poliakov, *The Aryan Myth: A History of Racist and Nationalist Ideas in Europe* (New York: Basic Books, 1974); George L. Mosse, *Toward the Final Solution;* Daniel Gasman, *The Scientific Origins of National Socialism: Social Darwinism in Ernst Haeckel and the German Monist League* (New York: American Elsevier, 1971); Hedwig Conrad-Martius, *Utopien der Menschenzüchtung: Der Sozialdarwinismus und seine Folgen (*Munich: Kosel, 1953); Loren R. Graham, "Science and Values: The Eugenics Movement in Germany and Russia in the 1920s," *American Historical Review,* 82 (1977), 1133–1164.

10.   Marc Hillel and Clarissa Henry, *Of Pure Blood* (New York: McGraw-Hill, 1976); Larry V. Thompson, *"Lebensborn* and the Eugenics Policy of the *Reichsführer SS,"* *Central European History,* 4 (1971), 54–77.

11.   Franz Stangl, the commander of Treblinka, began his SS career by working in the euthanasia program. His biographer discusses his increasing involvement in the death machinery and his attitudes toward it: Gitta Sereny, *Into that Darkness: From Mercy Killing to Mass Murder* (New York: McGraw-Hill, 1974).

12.   Poliakov, *Harvest of Hate,* pp. 185–186.

13.   Macdonald, *Memoirs of a Revolutionist,* p. 61.

14.   Peter Farb, *Man's Rise to Civilization as Shown by the Indians of North America from Primeval Times to the Coming of the Industrial Age,* (New York: Dutton, 1968), chap. 8.

# Chapter II

1.   We are indebted to Dr. John Mendelsohn of the Modern Military Branch, Military Archives Division of the National Archives and Records Service for information on the number of persons tried for war crimes. (Letter to George M. Kren, November 2, 1977.)

2.   The failure of Weimar democracy and the rise of Hitler and National Socialism have been the subject of many discussions and investigations. A few salient points: The military not only did not accept defeat, but never made a commitment to democracy. The new democratic government could not count upon the military for protection from right-wing subversion. The Weimar republic was associated—not altogether falsely—in the minds of many Germans with a humiliating defeat and a dishonorable peace treaty. Throughout its history it could never overcome the charge that it had signed the unacceptable Versailles agreement, including particularly the war guilt clause. The attempt to destroy German communism led to the creation in 1918 of the Free Corps—which meant arming the enemies of democracy. When German democracy reached a crisis after the depression of 1929, its democratic institutions proved unable to deal with it, and Adolf Hitler—employing a program dedicated to the destruction of democracy—readily gained power as well as substantial support from the German people.

3.   This has been challenged by David Irving in *Hitler's War* (New York: Basic Books, 1977) who argues from the absence of a written order by Hitler ordering the extermination of the Jews that Hitler not only did not order the extermination, but was not even aware that extermination of the Jews was taking place. The blame is put on Heinrich Himmler. Historians reviewing this book have been universal in their unconditional rejection of his thesis. Cf. the review by Bradley Smith in *German Studies Review* (October 1978) cited in chap. 1, note 1.

4. Friedrich Meinecke, *Die Deutsche Katastrophe* (Wiesbaden: Eberhard Brockhaus, 1946, English tr., Harvard University Press, 1950); Gerhard Ritter, *Europa und die Deutsche Frage: Betrachungen über die geschichtliche Eigenart des deutschen Staatsdenkens* (Munich: Münchner, 1948). The most important study of the political significance of German historicism is Georg Iggers, *The German Conception of History: The National Tradition of Historical Thought from Herder to the Present* (Middletown, Conn.: Wesleyan University Press, 1968). Also George M. Kren, "Political Implications of German Historicism," *Rocky Mountain Social Science Journal* 6 (April 1969), 91–99. Robert A. Pois, *Friedrich Meinecke and German Politics in the Twentieth Century* (Berkeley: University of California Press, 1972) is more critical than most other studies; Andreas Dorpalen, "Historiography as History: the Works of Gerhard Ritter," *Journal of Modern History,* 24 (March 1962), 1–18; George M. Kren, "Gerhard Ritter and the Interpretation of German History," *Wiener Library Bulletin* 18, (April 1964).

5. Erich Fromm, *Escape from Freedom* (New York: Holt Rinehart and Winston, 1941).

6. Wilhelm Reich, *The Mass Psychology of Fascism* (New York: Farrar, Straus & Giroux, 1970).

7. Theodore W. Adorno and others, in *The Authoritarian Personality* (New York: Harper, 1950), have attempted to construct a test for identifying an authoritarian personality in a work which combines a Freudian-analytic perspective with survey techniques.

8. Georg Lukács, *Die Zerstörrung der Vernunft* (Neuwid am Rhein, Berlin-Spandau: Herman Luchterhand, 1962); Hans Kohn, *The Mind of Germany: The Education of a Nation* (New York: Scribner's, 1960); Peter Viereck, *Metapolitics: The Roots of the Nazi Mind* (New York: Knopf, 1941). There are a legion of works seeking to document the intellectual sources of National Socialism.

9. Bruno Walter, *Mission Accomplished* (New York: Knopf, 1957).

10. The rejection of rationality has been a major theme of German culture. During the period of the Napoleonic wars the Enlightenment and rationalism were identified as an alien mode of thinking which led to the conclusion in much of German thought that democracy, liberalism, and rationalism were all somehow un-German. Thomas Mann's famous *Reflections of a Non-political Man (Betrachtungen eines Unpolitischen,* Frankfurt: S. Fischer Verlag, 1956) may be cited as the most famous example. Romanticism emerged in Germany at least partially as a counterideology to the French Enlightenment—a general European phenomenon, not restricted to Germany. But in Germany romanticism acquired a political and antidemocratic significance which did not exist elsewhere. Writers such as Jahn, Arndt, Wagner, Nietzsche, Stefan George, Spengler, Ernst Jünger are frequently cited in this connection.

11. See particularly chaps. 9 and 10 in Hugh T. Kerr, *A Compendium of Luther's Theology* (Philadelphia: Westminster Press, 1943).

12. Leonard von Muralt, *Bismarcks Verantwortlichkeit* (Göttingen: Musterschmidt, 1955).

13. The standard work in the substantial literature on the youth movement is now Walter Laqueur, *Young Germany: A History of the German Youth Movement* (New York: Basic Books, 1962). The relationship between the youth movement and the Free Corps is discussed by R. G. Waite, *Vanguard of Nazism: The Free Corps Movement in Germany 1918–1923* (Cambridge, Mass.: Harvard University Press, 1952).

14. This quotation from Hölderlin is cited by Laqueur, *Young Germany,* p. 5, to indicate the values of the second generation of the youth movement. Laqueur comments: "The youth movement wanted above all to be integrated human beings . . . and they were critical of a society that was not conducive to the development of such men and women."

15. R. H. S. Crossman, introduction to Walter Laqueur, *Young Germany,* p. xviii.

16. Laqueur, *Young Germany,* p. 41.

17. *American Historical Review,* 76 (December 1971):1457–1502.

18.   Rudolph Binion, *Hitler among the Germans* (New York: Elsevier, 1976).

19.   "The Legend of Hitler's Childhood." Reprinted in Erik H. Erikson, *Childhood and Society* (New York: Norton, 1963), pp. 326–358.

20.   Reich, *Mass Psychology,* p.5.

21.   Ernst Jünger, *The Storm of Steel* (London: Chatto & Windus, 1929).

22.   Friedrich Nietzsche, "On War and Warriors" in *Thus Spake Zarathustra,* translated by Thomas Common, in *The Philosophy of Nietzsche* (New York: Modern American Library, 1954), p. 48.

23.   Herman Hesse, *Steppenwolf* translated by Basil Creighton, updated by Joseph Mileck (New York: Bantam, 1969), p. 214–215.

24.   An important discussion of Hitler's role in National Socialism is provided by Karl Dietrich Bracher, "The Role of Hitler: Perspectives and Interpretations" in Walter Laqueur, ed., *Fascism: A Reader's Guide* (Berkeley: University of California Press, 1976), pp. 211–225.

25.   Waite, *Psychopathic God,* p. xvi.

26.   Some of the early anti-Semitic influences in Linz are discussed by Helmut J. Schmeller, *Hitler's View of History* (unpublished Ph.D. diss., Kansas State University, Manhattan, Kansas, 1975).

27.   Among the more important psychohistorical studies of Hitler are: Rudolph Binion, *Hitler among the Germans* (New York: Elsevier, 1976); Binion, "Hitler's Concept of *Lebensraum:* The Psychological Basis," *History of Childhood Quarterly* 1 (1973), 187–215; Binion, "Hitler Looks East," *ibid.,* 3(1975), 85–102; Helm Stierlin, *Adolf Hitler, A Family Perspective* (New York: Psychohistory Press, 1976); Gertrud M. Kurth, "The Jew and Adolf Hitler," *Psychoanalytic Quarterly,* 16 (1947), 11–32; Walter Langer, *The Mind of Adolf Hitler: The Secret Wartime Report* (New York: New American Library, 1972); James H. McRandle, *Track of the Wolf: Essays on National Socialism* (Evanston, Ill.: Northwestern University Press, 1965); Erikson, "The Legend of Hitler's Childhood"; Waite, *Psychopathic God;* Waite, "Adolf Hitler's Anti-Semitism" in Benjamin Wolman, ed., *The Psychoanalytic Interpretation of History* (New York: Basic Books, 1971), pp. 192–230; Waite, "Adolf Hitler's Guilt Feelings: A Problem in History and Psychology," *Journal of Interdisciplinary History* 1:2 (1971) 229–249; Bradley Smith, *Adolf Hitler: His Family, Childhood and Youth* (Stanford: Stanford University Press, 1967). Most recently William Carr, Hitler: *A Study in Personality and Politics* (London: Edward Arnold, 1978), reviews some of the psychohistorical literature. Peter Loewenberg, "Psychohistorical Perspective on Modern German History," *Journal of Modern History* 47 (1975), and George M. Kren, "Psychohistorical Interpretations of National Socialism," *German Studies Review,* 1:2 (May 1978) provide a survey of the psychohistorical literature. A detailed bibliography on the topic of psychohistory and National Socialism by Terry G. Mensch is scheduled for a forthcoming issue of the *Journal of Psychohistory.*

28.   The *Psychohistory Review* devoted most of an issue (Summer 1977) to a discussion by a number of scholars of Binion's work, followed by Binion's reply; and his *"Lebensraum"* article in the *History of Childhood Quarterly* is accompanied by comments on his thesis by a number of scholars.

# Chapter III

1.   Quoted in Gerald Reitlinger, *The SS: Alibi of a Nation 1922–1945* (New York: Viking, 1957), p. 72.

2.   The best narrative history of the SS to date is Heinz Höhne, *The Order of the Death's Head: The Story of Hitler's SS* (New York: Ballantine, 1971); Helmut Krausnick et al., *Anatomy of the SS State* contains a number of important analytical essays on the SS; also E. Neusüss-Hunkel, *Die SS* (Hanover and Frankfurt: Norddeutsche Verlagsanstalt O. Goedel, 1956). The unpublished Ph.D. dissertation by Gunnar C. Boehnert, "A Sociography of the SS Officer Corps, 1925–1939," (University of London, 1977) provides a detailed analysis of the

changing social composition of the SS; see also Manfred Wolfson, *The SS Leadership* (unpublished Ph.D. Diss., University of California, Berkeley, 1965); University Microfilms 65–13, 621).

3. *Hitler's Table Talk 1941–1944* (London: Weidenfeld and Nicholson, 1953), p. 167.

4. Cited in Höhne, *Order of the Death's Head,* p.26. This account of the origins of the SS follows Höhne's analysis in chap. 2 of the *Order of the Death's Head.*

5. Röhm's autobiography, *Die Geschichte eines Hochverräters* (Munich: Frz. Eher Nachf., 1934) describes his life until his return from Bolivia and is an important source for his ideas and character.

6. Erikson, "The Legend of Hitler's Childhood."

7. Tom Segev, *The Commanders of the Nazi Concentration Camps* (unpublished Ph.D. diss., Boston University Graduate School, 1977; University Microfilms, Ann Arbor, Mich., 77–21, 618).

8. Ibid.

9. Important studies on Himmler are Bradley Smith, *Heinrich Himmler: A Nazi in the Making, 1900–1926* (Stanford: Stanford University Press, 1971); Peter Loewenberg, "The Unsuccessful Adolescence of Heinrich Himmler," *American Historical Review,* 76 (1971), 612–641; Josef Ackermann, *Heinrich Himmler als Ideologue* (Göttingen: Musterschmidt, 1970).

10. On Heydrick, see Shlomo Aronson, *Reinhard Heyrdrich und die Frühgeschichte von Gestapo und SD* (Stuttgart: Deutsche Verlagsanstalt, 1971).

11. In addition to the discussion of the Röhm affair in Höhne's *Order of the Death's Head,* there is a popular, undocumented work by Max Gallo, *The Night of Long Knives* (New York: Harper & Row, 1972). An important analysis also appears in Martin Göhring, *Alles oder Nichts: Zwölf Jahres totalitärer Herrschaft in Deutschland I* (Tübingen: J. C. B. Mohr, 1966).

12. Ernst Niekisch, *Das Reich der Niederen Dämonen* (Hamburg: Rowohlt, 1953), provides an important assessment of the significance of Hitler's justification.

13. A good sketch of Eicke's early career is provided by Charles W. Sydnor, Jr., *Soldiers of Destruction: The SS Death's Head Division 1933–1945* (Princeton, N. J.: Princeton University Press, 1977).

14. Himmler himself recognized this: "I know that there are some people in Germany who become sick when they see this black coat; we have understanding for this and do not expect that we will be loved by too many." Heinrich Himmler, *Die Schutzstaffel als antibolschweistische Kampforganisation* (Munich: Zentralverlag der NSDAP, 1936), p. 29.

15. Hausser wrote his memoirs after the war. *Soldaten wie ander auch: Der Weg der Waffen SS* (Osnabrück: Munin, 1966).

16. Himmler's ideas are discussed in Josef Ackermann, *Heinrich Himmler als Ideologue* (Göttingen: Musterschmidt, 1970).

17. A detailed discussion of the "Fritsch crisis" is provided by Herman Foertsch, *Schuld und Verhängnis: Die Fritschkrise im Frühjahr 1938 als Wendepunkt in der Geschichte der Nationalsozialitsischen Zeit* (Stuttgart: Deutsche Verlagsanstalt, 1951).

18. Quoted in Gerald Reitlinger, *The SS: Alibi of a Nation* (New York: Viking, 1957).

19. Sydnor's *Soldiers of Destruction* includes specific evidence of personnel interchange between the Death's Head units in the concentration camps and the Waffen SS. The standard work on the Waffen SS is George H. Stein, *The Waffen SS: Hitler's Elite Guard at War, 1939–1945* (Ithaca, N.Y.: Cornell University Press, 1966). Other relevant sources include James Weingartner, *Hitler's Guard: The Story of the Leibstandarte SS Adolf Hitler 1933–1945* (Carbondale and Edwardsville, Ill.; Southern Illinois University Press, 1968); George M. Kren and Leon H. Rappoport, "The Waffen SS: A Social Psychological Perspective," *Armed Forces and Society,* 3 (November 1976).

20. Although some writers, such as Dawidowicz, argue that Hitler had intended to kill all the Jews as early as 1919, the evidence for this is weak—most notably because every effort was made until the invasion of the U.S.S.R. to force an expulsion of Jews from Germany. Eichmann first achieved recognition after the Anschluss when he arranged in Vienna for the wealthy Jews to pay for the emigration of the poorer ones.

21. Höhne, *Order of the Death's Head*, p. 405.

22. Ibid., p. 406.

23. Ibid., p. 409.

24. Ibid., p. 411.

25. Ibid., p. 414.

26. Nora Levin, *Holocaust*, pp. 311–314; Höhne, *Order of the Death's Head*, pp. 425–428; Saul Friedländer, *Counterfeit Nazi: the Ambiguity of Good* (London: Weidenfeld and Nicolson, 1969), chap. 5. Gerstein, who procured the zyklon B gas crystals, figures prominently in Rolf Hochhuth's *The Deputy* as the person who attempted to inform the papal nuncio of the genocide program.

27. Quoted in Friedländer, *Counterfeit Nazi*, pp. 116–121.

28. Gitta Sereny, *Into That Darkness: From Mercy Killing to Mass Murder* (McGraw-Hill, 1974). This biography of Franz Stangl, based on extensive interviews with him in a German prison, is one of the most important and, for some reason, least recognized studies of the Holocaust.

29. Ibid., pp. 113–114.

30. Rudolf Hoess: *Commandant of Auschwitz: The Autobiography of Rudolf Hoess* (Cleveland and New York: World, 1959), pp. 162–166, 208.

31. Ibid., p. 214.

32. Reitlinger indicates that Auschwitz received three quarters of a ton each month between February 14 and March 31, 1944, and cites Hoess to the effect that he had received ten tons of zyklon B from the "Degesch" company (Reitlinger, *Final Solution*, p. 147). According to a document left behind by Gerstein, who was for a time the officer assigned to supply zyklon B to Auschwitz, "the actual amount involved was approximately 9 tons 7 cwt., enough to kill eight million people" (quoted in Friedländer, *Counterfeit Nazi*, p. 181).

33. Ella Lingens, M.D., Ph.D., testified at the Auschwitz trial: "I know of almost no SS man who could not claim to have saved someone's life. There were few sadists. Not more than 5 or 10 percent were pathological criminals in the clinical sense. The others were all perfectly normal men who knew the difference between right and wrong." Quoted in Bernd Naumann, *Auschwitz: A Report on the Proceedings Against Robert Karl Ludwig Mulka and Others Before the Court at Frankfurt* (London: Pall Mall Press, 1966), p. 91.

34. Cf. Gerd Biermann, *Kinderzüchtigung und Kindesmisshandlung* (Munich, Basel: Ernst Reinhardt, 1969).

35. Helmuth Auerbach, "Die Einheit Dirlewanger," *Vierteljahrhefte für Zeitgeschichte*, 3 (1962), 250–263.

36. Höhne, *Order of the Death's Head*, pp. 577–609.

37. Simon Wiesenthal, *The Murderers Among Us: The Simon Wiesenthal Memoirs*, edited with an introductory profile by Joseph Wechsberg (New York: McGraw-Hill, 1967), p. 84.

38. A detailed discussion of SS veterans organizations, which also provides an excellent guide to the SS memoir literature, is Kurt P. Tauber, *Beyond Eagle and Swastika: German Nationalism since 1945* (Middletown, Conn.: Wesleyan University Press, 1967).

39. Hunter Thompson, *Hell's Angels* (New York: Random House, 1967).

40. Henry Dicks, *Licensed Mass Murder: A Soeio-psychological Study of Some SS Killers* (New York: Basic Books, 1972).

41.  Thomas Szasz, *The Myth of Mental Illness* (New York: Harper & Row, 1961). Stanley Milgram has produced extensive experimental evidence showing that normal people will frequently obey orders from legitimate authority figures to inflict severe pain on others: "With numbing regularity good people were seen to knuckle under to the demands of authority and perform actions that were callous and severe." Quoted in "Some Conditions of Obedience and Disobedience to Authority," *Human Relations*, 18 (1965), 74. Some interesting perspectives are also provided in Nevitt Sanford and Craig Comstock, *Sanctions for Evil* (San Francisco: Jossey-Bass, 1971), and Marc Pilisuk and Lyn Ober, "Torture and Genocide as Public Health Problems," *American Journal of Orthopsychiatry,* 46:3 (July 1976), 388–392.

42.  Hannah Arendt, *On Violence* (New York: Harcourt, Brace, 1969).

43.  Frantz Fanon, *The Wretched of the Earth* (New York: Grove Press, 1968).

44.  Herbert C. Kelman, "Violence without Moral Restraint: Reflections on the Dehumanization of Victims and Victimizers," *Journal of Social Issues,* 29 (1973), 29-61.

# Chapter IV

1.  There exists an extensive literature on anti-Semitism. Some important new perspectives appear in Richard L. Rubenstein, *After Auschwitz: Radical Theology and Contemporary Judaism* (Indianapolis: Bobbs-Merrill, 1966).

2.  Jean-Paul Sartre, *Anti-Semite and Jew,* translated by George J. Becker (New York: Schocken, 1948), p. 13.

3.  Leo Alexander, "War Crimes: Their Social-Psychological Aspects," *American Journal of Psychiatry,* 105 (August 1948), pp. 170–177.

4.  Sartre, *Anti-Semite and Jew.*

5.  Elie A. Cohen, *Human Behavior in the Concentration Camp,* translated by M. H. Braaksma (New York: Grosset & Dunlap, 1953), p. 144. Italics added.

6.  Roger Daniels, *Concentration Camps USA: Japanese-Americans and World War II* (New York: Holt, Rinehart and Winston, 1971), p. xxiv.

7.  This point is discussed in Bruno Bettelheim, *The Informed Heart: Autonomy in a Mass Age* (Glencoe, Ill.: Free Press, 1960); Bettelheim's "Individual and Mass Behavior in Extreme Situations," *Journal of Abnormal and Social Psychology* 38 (1943), pp. 417–452, based on his observation of behavior while a concentration camp prisoner, was to our knowledge the first work to discuss psychological changes in prisoners.

8.  Hilde O. Bluhm, "How Did They Survive? Mechanisms of Defense in Nazi Concentration Camps," *American Journal of Psychotherapy* 2 (January 1948), 32.

9.  Simon Wiesenthal, *The Murderers Among Us: The Simon Wiesenthal Memoirs* (New York: McGraw-Hill, 1967), p. 335.

10.  Frantz Fanon, *The Wretched of the Earth* (New York: Grove Press, 1968).

11.  Karl A. Schleunes, *The Twisted Road to Auschwitz: Nazi Policy toward German Jews* (Urbana, Ill.: University of Illinois Press, 1970).

12.  The following exchange between Dr. Georg Kareski, Leiter des Reichsverbandes jüdischer Kulturbünde (chairman of the Organization of Jewish Cultural Groups), and his interviewer, Goebbels, was reported in the newspaper *Der Angriff*, December 23, 1935:

*Frage:* Es ist Ihnen bekannt, Herr Direktor Kareski, dass unser Führer und Reichskanzler bei der Bergründung der Nürnberger Gesetze der Erwartung Ausdruck gegeben hat, dass durch diese einamlige säkulare Lösung, vielleicht doch eine Ebene geschaffen werden kann, auf der es dem deutschen Volke möglich wird, ein erträgliches Verhältnis zum jüdischen Volk finden zu können. Sie sind als führende Persönlichkeit der staatszionistischen Bewegung stets für eine scharfe Trennung zwischen deutschem und jüdischem Volkstum auf der Basis gegenseitiger Achtung eingetreten.

*Antwort:* Dar ist richtig. Ich habe seit vielen Jahren eine reinliche Abgrenzung der kulturellen Belange zweier miteinander lebender Völker also Voraussetzung für ein konfliktloses Zusammenleben angesehen, und bin für eine solche Abgrenzung, die den Respekt vor dem Bereich eines fremden Volkstums zur Voraussetzung hat, seit langem eingetreten.

*Question:* Are you aware, Director Kareski, that our Leader and Reichschancellor with the promulgation of the Nuremberg laws has expressed the expectation that through this onetime secular solution perhaps a basis may be created which would make it possible for the German nation to find an acceptable relationship to the Jewish nation? You, as a leading personality in the Zionist movement, have always advocated a sharp separation between German and Jewish national groups on the basis of mutual respect.

*Answer:* This is correct. For many years I have viewed a separation of the cultural concerns of two peoples living with each other as a prerequisite for a conflictless coexistence, and I support such a separation which respects the alien nationality.

Quoted in Klaus J. Hermann, *Das Dritte Reich und die Deutsch-Jüdischen Organisationen 1933–1934*, (Cologne: Carl Heymanns, 1969), p. 9.

13.  See Rita Thalmann and Emmanuel Feinermann, *Crystal Night: 9–10 November, 1938* (London, Thames and Hudson, 1974) and Lionel Kochan, *Pogrom: 10 November 1938* (London: André Deutsch, 1957).

14.  Cited in Helmut Krausnick et al., *Anatomy of the SS State* (New York: Walker, 1938), pp. 44–45. Hitler's anti-Semitism is extensively discussed in Eberhard Jäckel, *Hitler's Weltanschauung: A Blueprint for Power* (Middletown, Conn.: Wesleyan University Press, 1974) and in the chapter "The Jews in Hitler's Mental World," in Lucy Dawidowicz, *The War Against the Jews.*

15.  Krausnick, *Anatomy of the SS State,* pp. 84–85, quotes Heydrich as follows: "Those who remain alive . . . will be treated accordingly. If released . . . they would form a new cell from which the Jewish race could again develop."

16.  Ibid., p. 95.

17.  Hilberg, *Destruction of European Jews,* pp. 14–17.

18.  Hans Joachim Schoeps, *"Bereit für Deutschland!" Der Patriotismus Deutscher Juden und der Nationalsozialismus* (Berlin: Haude & Speneresche Verlagsbuchhandlung, 1970), p. 12.

19.  Quoted in Klaus J. Hermann, *Das Dritte Reich und die Deutsch-jüdischen Organisationen 1933–1945;* see also George L. Mosse, "The Influence of the Völkisch Idea on German Jewry," in *Germans and Jews* (New York: Grosset & Dunlap, 1970), pp. 77–115.

20.  Hilberg, *Destruction of European Jews,* p. 662.

21.  The appendix to Dawidowicz, *The War Against the Jews*, contains a brief discussion of the country-by-country fate of the Jews. Helen Fein, *Accounting for Genocide: National Responses and Jewish Victimization during the Holocaust* (New York: Free Press, 1979), provides a detailed bibliography of the fate of the Jews, country by country. Hannah Arendt, *Eichmann in Jerusalem,* chapters 9–13, also provides a discussion of the various national policies adopted by states directly or indirectly under German control during World War II.

22.  See Harold Flender, *Rescue in Denmark* (New York: Macfadden Bartell, 1964); Aage Bertelsen, *October 1943* (New York: Putnam's, 1954); Leni Yahil, *The Rescue of Danish Jewry: A Test of a Democracy* (Philadelphia, Pa.: Jewish Publication Society of America, 1969).

23.  Helen Fein, *Accounting For Genocide,* presents a detailed quantitative study of the numbers of Jews killed in the various Nazi-dominated countries analyzed according to three "predictor variables": (1) the degree of prewar (1936) indigenous anti-Semitism; (2) the reactions of local church authorities to information that "their" Jews were being deported to death camps; and (3) the degree of SS control over civil government authorities in 1941. As might be

expected, she reports that in general Jewish survival was highest in countries where anti-Semitism was low, church leaders spoke out against deportations, and SS control was low. Where these three variables were high, destruction of the Jews was also high.

There are, however, conceptual/methodological problems associated with this mode of analysis. For example (1) SS control was in most countries much less efficient and intense in 1941 than later on; (2) use of standardized techniques for quantifying the degree of prewar anti-Semitism and the reactions of church leaders to deportations is open to serious question; and (3) the predictor variables are in many instances treated separately, as if they were statistically independent of one another, when the burden of historical evidence shows that they were not. Thus, in most if not all of the German-conquered countries of Eastern Europe, the three predictor variables were all high, and Jewish destruction was also high. But Jewish losses were also high in Holland and Hungary, where historical evidence clearly shows that SS control was the single most significant factor. Considered as a whole, the Fein work presents much new, useful information, and her most specific quantitative finding, that SS control plus indigenous anti-Semitism accounts for 85 percent of the variance in the distribution of Jews killed throughout Europe, seems well founded. None of the data she presents, however, can be taken as substantial negation of the general historical and psychosocial thesis that SS domination was the most decisive factor in Jewish destruction.

24. Alexander Donat, *The Holocaust Kingdom* (New York: Holt, Rinehart and Winston, 1965), p. 542. A detailed discussion of these and other related points concerning survival in the camps is in Anna Pawelczynska, *Values and Violence in Auschwitz: A Sociological Analysis,* (Berkeley: University of California Press, 1979). A former prisoner at Auschwitz who worked as a Polish underground army courier until captured by the Germans, the author is professor of sociology in Poland, and notes in her introduction that thirty years had to pass before she was able to work on this material. The chapter "A Place in the Structure of Terror" (pp. 68–82) is especially relevant to the question of how people might survive in the camps. The work is very limited, however, and will surely seem questionable to some authorities in the field, because it gives only the most perfunctory attention to important differences between the situations of Jewish prisoners and others, including the non-Jewish Polish nationals. Many other sources indicate that in the latter group strong anti-Semitic attitudes were prevalent, and were sometimes brutally acted out, but Pawelczynska says nothing at all about this.

25. Alex Weissberg, *Desperate Mission: Joel Brand's Story* (New York: Criterion Books, 1958). Other works dealing with allied responses are Henry L. Feingold, *The Politics of Rescue: The Roosevelt Administration and the Holocaust, 1938–1945* (New Brunswick, N. J.: Rutgers University Press, 1970); Arthur D. Morse, *While Six Million Died: A Chronicle of American Apathy* (New York: Random House, 1967).

26. Levin, *Holocaust,* p. 126.

27. Elie Wiesel, *Legends of Our Time* (New York: Avon, 1970), p. 19.

28. Jacob Robinson, *Psychoanalysis in a Vacuum: Bruno Bettelheim and the Holocaust* (New York: Yad Vashem-Yivo Documentary Projects, 1970), p. 16.

29. Amos Elon, *The Israelis: Founders and Sons* (New York: Holt, Rinehart & Winston, 1971), p. 266.

30. Robert J. Lifton, *History and Human Survival* (New York: Random House, 1970); *Death in Life: Survivors of Hiroshima* (New York: Random House, 1967); *Home from the War* (New York: Simon and Schuster, 1973); *The Life of the Self* (New York: Simon and Schuster, 1976).

31. Leon Festinger, *A Theory of Cognitive Dissonance* (Evanston, Ill.: Row Peterson, 1957).

32. The best study of Auschwitz is Hermann Langbein, *Menschen in Auschwitz* (Vienna: Europa, 1972).

33. Edgar Schein et al., *Coercive Persuasion* (New York: Norton, 1961); see also Albert Biderman, "The Image of Brainwashing," *Public Opinion Quarterly,* 26 (1962), 547–563, and

his *March to Calumny: The Story of American POWs in the Korean War* (New York: Macmillan, 1963).

34.   Avery D. Weisman and Robert Kastenbaum, *"The Psychological Autopsy: A Study of the Terminal Phases of Life," Community Mental Health Journal,* Monograph No. 4 (1968). A detailed discussion of this work appears in Leon Rappoport, *Personality Development* (Glenview, Ill.: Scott, Foresman, 1972), pp. 428–430.

35.   Wiesenthal, *The Murderers Among Us,* pp. 9–10 and passim.

36.   Cohen, *Human Behavior,* pp. 277–278.

37.   Bettelheim, *The Informed Heart.*

38.   Viktor E. Frankel, *From Death Camp to Existentialism* (Boston: Beacon Press, 1959).

39.   The quotation is from the title of a 1920 novel by Franz Werfel: *Nicht der Mörderer, der Ermordete ist schuldig.*

# Chapter V

1.   George Orwell, "Politics and the English Language," in *Shooting an Elephant and Other Essays* (New York: Harcourt Brace, 1945), pp. 77–92.

2.   Frantz Fanon, *The Wretched of the Earth,* translated by Constance Farrington (New York: Grove Press, 1968).

3.   Zivia Lubetkin, "Warsaw: The January 1943 Uprising," in Meyer Barkai, ed., *The Fighting Ghettoes* (New York: Tower, 1962), p. 35.

4.   Ibid., p. 36.

5.   Tuba Belsky, "Jews of the Forest," in Barkai, *Fighting Ghettoes,* p. 175.

6.   *Time,* January 22, 1973, p. 21.

7.   Izhak Zuckerman, "The Jewish Revolt," in Barkai, *Fighting Ghettoes,* pp. 22–24. Zuckerman was in the Jewish Young Pioneers and was a combat group commander during the revolt.

8.   Ziphora Birman, "Grodna and Bialystok," in Barkai, *Fighting Ghettoes,* p. 108.

9.   Chaikia Grossman, "The Day of the Uprising," in Barkai, *Fighting Ghettoes,* pp. 116–117.

10.   Lucien Steinberg, *The Jews Against Hitler (Not as a Lamb)* (London and New York: Gordon & Cremonesi, 1978), p. 194, analyzed all of the available statistics on the Warsaw Ghetto revolt and concluded that only 3 percent of the seventy thousand Jewish inhabitants of the ghetto actually took part in combat against the Germans. When it is considered that at this point most of those left in the ghetto were able-bodied workers (the others had already been deported to death camps), and that they had all received warnings about the true purpose of deportation, it seems apparent that the vast majority either continued to hope for a miracle or chose not to risk the uncertainty of death or maiming in combat. In Vilna the United Partisan Organization had prepared a rebellion but in early September 1943 when the Germans made an offer of life in Estonian work camps, the population streamed out of the ghetto at their bidding, leaving the fighters alone among empty houses. See Ruzhka Korcok, *Lehavot ba Efer* (Tel Zviv: 1965), pp. 190–202.

11.   Eugene Heimler, ed., *Resistance against Tyranny* (London: Routledge and Kegan Paul, 1966), p. xi.

12.   Ibid., p. 152.

13.   Inge Scholl, *Students against Tyranny: The Resistance of the White Rose, Munich 1942–1943* (Middletown, Conn.: Wesleyan University Press, 1965), p. 37.

14.   In pre-Freudian language, one might have described this phenomenon in terms of simple self-respect. Today, Freudians could argue that since Scholl and his friends saw resistance as a "duty" or obligation, their behavior should be understood as resulting from a superego rather than

an ego process. But close study of the Scholl group suggests that they were consciously committed to resistance in a fully rational fashion. Their long planning sessions and careful preparation and distribution of leaflets, as well as their conduct following arrest, all offer evidence of serious ego functioning rather than the working out of guilt feelings usually associated with superego processes. They were, moreover, guilty of nothing.

15.    "The question remains whether this *action* by Jews within the resistance can properly be called Jewish resistance. It would seem that in Western Europe there was no such thing . . . the majority of Jews were completely assimilated and had no desire to be any different from their fellow-countrymen; many were no longer practicing Jews. In the Resistance, therefore, the behavior of the Jews in no way differed from that of other Frenchmen, Belgians or Dutchmen." Henri Michel, *The Shadow War: Resistance in Europe 1939–1945* (London, André Deutsch, 1972), p. 179.

16.    Leon Poliakov, "Jewish Resistance in France," *YIVO Annual of Jewish Social Science,* vol. 8 (New York: Yiddish Scientific Institute, 1953), pp. 252–263.

17.    Isaac Kabeli, "The Resistance of the Greek Jews," in *Yivo Annual of Jewish Social Science,* vol. 8, pp. 281–288.

18.    This conclusion is supported with new evidence presented by Steinberg, *The Jews Against Hitler,* and Yuri Suhl, ed., *They Fought Back: The Story of the Jewish Resistance in Nazi Europe* (New York: Schocken, 1967). Suhl in particular maintains that Jewish resistance throughout Europe has thus far been drastically underestimated by Holocaust scholars because relevant documents and testimony have been slow to emerge and remain quite scattered. We are, in this connection, very indebted to Jehuda Bauer and Malcolm Lowe for substantive help with all the reference material cited in Hebrew, and for their review of an earlier, shorter draft of this chapter.

19.    Michel, *The Shadow War,* p. 180. Reuben Ainsztein, *Jewish Resistance in Nazi Occupied Europe* (London: Paul Elek, 1974) provides a detailed study, including discussions of the relationship between Poles and Jews, and the essentially passive role of the Polish home army during the Warsaw ghetto uprising. The Polish resistance movement appears to have been the only one in occupied Europe which was also significantly anti-Semitic.

20.    For more details see Alfred Katz, *Poland's Ghettos* (New York: Twayne, 1970).

21.    The status of the Russian Jewish partisans remains debatable. Suhl, in *They Fought Back,* claims them as exemplars of Jewish resistance, and the account he presents of the revolt in Lachwa (pp. 165–167) is a good case in point. In August 1942 the two thousand Jews living in this small Byelorussian town attacked an *Einsatzgruppe* attempting to round them up. Using hand weapons, they broke through the SS cordon. Approximately six hundred reached shelter in the forests, but many were then killed by anti-Semitic peasants and native police acting as SS auxiliaries. It is stated that one hundred twenty of the Lachwa survivors were later able to join the partisans. Ainsztein in his *Jewish Resistance* also emphasizes the positive role of Soviet partisans. It may well be that the truth about the sympathetic Soviet partisans on the one hand, and the hostile Polish partisans, on the other, has become a casualty of the cold war.

22.    It has been estimated that there were as many as twenty-eight Jewish partisan units in central Poland, and that approximately one thousand Jews participated in the Polish Warsaw uprising in 1944. See Shmuel Krakowsky, *Lehimah Yehudit Be-Polin neged Ha-Natzim, 1942–1944* ("Jewish Armed Resistance in Poland"; Jerusalem, 1977).

23.    Few issues have been as controversial as that of the role of the Judenräte. Hannah Arendt's *Eichmann in Jerusalem: A Report on the Banality of Evil* (New York: Viking, 1965), which first raised this issue, has produced storms of angry denials and accusations. The standard work now is Isaiah Trunk, *Judenrat* (New York: Macmillan, 1972) which provides a thorough documentation of the various Judenrat-type organizations in Eastern Europe. Leonard Tushnet, *The Pavement of Hell* (New York: St. Martin's, 1972) provides biographical studies of Judenrat "leaders": Rumkowski of Lodz, Gens of Vilna, and Czerniakow of Warsaw. Czerniakow's diary has now been published in a superb edition edited by Raul Hilberg, Stanislaw Staron, and Josef

Kermisz, *The Warsaw Diary of Adam Czerniakow: Prelude to Doom* (New York: Stein and Day, 1979). Also see *Imposed Jewish Governing Bodies under Nazi Rule,* Colloquium, December 2–5, 1967. (New York: Yivo Institute for Jewish Research, 1972.)

24.   The following is from Louis De Jong, "The Netherlands and Auschwitz: Why Were the Reports of Mass Killings So Widely Disbelieved," in *Imposed Jewish Governing Bodies under Nazi Rule,* pp. 27–28:

> During all the years that European Jews were being driven into the gas chambers (not the only, but certainly the largest group to die in this way) the very idea of mechanized mass murder struck most people at home and abroad as utterly inconceivable. It represented an altogether novel factor in world history precisely because its monstrous and mechanical aspects differed so radically from earlier forms of what came to be known as genocide, and also from what those who were interested had been able to gather about torture and murder in German concentration camps before May 1940. The whole thing went so much beyond the powers of human imagination that, as I myself once put it: "Our mind, once having grasped the facts, immediately spews them out as something utterly alien and unnaturally loathsome." Remember the Jehovah's Witnesses who had lived by the side of the gas chambers and the crematorium in Birkenau: "One day we would believe our own eyes, the next day we would simply refuse to do so." This tallies with many postwar accounts, one from a man in Birkenau, who formed part of a group which saw the chimneys smoking day in and day out: "The people themselves," he wrote, "pretend that the place was a brickyard or a soap factory. This mass delusion lasted for four weeks." All that time, this man was the only one who dared to face what was, in fact, the unbearable truth.

25.   The story of twenty-four-year-old Mordechai Anielewicz who became commander of the Jewish Fighting Organization (ZOB) in Warsaw exemplifies this cruel dilemma. A leader of the left-wing Zionist youth group Hashomer Hatzair, he became committed to armed resistance only in 1942, when it became plain that a fighting death to preserve honor and provide a heritage for the Jewish people was all that remained as an alternative to the extermination camps. "The young but quickly maturing Mordechai understood that at present there was but one question: What kind of death would the Polish Jews select for themselves. . . . The moment Mordechai decided on struggle no other question existed for him." E. Ringelblum, "Comrade Mordechai," in Suhl, *They Fought Back,* pp.85–91.

26.   When fifteen-year-old Elie Wiesel arrived at Auschwitz with his father, they were accosted by an old prisoner as they waited for the selection:

> "What have you come here for, you sons of bitches? What are you doing here, eh?"
> Someone dared to answer him. . .
> "You shut your trap, you filthy swine . . . You'd have done better to have hanged yourselves where you were than to come here. Didn't you know what was in store for you at Auschwitz?"
> . . . His tone of voice became increasingly brutal.
> "Do you see that chimney over there? See it? Do you see those flames? (Yes we did see the flames.) Over there—that's where you're going to be taken. That's your grave, over there. Haven't you realized it yet? You dumb bastards, don't you understand anything? Your're going to be burned. Frizzled away. Turned into ashes."

Wiesel recounts this exchange in *Night* (New York: Avon, 1960) pp. 40–41. Later Wiesel himself began to be transformed. When his father contracted dysentery, he could do little except watch him sink slowly toward death. When his father finally died, Wiesel's sorrow was mixed with a feeling of relief, for a great burden to his own survival had been removed.

27.   Primo Levi, *Survival in Auschwitz* (London: Collier-Macmillan, 1961), pp. 80–81. A survivor from Treblinka expressed similar views while being interviewed by Gitta Sereny for her book about Franz Stangl, the commandant of Treblinka, *Into that Darkness.* "Did we become hardened, callous to the suffering, the horror around us? . . . One did, I think, develop a kind of dullness, a numbness where the daily nightmarish events became a kind of routine, and only special horrors aroused us, reminded us of normal feelings" (p. 192). And he indicates that

experience in the camps did not eliminate previously held biases: "The (Eastern) Polish Jews, they were people from a different world; they were filthy. It was impossible to feel any compassion, any solidarity with them." (p. 198).

28. The extraordinary transformation experienced by old prisoners is illustrated by the statement given to Sereny by a Treblinka survivor and quoted in *Into that Darkness*, pp. 212–213. After first explaining that the Jewish workers lived on the supplies stripped from incoming transports, the survivor described what happened when for a time the trainloads of victims ceased arriving:

> Things went from bad to worse that month of March. . . . There were no transports—in February just a few, remnants from here and there, and then a few hundred gypsies—they were really poor; they brought nothing. . . . In the storehouses everything had been packed up and shipped—we had never before seen all the space because it had always been so full. . . . You can't imagine what we felt when there was nothing there. You see, the *things* were our justification for being alive. If there were no *things* to administer, why would they let us stay alive? On top of that, we were, for the first time, hungry. . . . It was just about when we had reached the lowest ebb in our morale that, one day towards the end of March, Kurt Franz [a guard] walked into our barracks, a wide grin on his face. "As of tomorrow," he said, "transports will be rolling in again." And do you know what we did? We shouted "Hurrah, hurrah." It seems impossible now. Every time I think of it I die a small death; but it's the truth. That is what we did; and that is where we had got to. And sure enough, the next morning they arrived. We had spent all of the preceding evening in an excited, expectant mood; it meant life—you see, don't you?—safety and life. The fact that it was their death, whoever they were, which meant our life, was no longer relevant.

29. Hilberg, *The Destruction of the European Jews*, p. 586.

30. See Alexander Pechersky, "Revolt in Sobibor," in Suhl, *They Fought Back*, pp.7–50.

31. Isaac Kabeli, "The Resistance of the Greek Jews."

32. Sim Kessel, *Hanged at Auschwitz* (New York: Stein and Day, 1972).

33. Leon Wells, *The Janowska Road* (New York: Macmillan, 1963).

34. Shlomo Gul, "Escape from Punor," in Barkai, *Fighting Ghettoes*, pp. 241–251.

35. "Resistance in Ponyatov and Trabnik," in Barkai, *Fighting Ghettoes*, pp. 230–231.

36. Kessel, *Hanged at Auschwitz*, pp. 43–44.

37. For a more detailed discussion, see David Littlejohn, *The Patriotic Traitors* (London: Heinemann, 1972), and Margret Boveri, *Der Verrat im XX. Jahrhundert, I* (Hamburg: Rowohlt, 1956).

38. The "Thirteeners" are discussed in detail (with documentary material) in A. Rozenberg, "dos draytsentl," *Bletter far Geschichte* 5 (1952) 116–148; Katz, *Poland's Ghettoes*; Ainsztein, *Jewish Resistance*; Hilberg, *Warsaw Diary*.

39. Zelig Kalmanovitch, "A Diary of the Nazi Ghetto in Vilna," *YIVO Annual of Jewish Social Science*, 8 (1953), p. 31.

40. Ibid., pp. 65–67. The Vilna population handed over Itsik Witenberg to the Gestapo for fear of reprisals; a good description is in Ainsztein, *Jewish Resistance*, pp. 486–518. It was in the Vilna ghetto that apparently for the first time the much-repeated phrase "like sheep to slaughter" was used, in an appeal for resistance on January 1, 1942, by Aba Kowner of Hashomer Hatzair: "Let us not go to slaughter like sheep! Jewish youth, do not trust the deceiver. . . . Let us not go like sheep to slaughter! It is true that we are weak and we have nobody to help us. But our only dignified answer to the enemy must be resistance! Brothers, it is better to die like free fighters than to live by the murderer's grace. Resist until your last breath!" (Quoted in Ainsztein, *Jewish Resistance*, p. 489).

41. Jacob Presser, *The Destruction of the Dutch Jews* (New York: Dutton, 1969), p. 276.

42. See Steinberg, *Jews Against Hitler*, pp. 106–111; Leon Poliakov, "Jewish Resistance in France," *YIVO Annual of Jewish Social Science*, 8 (1953), pp. 252–263.

43.   In his memorial to the young Mordechai Anielewicz, commander of the Warsaw ghetto fighters Emmanuel Ringelblum spoke to the point under discussion here: "Mordechai and his fellows of the young generation knew too little about the history of freedom or they would have known that in such stormy times one had to give less consideration to the resolutions of committees and administrations and depend more on oneself, and one's own healthy instincts. . . . That truth was understood by the youth only when it was too late, when the majority of Warsaw Jews were already in Treblinka" (Quoted in Suhl, *They Fought Back,* pp. 90–91).

44.   Ibid., p. 90.

# Chapter VI

1.   George Steiner expresses the personal dynamics of serious feeling-reactions to the Holocaust by nonparticipants in an essay describing his fears for his children, "A Sort of Survivor," in *Language and Silence: Essays on Language, Literature, and the Inhuman* (New York: Atheneum, 1967); in a very different vein, Amos Elon has described the ambivalent feelings of Israeli youth toward their Holocaust heritage in *The Israelis: Founders and Sons* (New York: Bantam Books, 1972); the most extensive and valuable discussion of this general point, however, appears in Lawrence Langer's *The Holocaust and the Literary Imagination* (New Haven and London: Yale University Press, 1975).

Some personal eccentricities known to us are also noteworthy. One young scholar at an East Coast university occasionally gets drunk on brandy and pounds the floor in time to recordings of SS marching songs. Another older professor who fought in Germany as a young American soldier keeps a captured Luger in his desk for use when toying with the idea of suicide. A third writes anonymous accusatory poems; yet another has become a fanatic partisan of the state of Israel who claims to feel disgust at the mere sight of a Volkswagen.

2.   Samuel Hux, "The Holocaust and the Survival of Tragedy," *Worldview,* 20, no. 10 (Oct. 1977), 4–10. (Italics added.)

3.   Edmund Stillman and William Pfaff, *The Politics of Hysteria* (New York and Evanston: Harper & Row, 1964), pp. 30–31. Richard Rubenstein reached a similar conclusion: "We are more likely to understand the Holocaust if we regard it as the expression of some of the most profound tendencies of Western civilization in the twentieth century." *The Cunning of History: The Holocaust and the American Future* (New York: Harper & Row, 1975), p. 21. Herbert Marcuse wrote: "It may even be justifiable, logically as well as historically, to define Reason in terms which include slavery, the Inquisition, child labor, concentration camps, gas chambers, and nuclear preparedness. These may well have been integral parts of that rationality which has governed the recorded history of mankind." Herbert Marcuse, "A Note on Dialectic," in Andrew Arato and Eike Gebhardt, *The Essential Frankfurt School Reader* (New York: Urizen Books, 1978), p. 450.

4.   Primo Levi, *Survival in Auschwitz* (London: Collier-Macmillan, 1969), p. 118.

5.   There is an extensive clinical literature on the psychological effects of Nazi camp experience. See for example, A. Russell, "Late Psychosocial Consequences in Concentration Camp Survivor Families," *American Journal of Orthopsychiatry,* 44, no. 4 (July 1974), 611–619, and P. Matussek, *Internment in Concentration Camps and Its Consequences* (New York: Springer-Verlag, 1975).

6.   See Stanislov Grof, "Perinatal Roots of Wars, Totalitarianism and Revolutions; Observations from LSD Research," *Journal of Psychohistory* 4, no. 3 (1977), 269–308.

7.   See Amos Elon, *The Israelis:* "There is today no doubt that the resources of the Jewish community of Palestine, meager as they were . . . were not exhausted in effort to ward off the greatest disaster in the history of the Jewish people. Some Israelis argued in 1945 that, in deference to British sensitivities, these independent resources were hardly used. The question has haunted Israeli politicians ever since. Its moral dimensions are monstrous" (p. 276). "Dr.

Nachum Goldmann, former president of the World Jewish Congress, has publicly admitted that "we are all guilty of not having gone to all lengths. . . . We were too impressed with the argument that the [allied] generals should be left in peace to fight the war" (pp. 276–277).

8.   "Much of present sociology is illiterate. . . . It is conceived in a jargon of vehement obscurity." George Steiner, *Language and Silence,* p. 19. Thomas Szasz has made similar arguments about psychiatry, most concisely in the preface to his book *The Second Sin* (New York: Doubleday, 1973). Language is considered in more specific detail later in this chapter.

9.   In his authoritative *Political Theory* (Princeton: Princeton University Press, 1959) Arnold Brecht stipulates that toward the end of the nineteenth century the moral force of law had begun to decline drastically under the impact of analyses by G. Simmel and H. Rickert (pp. 136–211). These philosophers demonstrated that value judgments distinguishing between what is and what ought to be were simply arbitrary. And Simmel's fundamental argument was that "The logical inference from what is to what ought to be, is false in every case" (Brecht, p. 211). By 1914, moreover, according to Brecht, the philosopher of law G. Radbruch could argue that all concepts of law and justice were essentially matters of politics: "Philosophy of law is necessarily political philosophy, and vice versa. So perfect is this ultimate identity that we are justified in speaking of 'political and legal philosophy' in the singular form" (p. 138). A more contemporary formulation of these ideas appears in the work of Hans Kelsen, most notably in *The Pure Theory of Law* (translated by Max Knight; Berkeley: University of California Press, 1967). The notion of justice must be eliminated from "positive law," according to Kelsen, because it is a value not a scientific concept open to empirical investigation or determination. "Legal science" cannot be concerned with matters of ethics and politics because these matters are irrelevant to "pure knowledge." See H. Kelsen, "What Is Justice?" *Law Quarterly Review,* 51 (1957).

10.   See the works cited in chap. 1, note 9; also Robert Pois, who discusses implications of the Poliakov work in connection with the rise of German romanticism in his unpublished article "Historicity versus History: Some Reflections on the Philosophical Implications of the Holocaust" (available from the author at the University of Colorado). Daniel Gasman's *The Scientific Origins of National Socialism* posits that Haeckel and his science-oriented colleagues of the Monist League were specifically concerned with correcting or eliminating the Jewish racial characteristics they had "objectively" identified as sources of corruption in German society. Haeckel himself never called for actual physical destruction of the Jews but the idea of using physical force against them appears in the writings of at least one Monist League author, Heinrich Pudor.

11.   A number of psychohistorians have attempted to locate the psychological sources of Hitler's anti-Semitism in his childhood and adolescence. See chap. 2, notes 27 and 28.

12.   Michael Polanyi provides a very general discussion of this issue in his book *Personal Knowledge: Towards a Postcritical Philosophy* (Chicago: University of Chicago Press, 1958). After noting that a dehumanized "objective" science can allow humans to dominate nature, he concludes: "Then man dominates a world in which he himself does not exist. For with his obligation (to nature) he has lost his voice and his hope, and been left behind meaningless to himself" (p. 380). Similar views are expressed by the philosopher of science Ian Mitroff in the conclusion of his work *The Subjective Side of Science* (New York: American Elsevier, 1974), p. 271: "We have developed the kind of science (Apollonism) that knows how to reach 'the starry heavens above.' We have yet to learn how to develop the kind of science (Dionysian) that knows how to reach 'the moral law within.' " See also Floyd Matson, *The Broken Image* (New York: Anchor Books, 1966). The theme recognized in various ways by an increasing number of writers is essentially this: human affairs conducted according to a dehumanized science must ultimately reduce people to objects. Thus "the acceptance of living beings as machines, the domination of the modern world by technology, and the mechanization of mankind are but the extension and practical application of the mechanistic conception of physics" (Ludwig von Bertalanffy, *Problems of Life,* New York: Harper Torchbooks, 1960, p. 202).

13.   Quoted in A. Janik, and S. Toulmin, *Wittgenstein's Vienna* (New York: Simon and Schuster, 1973), p. 191.

14.   H. S. Hughes, *The Sea Change: The Migration of Social Thought 1930–1965* (New York: Harper & Row, 1975), p. 53.

15.   Quoted in Janik and Toulmin, *Wittgenstein's Vienna,* p. 195.

16.   Max Horkheimer and Theodore Adorno, *Dialectic of Enlightenment* (New York: Seabury Press, 1969), p. xii. Italics added.

17.   Probably the most radical exponent of this general viewpoint today is the philosopher of science Paul Feyerabend. In *Against Method* (London: NLB, 1975), he argues that all progress can only be understood as an expansion of human consciousness, and this being the case, any idea can only be evaluated by contrasting it with other, different ideas. One example he provides it that there is no "reason" for modern medical experts to ignore voodoo witchcraft as a means to medical knowledge. To the extent that studying voodoo is ruled out by established medical research methodology and the institutional norms of science in general, the exclusion is arbitrary and tends to impose conformity to the status quo while having nothing whatever to do with "the science" of medicine. Feyerabend's general view of scientific knowledge is as follows: "Knowledge so conceived is not a series of self-consistent theories that converges towards an ideal view; it is not a gradual approach to the truth. It is rather an ever increasing *ocean of mutually incompatible (and perhaps even incommensurable) alternatives,* each single theory, each fairy tale, each myth that is part of the collection forcing the others into greater articulation and all of them contributing, via this process of competition, to the development of our consciousness. Nothing is ever settled." (p. 30). Less dramatic but similar statements relevant to the view of science presented in this chapter may be found in Everett Mendelsohn, "The Social Construction of Scientific Knowledge," in E. Mendelsohn, P. Weingart, and R. Whitley, eds., *The Social Production of Scientific Knowledge* (Dordrecht, Holland: D. Reidel & Co., 1977), pp. 3–26; J. R. Ravetz, *Scientific Knowledge and Its Social Problems* (Oxford: Clarendon Press, 1971), especially the concluding section, "Critical Science: Politics and Morality," pp. 423–436.

18.   Richard Rubenstein, *The Cunning of History,* reached a very similar conclusion: "Thus, the Holocaust bears witness to *the advance of civilization,* I repeat, to the advance of civilization, to the point at which large scale massacre is no longer a crime and the state's sovereign powers are such that millions can be stripped of their rights and condemned to the world of the living dead" (p. 91). In a more general context of culture critique, Arianna Stassinopoulos has said: "It should have been obvious by now, even to the most fanatical believers in the 'locomotive of history,' that something has gone badly astray and the suspicion that the engineer is a homicidal maniac can no longer be ruled out. Instead, the belief persists that the locomotive is somehow chugging on in the direction of progress" (*After Reason,* New York: Stein and Day, 1978, p. 12). It may be presumed that these perspectives, and others like them, are what led Hannah Arendt to conclude: "In other words, I have clearly joined the ranks of those who for some time now have been attempting to dismantle metaphysics, and philosophy with all its categories, as we have known them from their beginning in Greece until today. Such dismantling is possible only on the assumption that the thread of tradition is broken and that we shall not be able to renew it." *The Life of the Mind, I: Thinking* (New York: Harcourt Brace Jovanovich, 1978), p. 212.

# Bibliographic Essay

The literature on the Holocaust has grown to almost unmanageable proportions. This essay makes no attempt to cite all the major works, nor all the works utilized in this study, but provides some general guidelines to sources available for further inquiry.

The best general bibliographic introduction is provided by the bibliographies in the *Vierteljahrhefte für Zeitgeschichte*. More specifically oriented toward the Holocaust are the catalog publications of the Wiener Library, *German Jewry: Its History, Life, and Culture,* ed. by Ilse R. Wolff, Catalogue series (London: Vallentine, Mitchell, 1958), and *Persecution and Resistance under the Nazis,* 2nd rev. and enl. ed., Catalogue series, 1 (London: Vallentine, Mitchell, 1960). These should be supplemented by the bibliographical entries in the *Wiener Library Bulletin* (1946—). Jacob Robinson and Philip Friedman's *Guide to Jewish History under Nazi Impact* (New York: KTAV, 1973; orig. publ. 1960) is unique for its inclusion of Yiddish and Hebrew works. Richard Rubenstein has prepared a course syllabus on the Holocaust, "Dimensions of the Holocaust Past and Future," which includes valuable bibliographies (restricted to English) appended to each chapter (New Haven, Conn.: National Humanities Institute, 1977; available free from the Institute, at 1 Hillhouse Avenue).

The earliest general accounts of the Holocaust, Gerald Reitlinger's *The Final Solution: The Attempt to Exterminate the Jews of Europe, 1939–1945* (London: Vallentine, Mitchell, 1953) and Leon Poliakov's *Harvest of Hate* (Syracuse: Syracuse University Press, 1954) have stood the test of time and the increased availability of new documentary evidence very well. Robert Manvell and Heinrich Fraenkel's able journalistic account, *The Incomparable Crime: Mass Extermination in the Twentieth Century: The Legacy of Guilt* (New York: Putnam, 1967) reproduces important documents and provides detailed sketches of persons involved in the death machinery.

More recently, both Nora Levin's *The Holocaust: The Destruction of European Jewry, 1933–1945* (New York: T. Y. Crowell, 1968) and Lucy Dawidowicz's *The War Against the Jews: 1933–1945* (New York: Holt,

A slightly different version of this essay, titled "The Literature of the Holocaust," first appeared in *Choice* 15:11 (January 1979). We wish to thank *Choice* for permission to use this material here.

Rinehart and Winston, 1975) recount the historical origins and development of the Holocaust in substantial detail. A major element in Levin's work is the examination of the failure of the "bystander," from the papacy to the Red Cross, to intervene actively on behalf of the Jews. Levin provides a detailed discussion of the so-called Brandt mission—the unsuccessful attempt of Joel Brandt of Hungary to ransom Hungarian Jews. Of particular importance also is the discussion of the Warsaw ghetto uprising, which focuses upon the unwillingness of the Polish Home Army under General Bor-Komorowski (AK) to support the uprising. The Polish underground was the only resistance movement in Europe that was anti-Semitic and that, as far as the extermination of the Jews was concerned, perceived a community of interest with the SS. A detailed examination of the Polish-Jewish relationship during the war is very much needed. Nora Levin's conclusion is that the establishment of the State of Israel as a Jewish homeland was *the* response to the Holocaust where Jews "no longer would petition or plead for their security or rely on legal rectitude and promises to achieve it"—the implication being that Jewish security would rest upon military prowess.

Helen Fein's *Accounting for Genocide: National Responses and Jewish Victimization during the Holocaust* (New York: Free Press, 1979) (discussed in the text) applies quantitative methods to the study of the Holocaust. This methodology adds little to what was known before, and the efforts made to define as quantitative variables such phenomena as "degrees of SS control" and "degrees of anti-Semitism" reveal the inappropriateness of statistical social science methods for study of the Holocaust. Fein's country-by-country narrative analysis of the "final solution," however, and her description of the role of the Christian churches, are significant contributions. Richard Rubenstein's *The Cunning of History: Mass Death and the American Future* (New York: Harper & Row, 1975), an essay about the meaning of the Holocaust, rather than an account of its history, has come closer to penetrating the sociocultural significance of the Holocaust than most other studies, not least because the author attempts to integrate the Holocaust into the main stream of contemporary history. His conclusion is that "the passing of time has made it increasingly evident that a hitherto unbreachable moral and political barrier in the history of Western civilization was successfully overcome by the Nazis in World War II and that henceforth the systematic, bureaucratically administered extermination of millions of citizens or subject people will forever be one of the capacities and temptations of government."

The response of individuals and institutions to the Holocaust is a matter of concern to almost all writers in the field. A detailed examination of the inadequate American response is provided by Henry Feingold's *The Politics of Rescue: The Roosevelt Administration and the Holocaust, 1935–1945* (New Brunswick, N.J.: Rutgers University Press, 1970) and a more popular critique along the same line by Arthur D. Morse, *While Six Million Died: A Chronicle of American Apathy* (New York: Random House, 1968). A work which appeared too late to be considered in this study is Bernard Wasserstein's *Britain and the Jews of Europe, 1939–1945* (London: Oxford University Press, 1979). It suggests that British action was predicated on a lack of sympathy for the Jewish fate, quoting one foreign office official as saying that "in my opinion, a disproportionate amount of time of this office is wasted in dealing with the wailing Jews." The role of the Vatican has been dramatized in the controversial play by Rolf Hochhuth, *The Deputy* (New York: Grove, 1964). Eric Bentley has edited an anthology, *The Storm over "The Deputy"* (New York: Grove, 1964), which provides a variety of comments on the issues raised by Hochhuth. Günter Lewy in *The Catholic Church and Nazi Germany* (New York: McGraw Hill, 1964) focuses on the German episcopate. The controversial role of Pius XII is examined by Saul Friedländer's *Pius XII and the Third Reich: A Documentation* (New York: Knopf, 1966).

Anti-Semitism has been endemic to Western civilization, but is in itself an insufficient cause for explaining the Holocaust, which was vastly more than a simple "harvest of hate." In the latter part of the nineteenth century, anti-Semitism was transformed from prejudice into a political ideology. Hannah Arendt argued in her *The Origins of Totalitarianism* (New York: Harcourt, Brace, 1951) that anti-Semitism is central to modern totalitarianism. Despite some weaknesses—most noticeably in its treatment of Soviet totalitarianism, which is compared with the Nazi model—this is one of the most brilliant works on the nature of totalitarianism to have appeared within the last quarter of a century. Arendt perceived the Dreyfus affair in France as the central turning point in the origins of the "new" anti-Semitism: for the first time anti-Semitism became a major political force and was used in an unsuccessful attempt to destroy French democracy.

Although anti-Semitism existed before Christianity in the ancient world, Christianity legitimized acts against the Jews by appealing to the charge of deicide—the murder of God. In his examination of medieval anti-Semitism, Joshua Trachtenberg in *The Devil and the Jews: The Medieval Conception of the Jew and Its Relation to Modern Anti-Semitism* (New Haven: Yale University Press, 1943) shows how the Jew was perceived as a Christ killer in league with the devil, who constantly seeks to repeat the crime by attempting to desecrate the host. A major virtue of this work is the inclusion of important contemporary cartoons that illustrate the popular image of the Jew and the frequency with which Satan is portrayed as a Jew. In the psychoanalytically informed essay *After Auschwitz: Radical Theology and Contemporary Judaism* (Indianapolis: Bobbs-Merrill, 1966) Richard Rubenstein shows the persistence of this theme of deicide in the modern world and its transmutation by modern anti-Semitic propaganda.

The latter part of the nineteenth century saw anti-Semitism transformed in at least two important ways: the definition of the Jew changed from a religious to a racial one, and anti-Semitism became a political ideology, with the development of anti-Semitic political parties in many European countries. The Jew was then viewed as part of an international conspiracy seeking world domination. This conspiracy thesis was articulated in one of the most important of all historical forgeries, the *Protocols of the Elders of Zion.* Created in Czarist Russia, it enjoyed a long history and even today is available in many languages from Spanish to Egyptian, and still serves as a major source for all radical anti-Semitic agitation. Its origins and strange fate have been brilliantly described by Norman Cohn in *Warrant for Genocide: The Myth of the Jewish World-Conspiracy and the Protocols of the Elders of Zion* (New York: Harper & Row, 1967). Peter Pulzer in *The Rise of Political Anti-Semitism in Germany and Austria* (New York: Wiley, 1964) analyzes the development of the political anti-Semitic parties in Germany and Austria. His study is particularly valuable for its discussion of Austrian anti-Semitism, which, in contrast to the much-studied German variety, has been generally slighted by historians. Not the least merit of the work is that it focuses upon the specific Austrian origins of National Socialism. This study should be supplemented by Andrew Whiteside's history of Austrian National Socialism, *Austrian National Socialism before 1918* (The Hague: Nijhoff, 1962).

A substantial body of literature on Germans and Jews during the German imperial period and the Weimar Republic is now available. Paul W. Massing's *Rehearsal for Destruction: A Study of Political Anti-Semitism in Imperial Germany* (New York: Howard Fertig, 1967; orig. pub. 1949) concentrates on the formation of German anti-Semitic parties. His section on the relationship of socialism in Germany to anti-Semitism is of particular importance. Jehuda Reinharz's *Fatherland or Promised Land: The Dilemma of the German Jew, 1893–1914* (Ann Arbor, Mich.: University of Michigan Press, 1975) focuses on the Jewish response to anti-Semitism, based particularly on the documents of the *Centralverein,* the union of citizens of Jewish faith, as well as the emerging Zionist organizations. George L. Mosse's *Crisis of German Ideology: Intellectual Origins of the Third Reich* (New York: Grosset and Dunlap, 1964) examines the murky ideology of the German *völkisch* movement—an amalgamation of racist, antisocialist, anticapitalist, and nationalist thought, coupled at times with mysticism, sun worship, and the like. This movement—not unified except for its emphasis on racial purity and the perception of the Jew as the archenemy—was a direct source of National Socialism. In contrast to the apologetic view of many German historians, Mosse analyzes the specific and uniquely German sources for the Holocaust. Uriel Tal in *Christians and Jews in Germany: Religion, Politics and Ideology in the Second Reich, 1870–1914* (Ithaca, N. Y.: Cornell University Press, 1975) looks at the specific character of anti-Semitism during the German imperial period. He provides a new analysis of the Christian element of anti-Semitism as well as the sources for "scientific" anti-Semitism that, despite its opposition to Christianity, was nevertheless strongly influenced by Christianity. "Christian anti-Semitism stigmatized Jewish perfidy but it permitted the Jew to exist . . . as a living witness to the truth of Christianity. The Jew must remain to act out his preordained ignominious role as villain in the drama of salvation. . . . But he was always free to abrogate his covenant with Jehova and accept the benevolent efforts of the church to redeem him. According to racial theory, however, baptism could not penetrate the tainted Jewish seed; the deep stain could only be removed by destroying the source of infection and its bearer, the physical Jew."

Sidney M. Bolkosky's *The Distorted Image: German Jewish Perception of Germans and Germany, 1918–1935* (New York and Amsterdam: Elsevier Scientific Publishing Co., 1975) traces the mutual perceptions of Germans and Jews between 1918 and 1935. Jews thought of themselves as good patriotic Germans and believed that they were perceived as such. In fact, however, they were generally seen as unwanted aliens.

The Holocaust is incomprehensible without understanding National Socialism and its leader, Adolf Hitler. The literature on both apperars almost boundless; yet, as far as National Socialism is concerned, Karl Dietrich Bracher's *The German Dictatorship: The Origins, Structure, and Effects of National Socialism* (New York: Praeger, 1970) is about as definitive a work as is likely to appear. This major achievement, not likely to become outdated, approaches the Nazi movement through the methodologies of history, political science, and sociology. If it has any limitation, it is a failure to apply the insights of psychoanalysis and psychology to the Nazi phenomenon. The application of these perspectives has been of major significance in recent decades—perhaps the very irrationality of Nazism has attracted psychohistorians to this subject. Certainly psychohistorians have been drawn to this as to no other subject; see the bibliographical review essay by George M. Kren, "Psychohistorical Interpretations of National Socialism," *German Studies Review* 1, no. 2, (May 1978). A detailed bibliography, "Psychohistory of the Third Reich," is provided by Terry G. Mensch in the *Journal of Psychohistory* (in press).

Robert G. L. Waite began his recent biography of Hitler, *The Psychopathic God: Adolf Hitler* (New York: Basic Books, 1977), by noting that more will be written about Hitler than about anyone else in history with the exception of Jesus Christ. It is dubious that the riddle of Hitler's personality and nature can ever be definitively solved.

The relationship between Hitler and the Holocaust is more direct than that encompassed in his role as head of an anti-Semitic government. While anti-Semitism was popular in Imperial Germany and the Weimar period, it is doubtful that many wished to kill all the Jews. Even after David Irving's attempt to refute Hitler's involvement with the Holocaust in *Hitler's War* (New York: Viking, 1977), a work almost universally rejected by the scholarly community, it appears evident that the source of the Holocaust may be traced directly to Hitler and that the extermination of the Jews seems to have been the basic dynamic that motivated his whole career. The standard political biography remains Alan Bullock's *Hitler: A Study in Tyranny* (New York: Harper & Row, 1964). More directly relevant for illuminating the relationship between Hitler and the Jews are the recent psychohistorical studies, which, seeking to find the sources for Hitler's murderous hatred of the Jews in unconscious processes, have added a new dimension to our understanding. There is of course no consensus about the legitimacy of psychohistory within the historical profession, and the controversy surrounding its status as a mode of historical understanding is likely to continue unabated. Every psychoanalytically oriented study of Hitler remains controversial—comments on all of them have ranged from praise to extreme condemnation. Yet, the directions of these studies appear with all their problems to be the most promising approach to the phenomenon of Hitler, who is clearly not comprehensible by the traditional modes of biographical study.

The most important psychobiographies of Hitler are those by Langer, Waite, Binion, and Stierlin. Langer worked for the OSS during the war and was asked to prepare a study of Hitler. The resulting *The Mind of Adolf Hitler: The Secret Wartime Report* (New York: Basic Books, 1972) emphasizes Hitler's childhood and his unsatisfactory relationship with his father. Considering the limitations under which the study was done it has held up relatively well. Waite's very long study, which is a combination psychobiography and life-and-times history, examines the various reports of Hitler's sexual perversions (which Waite tends to accept) and attempts to assess the significance of Hitler's monorchism (one undescended testicle, which has led at least one reviewer to speak irreverently of "the great ball game"). In sharp contrast to Waite's broadly conceived biography, Rudolph Binion's remarkably short work *Hitler Among the Germans* (New York: Elsevier, 1976) seeks to isolate the fundamental psychological causes which explain Hitler. Binion's work is grounded on the premise of Freudian psychology that early traumatic experiences may be worked out by compulsive repetition in adult life. Binion concentrates on two episodes in Hitler's life: the death of his mother and his being gassed in the last months of World War I. Overcoming some of his early hesitations about psychohistory, Allan Bullock has written a substantial review of Waite and Binion, "The Schickelgruber Story," *New York Review of Books,* 24 (May 26, 1977), 10–15. Other reviews are more polemical. Extended discussions of Binion's work by George H. Stein, Bradley F. Smith, George L. Mosse, Norbert Bromberg, Gertrud M. Kurth, Andreas Dorpalen, Dietrich Orlow, with a reply by Binion, are found following his article "Hitler's Concept of *Lebensraum*" in the Fall 1973 *History of Childhood Quarterly* 1, no. 2, pp. 187–215, and in a symposium on Binion's work in the Summer 1977 issue of the *Psychohistory Review.* Helm Stierlin's study *Adolf Hitler, A Family Perspective* (New York: Psychohistory Press, 1976) emphasizes the central role of Hitler's mother and sets forth the thesis that Hitler came to act as his mother's delegate and avenger.

Next to Hitler the most important person involved in the Holocaust was Heinrich Himmler. Aided by the publication of his adolescent diaries, historians have attempted to explain what made this mild-mannered man, who created in the SS one of the most terrible instruments of destruction ever fashioned, a mass murderer of hitherto unimaginable magnitude. Bradley F. Smith in his *Heinrich Himmler: A Nazi in the Making, 1900–1926* (Stanford, Calif.: Hoover Institution Press, 1971) succeeds in showing the interaction of personal and social-political forces. Peter Loewenberg's article "The Unsuccessful Adolescence of Heinrich Himmler," *American Historical Review,* 76 (June 1971), which comes close to being a clinical diagnosis, presents evidence leading to the conclusion that Himmler was a "schizoid personality who was systematic, rigid, controlled and restricted in emotional expression . . . [an] obsessive-compulsive character."

Hannah Arendt reported the Eichmann trial in Jerusalem for the *New Yorker,* and then published her study under the title *Eichmann in Jerusalem: A Report on the Banality of Evil* (New York: Viking, 1964). A brilliant work, it gave much offense and raised a series of heated commentaries. Critics opposed her interpretation of Eichmann as a rather weak bureaucrat, banal, concerned with the advancement of his own career. Somehow that much evil seemed to demand a Faustian, possessed, daemonic personality rather than a faceless bureaucrat simply doing his job. Arendt also suggested that cooperation of Jewish community leaders with the Nazis made their job easier.

Rudolf Hoess, who commanded Auschwitz for most of its life, wrote his autobiography, *Commandant of Auschwitz* (Cleveland and New York: World, 1959), while in a Polish prison waiting to be hanged. It is a valuable document which shows Hoess to have been an average dutiful man who acted out of what he termed idealism. The autobiography shows all sorts of sentimentality and self-pity, but above all, even after the events, Hoess clearly had no realization of what he had done. The German edition, *Kommandant in Auschwitz* (Deutsch Verlags-Anstalt, 1958), contains a valuable commentary and introduction by Martin Broszat that deserves to be translated. It is clear that Hoess was not a sadist in any clinical sense, or even personally brutal. He was an average law abiding citizen—and it was exactly his willingness to abide by laws and rules that made Auschwitz possible and that made him such a frightening person—an ordinary individual who allowed himself to be persuaded that the elimination of millions was a service to his country and that he could not question the orders of his superiors.

Whereas Arendt's *Eichmann* was based on publicly available evidence, Gitta Sereny's unique biography of the commandant of Treblinka, Franz Stangl—*Into that Darkness: From Mercy Killing to Mass Murder* (New York: McGraw-Hill, 1974)—is the result of Sereny's seventy hours of interviews with Stangl in a German prison where he was serving a life sentence after his extradition from Brazil. Stangl came from a working-class background, with a typical authoritarian father and subservient mother. During 1931 he joined the Austrian police force, which was absorbed by the Nazi organization after the Anschluss. In 1940 Stangl was assigned to Hartheim, the hospital where euthanasia of mentally defective and ill Germans was carried out. Later he was assigned to Poland, building up the extermination camp in Sobibor. By his accounts—which appear trustworthy—he made every effort to get out of this, but lacked the strength to do so, and thus ended up as commandant of Treblinka. There, as in the euthanasia program, he participated "as little as possible" in the killings, which he left to others, while he concerned himself with running a smooth organization. Apparently he had no strong hatred of Jews but saw himself only as doing his job as he was ordered to do, feeling little responsibility for his actions, which appeared to him to be not really his own.

Sereny is a sensitive writer. Her conversations with Stangl were a real dialogue. The work compels a radical rejection of the stereotyped view of the SS in the camps as brutes and sadists—Stangl was far from that—and its replacement by a perception of these individuals as weak and lacking the capacity to recognize that their actions, carried out in response to orders, were wrong. As Dwight Macdonald pointed out in 1945 when the news of the camps reached the United States, we must now fear the person who obeys the law more than the one who breaks it (*Memoirs of a Revolutionist,* New York: Farrar, Straus, 1957).

The nature of the individuals involved in the camp system is further documented in a remarkable Ph.D. dissertation by Tom Segev, *The Commanders of the Nazi Concentration Camps* (Boston University, 1977; University Microfilms, 77–21, 618). Segev, a young Israeli historian (in what surely must have been a difficult undertaking), interviewed many of the remaining commandants of concentration camps. The image of their personality that emerges is that of individuals who show little signs of pathology, who carried out orders, and who—and here Segev differs from other accounts— were tremendously enthusiastic about their being chosen to participate in a new order, swept away by a euphoria that led them to do whatever was necessary, and who still look back nostalgically to "the good old days."

Henry V. Dicks, a British psychiatrist and author of *Licensed Mass Murder: A Socio-Psychological Study of Some SS Killers* (New York: Basic Books, 1972) interviewed a number of former SS officers and men serving time in German prisons for having participated in various mass killings. He emphasizes as a common element among them an unsatisfactory childhood, almost always with authoritarian fathers who believed in the virtues of corporal punishment. Dicks' interviews confirm Peter Loewenberg's thesis, advanced in "The Psychohistorical Origins of the Nazi Youth Cohort," *American Historical Review,* 76 (Dec. 1971), that the experience of World War I, the deprivation of food during the latter years of the war, and the absence of the father and his return home, defeated and unable to adjust after the war, were decisive in molding the generation that formed the main followers of the Nazi movement. Dicks' work indicates how little pressure it took to persuade individuals to commit atrocities (never perceived as such) and destructive acts when these were authorized by a superior legal authority. The real horror is not to be found in pathological and sadistic excesses— which certainly did take place in the camps—but in the bureaucratically organized mass destruction of people defined by the rulers of the state as nonpersons. The question is how so many individuals came to believe that the welfare of the country required the extermination of millions of individuals and why the restraints against violence could so readily be abandoned.

The essential effective cause for the Holocaust lies in the conjunction of Hitler's murderous hatred for the Jews with the availability in the SS of an instrument that was able and willing to translate his fantasies of a world purified from Jews into reality.

Study of the SS requires more than an analysis of the personality of its leadership. It bears a striking resemblance to other twentieth century military forces, but also embodied some unique elements. Heinrich Himmler wished to make it into an order modeled after the Jesuits, endowed with a sense of mission. Beneath the daemonic imagery of the SS appears the reality of an organization with a core leadership of men able to operate with ruthless efficiency in the service of ideas which gave meaning to their lives. Heinz Höhne's *The Order of the Death's Head: The Story of Hitler's SS* (New York: Coward-McCann, 1970) provides a thoroughly detailed analysis of this organization; his examination of the infighting should go far toward modifying the image of a monolithic organization. It is significant that except for the group of young historians associated with the Institut fur Zeitgeschichte, German academic historians—Hohne is a journalist—have generally chosen to avoid dealing with the SS. The essays from the Institut für Zeitgeschichte by Helmut Krausnick and others, *Anatomy of the SS State* (New York: Walker, 1968) examine several aspects of the history of the SS, particularly the concentration camp system and the administration of the genocide program.

The Holocaust evolved bureaucratically. From "wild" anti-Semitic acts in 1933 to the Nuremberg laws of 1935, which gave anti-Semitism a legal foundation, to the decision to kill all Jews, there was a steady development of institutions and laws to legalize and facilitate this course. Karl A. Schleunes in *The Twisted Road to Auschwitz: Nazi Policy toward German Jews* (Urbana, Ill.: University of Illinois Press, 1970) examines this development from 1933 until the outbreak of the war. He demonstrates how some members of the civil service bureacracy attempted, working from within the system, to restrain the extremists, particularly on the question of the racial definition of a Jew, which was codified in 1935. Raul Hilberg's brilliant, magisterial study, *The Destruction of the European Jews* (New York: Octagon Books, 1978; orig. pub. 1961) examines how the Germans moved from a policy of expulsion to one of physical killing. His detailed, thoroughly documented record shows that many individuals and official agencies outside the SS and the party were involved and cooperated with the genocide policy. Hilberg, together with Arendt and Bruno Bettelheim (*The Informed Heart*, Chicago: The Free Press, 1960), has been violently attacked because he too has emphasized Jewish collaboration with the SS. "The mass of Jews," Hilberg wrote, "reacted to every German order by complying with it automatically. . . . The successful execution of the German demands depended on the actions by Jews. Only when one realizes how large a part of the destruction process consisted of the fulfillment of these measures can one begin to appraise the role of the Jews in their own destruction." Hannah Arendt specifically noted the role of the leaders in the Jewish communities. She cites as one example Leo Baeck, the highly respected former chief rabbi of Berlin who (according to the account of Eric Boehm's *We Survived: Fourteen Histories of the Hidden and Hunted of Nazi Germany,* Santa Barbara, Calif: American Bibliographical Center—Clio Press, 1966), while interned in Thereseinstadt, learned of the gassings in Auschwitz, but refused to make this known to his fellow prisoners on the grounds that nothing could be done about it, and that this knowledge would only create more unhappiness.

The institution associated with Jewish collaboration (not an ideal term) was the *Judenrat,* a German-appointed "self-government" of the ghettos with members frequently, though not always, drawn from the leadership of the former Jewish community. Isaiah Trunk's *Judenrat: The Jewish Councils in Eastern Europe Under Nazi Occupation* (New York: Macmillan, 1972), a work based on a thorough knowledge of the sources, examines in detail the various Jewish councils in the occupied areas of Eastern Europe, and the institutions connected with them, including the role of the Jewish police in the ghettos. While condemning the role of the police, Trunk's very informed judgments of the motives of those who served on the councils emphasizes their attempt—albeit largely unsuccessful—to help the ghetto population as much as possible and to save some Jews by various kinds of bargaining with the Germans. His view is less judgmental than that of most other writers. Adam Czerniakow's diary of the period when he was head of the Warsaw ghetto *Judenrat* is now available in an English translation, *The Warsaw Diary of Adam Czerniakow: Prelude to Doom,* ed. by Raul Hilberg, Stanislaw Staron, and Josef Kermisz (New York: Stein and Day, 1979).

The whole question of Jewish resistance has become a major polemical issue. Since the publication of the works of Arendt, Hilberg, and Bettelheim, more information has come to light, and older views which denied the existence of any Jewish resistance clearly must be rejected. The best-known event is the Warsaw ghetto uprising. Ber Mark's detailed history, originally in Polish, is now available in an English translation: *Uprising in the Warsaw Ghetto* (New York: Schocken, 1975). Dan Kurzman provides a popular account of the fighting in *The Bravest Battle: The Twenty-Eight Days of the Warsaw Ghetto Uprising* (New York: Putnam, 1976). Reuben Ainsztein's *Jewish Resistance in Nazi-Occupied Eastern Europe* (New York: Barnes & Noble, 1974) is a very detailed account based on sources in various European languages—Polish, Yiddish, Russian, Lithuanian, among others—which brings together a substantial body of evidence. Although Jews resisted, there was no unified Jewish resistance movement, primarily because the nature of the German occupation made the organization of a unified movement impossible. And Jewish disunity—with views ranging from those of orthodox religious Jews who accepted whatever happened as divine punishment, to Zionists, to Bundists—created further problems. But above all, the failure of a Jewish resistance movement in Eastern Europe must be ascribed to the fact that the Polish home army and the London government in exile had no desire to make a common front with the Jews. Polish partisans frequently betrayed Jews and a large segment of the Polish population agreed with the Germans in seeking to make Europe *judenrein.*

Although Jews participated in disproportionately large numbers in the resistance movements in Western Europe, Henri Michel—the historian of European resistance movements—argues that "the question remains whether this action by Jews with the resistance can properly be called Jewish resistance. . . . Jews participated as Frenchmen, or communists, and rarely as Jews" in *The Shadow War: Resistance in Europe 1939–1945* (London: Andre Deutsch, 1972), pp. 178–179.

Lucy Dawidowicz in "The Holocaust as Historical Record," in *Dimensions of the Holocaust: Lectures at Northwestern University* (Evanston, Ill.: Northwestern University, 1977) describes the attempts by Jews in the ghettos to provide a historical record of the events they were experiencing. Under incredible conditions they generated archives and records, the most significant one being the Oneg Shabbat, the code name Emmanuel Ringelblum gave the attempt to preserve a historical record. "When the time comes," one person wrote, "and indeed it will surely come—let the world read and know what the murderers perpetrated. This will be the richest material for the mourner when he writes the elegy for the present time" (p. 25).

Two works almost miraculously surviving the destruction of the ghetto (though their authors did not), from which in some sense we are able to comprehend what it was like, are *Scroll of Agony: The Warsaw Diary of Chaim A. Kaplan,* translated and edited by Abraham I. Katsch (New York: Macmillan, 1965) and *Notes from the Warsaw Ghetto: The Journal of Emmanuel Ringelblum,* translated and edited by Jacob Sloan (New York: Schocken, 1974; orig. publ. 1958). German film provides the basic footage for the BBC film *The Warsaw Ghetto,* which adds an important visual dimension to the ghetto reality described in the written accounts.

There are numerous descriptions of Auschwitz by survivors. The best account of its history is given by Hermann Langbein, an Austrian veteran of the Spanish Civil War and former communist, in *Menschen in Auschwitz* (Vienna: Europa-Verlag, 1972). This provides a detailed analysis based on personal experience as an inmate of Auschwitz and other camps, and discussions with numerous other survivors, supplemented with a wide knowledge of the relevant literature.

All the available survivor accounts by former inmates have something unique and valuable to say. All refract the camp experience through their own perceptions. Any selection from among these accounts is purely arbitrary. Elie Wiesel's *Night* (New York: Avon, 1960) describes his experiences from the time he entered Auschwitz as a boy with his father until his liberation. More than a factual account, it also describes Wiesel's spiritual odyssey from a believer who thought that as long as Jews were pious and studious no evil would touch them, to one who would end his journey crying out: "Why should I bless His name?" Wiesel, in a series of works written afterward, has attempted to come to terms with this experience.

Primo Levi's *Survival in Auschwitz: The Nazi Assault on Humanity* (New York: Macmillan, 1977; orig. pub. as *If This Man Is a Man*, 1961) is a very different work, by an Italian who survived largely because his previous experience as a chemist got him employed in the Buna works in Auschwitz. Here are descriptions of what it took to survive, the kinds of compromises that had to be made, and some analysis of why some survived and others did not. Terrence Des Pres' *The Survivor: An Anatomy of Life in the Death Camps* (New York: Oxford University Press, 1976) attempts to use the language and concepts of sociobiology to create a philosophy from the survival experience, which leads him to a kind of vitalism. It provides a convenient bibliography of survivor accounts. A one-sided controversial work, *The Survivor* has contributed significantly to the debate about the meaning of survival in the camps. For some of the prisoners survival also meant new beginnings. Leo Eitinger's *Concentration Camp Survivors in Norway and Israel* (Oslo: Universitetsforlager, 1964) presents a scholarly examination of the psychological costs and permanent scars that the camps inflicted. Robert Jay Lifton, in a number of works, has theorized about a "survivor guilt complex" and attempted to analyze its psychological meaning; see his *Death in Life: Survivors of Hiroshima* (New York: Random House, 1967) and *History and Human Survival* (New York: Vintage Books, 1971).

As the Holocaust recedes in time the question of its meaning seems to grow more rather than less urgent. Consequently it may be expected that both the substantive and interpretative literature will continue to grow.

Since this book was completed, the following important studies have appeared: Charles W. Sydnor, Jr., "The Selling of Adolf Hitler; David Irving's *Hitler's War*," *Central European History* XII, 2, 1979, pp. 169–199, is an excellent review of the Hitler literature which should dispose of any myths about Hitler's innocence. Andreas Hillgruber, "Die Ideologisch-Dogmatische Grundlage der Nationalsozialistischen Politik der Ausrottung der Juden in den besetzten Gebieten der Sowjetunion und Ihre Durchführung 1941–1944" (The ideological-dogmatic foundations of national socialist policy of the extermination of the Jews in the occupied territories of the Soviet Union and its implementtion 1941–1944) *German Studies Review* II, 3, 1979, pp. 263–296, provides an important analysis. Alexander Donat, whose *Holocaust Kingdom* is one of the more salient survivor accounts, has edited an important anthology, *The Death Camp Treblinka: A Documentary* (New York: The Holocaust Library, 1979). It presents very significant and hitherto unavailable survivor testimony, including a history of the camp, photographs, and bibliographic material. *The Stroop Report: The Jewish Quarter of Warsaw Is No More* (New York: Random House, 1979) makes available for the first time in English (a German edition had appeared in 1960), action reports by the SS commander responsible for the destruction of the Warsaw Ghetto. It contains facsimile reproductions, English translations, photographs, and an excellent introductory discussion by Andrzej Wirth.

# Index